Mistaken IDENTITY
THE TRIALS OF JOE WINDRED

STEPHEN DANDO-COLLINS
Mistaken IDENTITY
THE TRIALS OF JOE WINDRED

VINTAGE BOOKS
Australia

A Vintage book
Published by Random House Australia Pty Ltd
Level 3, 100 Pacific Highway, North Sydney NSW 2060
www.randomhouse.com.au

First published by Vintage in 2012

Copyright © Fame and Fortune Pty Ltd 2012

The moral right of the author has been asserted.

All rights reserved. No part of this book may be reproduced or transmitted by any person or entity, including internet search engines or retailers, in any form or by any means, electronic or mechanical, including photocopying (except under the statutory exceptions provisions of the Australian *Copyright Act 1968*), recording, scanning or by any information storage and retrieval system without the prior written permission of Random House Australia.

Addresses for companies within the Random House Group can be found at www.randomhouse.com.au/offices

National Library of Australia
Cataloguing-in-Publication entry

Dando-Collins, Stephen, 1950–
Mistaken identity: the trials of Joe Windred/Stephen Dando-Collins.

ISBN 978 1 74275 517 5 (pbk)

Windred, Joseph.
Mistaken identity.
Judicial error.
Mayors–New South Wales–Orange–Biography.
Fugitives from justice–California–San Francisco–Biography.

994.45092

Cover design by Christabella Designs
Cover photograph by iStockphoto
Typeset in 11.5/14 pt Bembo by Post Pre-press Group, Brisbane, Queensland
Printed in Australia by Griffin Press, an accredited ISO AS/NZS 14001:2004 Environmental Management System printer

Random House Australia uses papers that are natural, renewable and recyclable products and made from wood grown in sustainable forests. The logging and manufacturing processes are expected to conform to the environmental regulations of the country of origin.

'The best that fate can bring is wealth joined with the happy gift of wisdom'

Pindar, *Pythia II*, 5th century BC

TABLE OF CONTENTS

ACKNOWLEDGEMENTS ix

CHAPTER 1 – The Lynch Mob 1
CHAPTER 2 – Eleven Years Earlier 4
CHAPTER 3 – The Watch 12
CHAPTER 4 – The Informer 15
CHAPTER 5 – The Sydney Trial 20
CHAPTER 6 – The Verdict 42
CHAPTER 7 – The Sentence 48
CHAPTER 8 – Joe's Big Fight 52
CHAPTER 9 – The Love of Joe's Life 62
CHAPTER 10 – The Crash 71
CHAPTER 11 – The Lure of Gold 76
CHAPTER 12 – To California 80
CHAPTER 13 – Welcome to California 85
CHAPTER 14 – The Gold Country 92
CHAPTER 15 – The Jansen Job 101
CHAPTER 16 – A Golden Madness 108
CHAPTER 17 – The Kangaroo Court 123
CHAPTER 18 – The New Jansen Trial 140
CHAPTER 19 – The Prison Break 153
CHAPTER 20 – An Escape, a Lynching 166
CHAPTER 21 – Tom Burdue's Murder Trial 177
CHAPTER 22 – The Hanging of 'English Jim' 192
CHAPTER 23 – Life and Death 203
CHAPTER 24 – Hiding Out 213
CHAPTER 25 – The Racehorse Owner 230
CHAPTER 26 – A Wedding Ring, a Horse Thief and a
  Gold Strike 234
CHAPTER 27 – The Price of Success 245
CHAPTER 28 – Another Narrow Escape 250
EPILOGUE – The Orange Days 258

BIBLIOGRAPHY 263
NOTES 269
INDEX 279

ACKNOWLEDGEMENTS

The author extends his special thanks for expert help to Bill Riddle, Senior Librarian, California Documents, Government Publications Section, California State Library, Sacramento, California. Thanks also to Peter Douglass, Local Studies Librarian with Central West Libraries, Orange, NSW, Alison Russell of Orange City Council, Orange historians Phil Stevenson and Ross Maroney, and Kevin McGuinness of History Services, Sydney, for their invaluable help in the research for this work. To my publisher at Random House Australia, Meredith Curnow, and editor, Patrick Mangan, and my New York literary agent, Richard Curtis, my sincere gratitude for their ongoing advice and support.

This book is for my wife, Louise. Just as Mary Windred loyally stood by her man through thick and thin, Louise has enjoyed and endured the vicissitudes of fortune with me for three rollercoaster decades.

1

THE LYNCH MOB

Saturday, February 22, 1851. San Francisco, California

'Hang the Australians!' bayed men in the crowd of ten thousand filling the streets around San Francisco's City Hall. 'Have them out! Hang them!'

This mob was in the mood for a lynching, and just the fifty men of the Washington Guard militia stood between them and the two Australians being held in the cells in the City Hall basement.

Pushing through the clamouring throng came a clean-cut twenty-nine-year-old. 'Make way!' he called. 'Make way there!'

Despite his youth, William Taylor was the most senior of the eight Methodist ministers in San Francisco. Born in Virginia to Scots–Irish parents, like many of the men in this crowd today Taylor had only landed in San Francisco in 1849, drawn by the 1848 discovery of gold in California. And, like Taylor, the men in the crowd were all young, in their thirties, their twenties, their teens. Some were even pre-teenage boys. It was young men who had the strength and fortitude to survive the sea journey or the overland trek to reach gold-rush California from the eastern United States. Here, a man of forty was considered an old-timer. Here, too, with men outnumbering women twenty to one, the tempering influence of mothers or wives was largely absent, and there was no holding back many of these youths.

For eighteen months, from his pulpit in the Methodist Episcopal

Church on Powell Street and preaching outdoors in the city's Plaza and elsewhere, the Reverend Taylor had been fighting an uphill battle to bring God into the lives of young men driven by greed, drink and testosterone.

'The courts are sure to let them go!' bellowed an agitator close by Taylor as he fought his way through the serried ranks.

'Hang them now!' yelled another youth near the minister.

'Hang them! Hang them! Hang them!' It grew into a chant repeated by a chilling choir of thousands of voices.

The Reverend Taylor had become widely known in San Francisco. Recognising his face, the militia guards permitted him to reach the cellblock's basement door. The anxious face of Abraham Bartol, captain of the militia company, appeared on the other side of the grilled door.

'I wish to see the Australians,' said Taylor firmly to Bartol.

Taylor's reputation, combined with his air of self-importance, gained him entry. In adjoining cells he found two prisoners whose downcast eyes raised at his approach.

'Which one of you is Joseph Windred?' the clergyman asked. When neither replied, eyeing him suspiciously, Taylor added, 'I am the Reverend William Taylor. I have been sent to you by your wife.'

'I'm Joe Windred,' one now said, coming to his feet and walking to the bars that separated them. More than six feet tall, well built, Windred had a pleasant, intelligent face. Aged twenty-eight, he was just a year younger than the minister. Now, he added, 'But I'm not who they say I am.'

The shorter of the two prisoners, a bearded man, also rose and came to the cell bars, as the chanting voices could be heard from the streets outside: 'Hang them! Hang them! Hang them! Hang them!'

'There has been a terrible mistake,' the second man told the minister, his eyes betraying his fear. 'They say I'm the murderer James Stuart. But I am Tom Burdue. You must help us, reverend!'

'It's true,' said Windred. 'They accuse Tom of being Stuart, and me of being his accomplice.'

'They want to lynch us!' Burdue said, sounding increasingly desperate.

'Can you convince them that we are not who they say we are, reverend?' Joe implored.[1]

Joe Windred's future was hanging by a thread. Yet it was neither the first nor the last time he'd find himself in such dire straits. By any measure, Joe led an amazing life, defined as it was by a series of extraordinary coincidences. Overcoming physical disability, this indomitable Australian would become a renowned boxer and racehorse trainer, be hailed a hero for saving children's lives, feature in a landmark case in American legal history, find himself in a cell alongside a future President of Nicaragua, help build California's notorious San Quentin Prison, make a daring prison break, and strike it rich digging for gold. Joe's destiny was shaped by two remarkable and cruel twists of fate. For, his 1851 incarceration in San Francisco was mirrored by an identical crime he'd been accused of committing just over a decade earlier, back home in Australia. Then, too, Joe had been mistaken for someone else. The most astonishing thing of all was that this latest crime had been committed eleven years *to the day* since that first injustice.

2

ELEVEN YEARS EARLIER

Wednesday, February 19, 1840. Outside Windsor, New South Wales

AT THE STROKE OF midnight, as seventeen-year-old Joe Windred lay in his bed, asleep, a crime was being committed two kilometres away from his Windsor home. A crime that would dramatically change the life of this young man.

Sefton Cottage, a secluded farmhouse a kilometre and a half outside Windsor on the Richmond road, was in darkness. The rustic silence was broken by the eruption of a barking dog. Like a hound from Hell, the dog alternately barked and snarled, and, baring its teeth, strained at its chain, striving to reach three intruders. The men who had disturbed the dog fearfully backed away. Cursing the animal, and the racket it made, the trio retreated from the back door and made their stumbling, bumbling way through the midnight blackness to the front of the house.

All three wore dark clothing. Their hats were pulled down tightly. And, like women at a funeral, their faces were covered by black gauze veils. One member of the band, the tallest, carried a gun, a long-barrelled fowling piece. Of the other gang members, one was stouter and of middling height, while the third man was a slight figure. The stout one was armed with a thick, short club, the other with a walking stick.

One of the younger members of the band worried aloud that the dog would be heard by neighbours, but the leader, the man carrying the gun, only scoffed. There was nothing new about a barking dog on a dark February night. Besides, Sefton Cottage's nearest neighbours were well out of earshot. Solitude was one of the great attractions to those who enjoyed country life, and to thieves who preyed on them.

The leader of the band bashed on the front door with the butt of his gun. 'Open up!' he called. 'Open up the door, damn you!'

A candle flickered to life in a front room, and in its eerie light a man's face appeared in the room's window. 'What is it you want?' called the fearful owner of the face as he tried to make out the shadowy figures by the door.

'Open up, or it'll be the worse for you!' the gang's leader demanded.

'I cannot! Unless I have my mistress' leave to do it.'

'Then, get her leave, you bloody fool!'

The face disappeared from the window. But the door didn't open. Cursing, the middle-sized intruder bashed on the door with his club and demanded admittance. After fifteen minutes, the bashing terminated. The dog at the back of the house ceased to bark. Silence reclaimed the night around Sefton Cottage, falling like a cloak over the farmhouse. In the sidelight window beside the front door, the anxious face appeared, this time lit from below by the glow of his candle. Peering out into night, he sought to assure himself that the three men had departed.

'Aha!' Triumphantly, the gang's leader sprang up from where he had been skulking outside the door. Jamming the end of his gun up against the window glass opposite the frightened face, he growled, 'Open the door, or I'll blow your bloody head off!'

'Mistress!' the terrified servant called back over his shoulder. 'They will kill me! I have no choice. I must open the door to them.'

'Yes, open the door, Thomas,' came the resigned voice of a woman from the rear of the house.

A key was turned in the lock by Thomas the servant. Slowly, the door was opened. The gang's leader stormed in through the opening. His two colleagues followed close behind. 'You bloody wretch!' snarled the leader. 'Why have you kept us waiting so long?'

The servant, Thomas Keane, was relieved of his candle by the shortest member of the robber band, who was dressed all in blue.

Roughly, the gang's leader pushed Keane into the front room. A native of Ireland, Keane had come to New South Wales a convicted petty criminal. He had been a free man and in the employ of John Barker for the past few years. There was a blanket on the sofa in the front room. This was where Keane slept whenever his employer was away from home on business, with instructions to protect the house and its mistress, Mrs Barker. Ever since John Barker had departed on business on February 10, Keane had fulfilled his orders. But this night he had failed his master.

The gang's leader used his free hand to lift the blanket from the sofa and pass it to the taller of his accomplices. 'Roll him up in it, Paddy,' he instructed.

Laying his club aside, Paddy spread the blanket on the floor. He then forced Keane to lie full length on the blanket, before kneeling beside him and rolling him over and over.

With Keane protesting and struggling, Paddy said coldly to his leader, 'Ram the piece down his throat, why don't you?'

The leader moved to stand over the servant. Putting the tip of the fowling piece's barrel to Keane's head, he said, matter-of-factly, 'If you keep quiet, we won't hurt you. If you are not, we will.'

The terrorised servant gave up his resistance, and lay quiet, now effectively and securely restrained with his arms pinioned by his side.

'Where does your mistress keep the money?' the leader now demanded.

'I don't know,' Keane responded, looking up at the gang leader. He didn't recognise the man's voice, while a floppy cabbage tree hat on his head and the black veil over his face protected his anonymity.

'Which room is your mistress' bedroom?'

Keane didn't reply.

'Which room?'

Still, the servant remained mute.

'Bloody wretch!'

The man with the gun turned away and led his companions out into the hall. With a finger to his black-gauzed mouth he urged quiet, then tiptoed along the hall, putting an ear to each closed door. At a door toward the back of the house, he cupped a hand to his ear, indicating that his accomplices should listen intently. Sure enough, from inside the room they could all hear the whisperings of two females, one just a girl, the other older. Trying the door handle, the leader found the door locked. 'Open up in there, mistress!' he loudly commanded. 'We know you're in there. Open, I say, or we'll burst it open!'

After a pause, the door was unlocked from within, and opened. The three men strode into the room. Eliza Barker, with a robe hastily thrown over her nightgown, withdrew from the door, retreating toward her ruffled bed. A servant girl in her teens clutched at her mistress. The girl was terrified, but the lady of the house was remarkably calm as she looked at the shadowy figures confronting her in the low light of their candle. Twenty-nine-year-old Eliza Barker, the former Eliza Dargin, had been married to forty-seven-year-old John Barker for the past six years. Eliza's late father, Thomas Dargin, had come to New South Wales in 1792 as a seaman, and after receiving government land grants in the Windsor area had gone on to do well in the tavern trade. Thomas and his colonial wife, Mary, had produced a large brood of little Dargins. The Dargin daughters, in particular, had proven to be of strong character. Eliza, third eldest of the five Dargin girls, was no exception.

'What do you want?' Eliza now bravely demanded.

'Well, mistress,' said the gang's leader, standing in the doorway and cradling the gun in his arms, 'all we want is your money.'

'I have very little money in the house,' she returned.

'We know that. But, if you give it up, it will save trouble.'

As the servant girl pleaded with Eliza to do as the robbers said, the mistress of the house thought for a moment. Then, with a sigh, she reached beneath her pillow and brought out a pocketbook. The middle-sized robber, Paddy, stepped forward and snatched the pocketbook from her. He found no money in it, but he did find the house-keys. As the leader stood at the door brandishing his gun and the short robber lit proceedings with the candle, Paddy unlocked a bedside drawer. With a cry of glee, he emptied it of cash he found there. He counted out pound notes and coins for the benefit of the others before stuffing them in his pocket.

But the leader, unimpressed by the meagre haul, instructed Paddy to keep looking.

Moving to a chest of drawers, Paddy rifled each drawer in turn, taking out Eliza's favourite gold-drop earrings, several silk shawls and a brown handkerchief. Removing his hat, taking care to make sure that his veil remained in place, the thief stuffed the items into it, then put the hat back on his head. Now, he spied a fob watch hanging by its chain from a nail on the wall. 'There's a silver watch,' he said.

'Oh, don't take that,' the leader responded, aware that quality watches were easy to trace via their makers' numbers and markings, making them hard to sell and easy to trace.

Paddy resumed his search of the room, but after he failed to turn up any more valuables, his leader escorted Eliza and the trembling servant girl to the front room. Paddy, lingering behind, quickly snatched the watch from the wall and slipped it under his hat. He joined the others to find the females sitting on the sofa. With the helpless Thomas Keane lying rolled up before them, the gang's leader ordered the candle-bearer to manipulate Keane into a sitting position in his blanket, with his back to the sofa. While this was going on, Paddy scoured the front room for money, without success.

The leader was displeased with the night's work. Farmer Barker was reputed to keep hundreds of pounds in the house after selling wool. And hadn't Barker only recently returned from a wool sale? 'We thought you had more money, mistress,' the leader now confessed, 'or we would not have troubled you.'

The robber band withdrew into the night, dowsing the candle as they went, leaving their traumatised victims in the dark. Thomas Keane, trussed up like a Christmas turkey, had not recognised any of the thieves, but, as the trio departed, he heard the leader use a term which he recognised as distinctly Scottish.[2]

Eliza Barker helped Keane from the blanket. But her ordeal had only just begun.

At 7.00 a.m. that same morning, there was a knock at the Barker door. When Eliza, her eyes red from lack of sleep, and half fearing the return of the robbers, tentatively answered the knock, she found her smiling nephew Joseph Windred standing on her doorstep.

Then close to five feet eleven inches tall, Joe Windred was a strapping teenager. He had been born here at Windsor, a village of several hundred inhabitants located fifty-five kilometres west of Sydney. Beside the broad Hawkesbury River, Windsor was the regional centre for a lush farming district where sheep and crops did equally well. Joe's tradesman father, Joseph Windred senior, a former English convict, had quietly prospered here in recent years. Joe's mother, Sophia, was Eliza Barker's elder sister. A much-loved nephew and welcome visitor, young Joe frequently came to the Barker house. Today, he was making a prearranged call, having walked out from the village, to collect one of his Uncle John's horses to take it to the blacksmith shop owned by his employer, Windsor businessman James Cullen – another of Joe's uncles by marriage.

Eliza and her husband were especially fond of Joe, admiring his industry and the way he'd never let a childhood physical disability, a lame foot, hold him back. Despite that disability, Joe never uttered a word of complaint or self-pity, and never asked for special treatment. Grateful to see Joe's friendly and trusted face, Eliza ushered him indoors. Thomas Keane had already gone for the police, who were yet to put in an appearance, and, to Joe, over a cup of tea, Eliza gushed out the details of the robbery she and her two servants had just endured. As Joe listened, he was sympathetic, yet, he did not look entirely surprised by the news. Now, he questioned his aunt, asking her to describe the robbers, and after Eliza had told him all she could remember of the three masked men, including the fact that one of them was called Paddy, she thought that Joe looked strangely embarrassed.

'Must have been some of the neighbours' men,' Joe remarked.[3]

After half an hour, Joe bade his aunt good morning and went out to the barn to saddle up the horse he had been sent to collect. As Eliza watched him go, Joe walked with his habitual limp. While growing up, recognising he would never be able to run as fast as his brothers and schoolmates, Joe had made determined efforts to excel in other physical activities. In the Hawkesbury River, Joe had become a strong swimmer. On the river, he'd made himself a powerful oarsman. Both pursuits had built up his shoulders and arm muscles. He was also one of the best young riders in the district. It helped that he had a natural affinity with horses. That skill had won Joe his job as a farrier, shoeing horses for his Uncle James.

With a wave to his Aunt Eliza, Joe rode out the gate and headed off down the Richmond road toward Windsor. Joe didn't stop when he reached his employer's premises in George Street, Windsor's high street. Instead, he continued on into the heart of the village. Turning into Fitzgerald Street, he rode up to a tall figure standing on the doorstep of a double-storey residence halfway along the block, opposite Hangman's Row.

This was Henry Nichols, one of Windsor's most unsavoury characters. Transported to New South Wales for petty theft in 1831, Nichols had been a free man for the past eighteen months. He was a shoemaker by trade, but Joe knew for a fact that Nichols used his house as an illegal gambling den out of hours. Nichols was also said to be involved in a variety of other illegal dealings, and had escaped conviction on charges ranging from cattle and sheep stealing to assault, with witnesses suddenly having lapses of memory when the cases came to court. Ordinarily, Joe would have had nothing to do with the man, but Joe's best friend Andy Garven worked with Nichols in the shoemaking business, so, if Joe wanted to see Andy, he couldn't avoid Nichols. But it wasn't Andy that Joe was seeking today.

'Where's Robinson?' he angrily called to Nichols from the back of the horse. John Robinson, who boarded with Nichols, was another shoemaker who, like Nichols and Garven, worked at the Windsor shoe store owned by local businessman Thomas Bridges.

'Gone to work at Bridges',' Nichols replied, his accent exhibiting the rolling 'r' typical of Scottish natives.

With the Bridges shoe store just fifty metres further along Fitzgerald Street, Joe urged his mount forward and trotted in that direction. At this early hour the store was not yet open. Three young men now appeared around a corner and came strolling along the street toward Joe. Chattering and laughing, they gave Joe a cheery greeting. One, John Cheeke, also boarded with Henry Nichols. Another was Joe's best mate, the five feet five inches Andy Garven. An eighteen-year-old Irish imp with a round face and freckles, Garven hailed from Waterford. He and Joe were as close as brothers. Where Joe was shy and slow to make friends, cheeky Garven was the life of any party. The third youth was the same age as Garven, but taller, stouter. He was John Robinson, the object of Joe's quest. Also possessing a criminal record and also originally from Ireland, Robinson had a nickname among his Windsor cronies: Paddy.

Henry Nichols, standing on his doorstep still, watched the group pass. They were heading toward the inn on the corner of Fitzgerald and George streets run by George Freeman. Joe, on horseback, was quizzing Robinson, and Robinson was casually tossing off each question with a grin and denying everything that Joe put to him. Turning, Nichols went back inside. A little while later, he re-emerged, closed the door behind him, and began walking toward Bridges' store to start work for the day. As Nichols walked, he heard voices around the back of his rented house. Looking to his right, he saw young Joe Windred, still mounted, arguing with Paddy Robinson. Smiling to himself, Nichols kept walking.[4]

3

THE WATCH

Sunday, February 23, 1840. Windsor, New South Wales

GALES OF LAUGHTER COULD be heard coming from Henry Nichols' house. To some, this was an ungodly sound on a Sunday. To others, it was a beacon. It was five minutes after 4.00 in the afternoon when Thomas Wilson ambled into the Nichols parlour. Damp from summer rain, with a clay pipe jutting from the corner of his mouth, Wilson was eager to join the revelry. An English petty criminal serving a seven-year sentence, Wilson was one of fifty convicts working at John Teale's Endeavour Mill in Windsor's George Street. This was the largest flour mill in New South Wales, with its sixty-four horses turning the grinding wheel around the clock in sixteen-horse shifts.

Every Sunday, Tom Wilson was permitted by Teale his master to 'walk out' for an hour between 4.00 and 5.00. And Wilson liked nothing better than spending that hour at Nichols', enjoying a hand of cards and downing a tot or two of rum. There were four men at the table, playing All Fours, a game involving two pairs of players. Money lay on the table. The players were watched by Nichols' eighteen-year-old wife, Elizabeth, who poured tumblers of rum. Nichols himself was playing, along with boarders John 'Paddy' Robinson and John Cheeke. The fourth player was John Smith, a young local cook.

Lighting his pipe, Wilson joined Elizabeth Nichols watching the game, hoping that a place would soon open up for him at the table. That place seemed imminent, for, Paddy Robinson, who had downed too much rum, was on a losing streak. The hand ended. Nichols laughed, and raked in the money. With Robinson cursing and declaring that he had lost his last four half crowns, Wilson edged closer to his chair. But Robinson lifted his hat and produced a fine silver watch from beneath it.

He held out the watch. 'Who will lend me five shillings on this?'

Across the table, Nichols was glowering at him, but Robinson was too drunk to notice, or to care.

'Let me have a look at that, Paddy,' said Smith the cook, taking the timepiece and inspecting it.

Now Nichols, saying that Robinson was a fool, and that he had a good mind to turn him out into the street, discouraged Smith from advancing the money. Smith handed the watch back to Robinson, who, cursing, vacated his chair in favour of Wilson and slouched away. Wilson quickly took the empty chair and lay his money down. As the six cards for the next hand were being dealt to each player, Elizabeth Nichols leaned close to her husband and venomously warned that Robinson was a liability, and urged him to turn the youth out. While Nichols agreed that Robinson was a young fool and deserved to be turned out, he calmed his wife by saying that he would sort out their unreliable lodger without having to go to that extreme.[5]

Friday, February 28, 1840. Windsor, New South Wales

It was in the middle of the evening when Paddy Robinson came staggering home to the Nichols house, rolling in the door from George Freeman's pub, drunk. Collapsing into a chair as his landlord and others played cards, Robinson was soon fast asleep where he sat. He was followed in the door shortly after by Andrew Garven and Joe Windred. Both were highly agitated.

When Nichols asked Garven what the problem was, Garven answered, 'It's the things in his hat. Paddy is showing them about.'

Nichols got up, went to the snoring Robinson, and lifted the hat from his head. Silk shawls and a brown handkerchief spilled out. A silver watch tumbled to the floor with a clunk. It was the same watch that Robinson had produced days earlier, at the card game, but now it was minus its engraved silver case.

Frowning, Joe Windred bent and picked up the watch. Looking at it, and recognising it, he angrily declared, 'Robinson shall not have it!' He slipped the watch into his pocket.

'What will you do with it?' Nichols demanded, suddenly anxious.

'I'd rather break it, or throw it in the river, before Robinson had it,' Joe declared, turning and leaving.

Garven, throwing Nichols a worried look, hurried after his friend.[6]

4

THE INFORMER

Wednesday, March 4, 1840. Windsor, New South Wales

THE WORKING DAY WAS at an end, and Nichols, Robinson, Cheeke and Garven were walking out of Bridges' shoe store. From along the street, a voice called on them to stop. The Windsor watch-house keeper and two constables came hurrying up.

'John Cheeke, I have a warrant for your arrest!' declared Watch-house Keeper John Horan.

'For what?' Cheeke fearfully asked, as the policemen secured him by the arms.

'In connection with the burglary at the premises of Samuel Ashcroft, the tailor,' was the reply, before Cheeke was led away toward Court Street and the town's watch-house.

Nichols, Robinson and Garven looked at each other with trepidation, before Nichols and Robinson set off for Nichols' nearby house at the trot, leaving Garven to head to his own lodgings. When Nichols and Robinson arrived home, Elizabeth Nichols greeted them carrying her two-month-old baby. Her husband had no time for pleasantries. Angrily, Nichols instructed Robinson to get rid of all incriminating evidence, at once. Robinson hurried upstairs to his room, and before long returned with a bundle.

The pair went outside, to a lavatory behind the house. There, Nichols watched as Robinson dumped the silver case to John Barker's stolen watch into a toilet, followed by two silk shawls and a handkerchief. There was no dividing fence between the Nichols property and that next door, so Robinson also dumped several remaining items of clothing into the neighbours' lavatory.

Returning to the house, Nichols and Robinson sat down with Elizabeth Nichols to the evening meal. They were eating when there was a loud bashing on the front door. The three of them looked at each other; then, as the knocking continued, Nichols came to his feet and answered the knock. On opening the door, he found constables standing there.

'Henry Nichols, we have a warrant for your arrest.'

Nichols was hustled away, leaving his wife and boarder shocked and alarmed. Like Cheeke, Nichols was taken to the Windsor Watchhouse. Watch-house Keeper John Horan looked up from his desk as the prisoner was brought in. Horan knew Henry Nichols well enough. Over the seven years that he had been in this job, Horan had seen Nichols brought in on a number of occasions, on a variety of charges.

'You are charged with the burglary at the premises of Samuel Ashcroft the tailor on Saturday last,' Horan informed the prisoner, as he wrote Nichols' details in his day book.

'That bloody wretch Cheeke has split on me, hasn't he?' Nichols sourly responded. When the watch-house keeper made no comment, Nichols went on, 'What if I were to give information? What if I were to tell the chief constable who robbed John Barker's place the other week? Would that get me off the Ashcroft charge?'

Horan looked up, and replied that Nichols could give his information to him, and need not trouble the chief constable. But, he said, the police would need more than just an accusation. They would need solid proof. When Nichols agreed that he could provide that proof, Horan asked him to name names.

'Cheeke was involved in the Barker robbery,' Nichols announced, 'and John Robinson.' He then offered to lead the police to where loot from both the Barker and Ashcroft robberies had been hidden by Robinson.

Taking Nichols at his word, a party of constables escorted him back to his Fitzgerald Street home. Robinson was still there, and on the strength of Nichols' information he too was arrested. Nichols then led the police outside, to the lavatory. Lanterns were brought, and Nichols rolled up his sleeve. Then, without hesitation, Nichols, on his knees, reached down into the stinking faeces and urine, felt about, and came out with a saturated silk shawl. A second exploration brought out another shawl, and a handkerchief. A third delve into the muck found the silver watch case. These, said Nichols, were all from the Barker robbery, and with his own eyes he had seen Robinson hide them here.

Nichols then led the constables to the neighbouring property, and likewise went fishing in the lavatory there. This time, he came out with a handkerchief, a vest and men's underwear, all of which were on the list of stolen items provided by Ashcroft the tailor. The goods retrieved by Nichols were bagged, and Nichols, reeking of excrement, was taken back to the watch-house. There, he made a statement. According to Nichols, Robinson had told him all about the Barker robbery the day after it had taken place, revealing everything about the crime, he said, from the barking dog at the back door of Sefton Cottage to the disappointing financial reward for the robbers' criminal effort.

Nichols added: 'Robinson said to me, "If I had known as much before I went, as I do now, I would not have gone out there."'

When reminded that three men had carried out the Barker robbery, Nichols said that, apart from Cheeke and Robinson, Andrew Garven had participated in the crime. Constables were sent back out into the night, to Garven's lodgings. Soon, protesting his innocence, the Irish teenager was brought in the watch-house door.[7]

As the police questioned people around the town about items stolen from the Barker farmhouse, it became clear that in the days following the robbery John Cheeke had attempted to sell some of those items to various townspeople. But when questioned, Cheeke vehemently denied taking part in the robbery itself. He had not been the third man, he declared. The police believed him, for, according to Eliza Barker and Thomas Keane, that third man, the one carrying the gun, had been by far the tallest member of the band – and Cheeke was no taller than Robinson.

The police were convinced that John Robinson was the 'Paddy' who had been at the forefront of the crime. Apart from the fact that his nickname had been used during the robbery, at the scene of the crime the police had found the club that 'Paddy' carried that night. After laying the weapon aside to roll Thomas Keane in the blanket, Paddy had forgotten to retrieve it. This was an era long before fingerprinting, but the Windsor police had another way to link Robinson to the club. Nichols, in his statement, had said that Robinson originally left his house at 8.00 on the night of the robbery. At around 11.00 p.m., Nichols went on, Robinson had returned, equipped with a walking stick. After fossicking in rubbish beneath the stairs of the Nichols house, he had come out with a wooden club. Taking stick and club with him, Nichols claimed, Paddy Robinson had again departed into the night, not returning until 3.00 a.m.

The police were also certain that Andrew Garven had been the shortest member of the band, the one who had held the candle during the robbery. But, if Cheeke was not the third man, who was? Both Robinson and Garven were claiming they'd had nothing to do with the robbery, so neither was going to name the third man. Nichols was questioned again. Now, the police suggested that *he* had in fact been the third man. Nichols vehemently denied it, and when pressed to identify the third man and leader of the band, he gave the police a name. It was a name that surprised the constables and Watch-house Keeper Horan.

With perspiration running from his brow, Joe Windred was shoeing a horse. Looking up, he saw a party of constables advancing toward him.

'Joseph Windred,' said the leading constable, 'we have a warrant for your arrest, in connection with the robbery of your uncle, John Barker.'

Henry Nichols had named Joe as the third man. According to Nichols, Joe had not only taken part in the robbery, he had been the one carrying the gun on the night. Even though Joe had never before been in trouble with the law, Windsor police magistrate Samuel North, who would commit Joe for trial in Sydney before the Supreme Court, would be satisfied that there was sufficient evidence for a conviction to be obtained against him. Joe was tall, as the man with the gun on the night of the robbery had been. Joe was known to be a close associate of Garven, and, to a lesser extent, an associate of Robinson and Cheeke. Joe admitted having been at the Nichols house, with all three, early on the night of the robbery. And Joe had an intimate knowledge of John Barker's home and business affairs. Charged with leading the robbery, Joe was thrown into Windsor Gaol, which stood behind the watch-house on Court Street, to await transfer to Sydney for trial.

5

THE SYDNEY TRIAL

Friday, May 8, 1840. Sydney, New South Wales

'COME OUT, WINDRED, GARVEN, Robinson and Cheeke,' bellowed the turnkey of Sydney Gaol, reading from the court docket in front of him.

Joe Windred passed through the open cell door and stood in the corridor, glumly waiting for the other three men who had been called out to join him.

Sydney Gaol was at this time on lower George Street, close to the Rocks and Circular Quay. Like most of Sydney's public buildings, the cold, damp stone gaol was inadequate for its purpose. 'The gaol in its present crowded state, without classification or labour, is a moral pestilence,' New South Wales Governor Sir Richard Bourke had written seven years earlier, 'and from its confined and low situation in the populous part of the town, appears likely at any moment to generate a physical one'.[8] Bourke had pushed through the construction of a new gaol for Sydney. That gaol was still under construction at Darlinghurst; it would open in June the following year, along with a new courthouse.

In the meantime, the George Street gaol that had been deemed crowded and unhealthy in 1833 was still serving the colony, and was even more crowded and unhealthy. One community cell inside the prison was devoted to debtors. Six other large cells were filled with convicted criminals doing hard labour in the gaol's rock-breaking yard and with men awaiting trial. Joe had been thrown in with the worst of humanity, for the authorities made no attempt to separate murderers from pickpockets, rapists from horse-thieves, or hardened 'lags' from innocent men awaiting their day in court. To make matters worse, apart from the men undergoing rock-breaking punishment, there was no work to make the hours pass more quickly for inmates, no opportunity or room to exercise in the crowded cells. And ablutions had to be done in a bucket in front of the prisoners' cellmates.

Joe had been transferred here from Windsor Gaol just a week earlier, not long after celebrating his eighteenth birthday on April 27. Any man who spent any length of time here in Sydney Gaol could expect to obtain an education from the practitioners of the various criminal arts who shared his cell. Graduates of Sydney Gaol's academy of crime could learn the tricks of the trade from the colony's Flash Men ('fences', or dealers in stolen goods, and pimps, who managed prostitutes), Turf Men (illegal 'turf accountants', or bookmakers), Lock Men (break-and-enter specialists), Packet Men (forgers), Hocus Pocus Men (deception/confidence tricksters), and *Leger-de-Main* Men (sleight-of-hand artists).[9]

Now, Joe stood, humiliated, as gaolers roughly attached chains to chafing fetters – which circled his ankles – and the heavy manacles on his wrists, linking him with the man behind. He was not permitted to talk with the others in his group. Not that he wanted to. Like Joe, Garven, Robinson and Cheeke were pleading 'not guilty'. All three were pretending complete ignorance of the crime. Yet, Joe knew very well that all were implicated.

Not even Joe's best mate, Andy Garven, had offered a good word for him, despite the fact that Joe had gone out of his way to try to protect Andy once he learned of the robbery, hiding his uncle's stolen watch to prevent it being traced to Garven via his motley associates. Joe was like that; loyalty was everything to him, and he stuck by his mates. It would later be said of him that he 'never failed a friend or deceived a foe'.[10] Not only had Andy failed to do the right thing by Joe, he had deceived him. For, Andy was not who he'd said he was. As Joe had only discovered since his arrest, Garven's real name was Hogan, and he had come out to New South

Wales as a child, convicted of theft. He had served out his time, but when he moved to the Windsor district, Garven had changed his name. No one knew why. This gave rise to the suspicion that he'd committed other crimes under his real name.

'Move off!' bellowed the chief turnkey, himself a former convict.

Out through the gaol's arched gateway and into lower George Street the quartet shuffled, their chains clanking with every step. Here, in the busiest part of this thriving port city of 50,000 inhabitants, a nonstop cavalcade of carriages, wagons, horses and pedestrians was passing. Directly in front of him Joe could see the shops of the appropriately named William Stone the stair cutter, and J. C. Raphael the clothier. Over Joe's shoulder, the masts and spars of ships docked at Circular Quay and sitting out in the harbour rose above the rooftops. How Joe would love to be aboard one of those ships right now, and sailing away to adventure in some exotic place.

'Pick up your feet!' growled a guard.

With Joe in the lead and carrying his slight limp, the quartet set off. Joe, Andy Garven/Hogan, Paddy Robinson and John Cheeke traipsed up George Street, clutching their chains, and with heads hung low. Children they passed jeered them, and ladies and gentlemen of 'the Fancy', as New South Wales' well-to-do elite were known colloquially, disdainfully looked the other way as they were driven by in their carriages. Turning left out of George Street, the gaol party came down King, crossing Pitt and Castlereagh. On the far corner of Elizabeth and King streets stood the red-brick courthouse, their destination, where the fates of all four would soon be decided.

Sydney's first permanent Supreme Court building was not grand. It had started out promisingly, with a fine design by noted colonial architect Francis Greenway. But the building thrown up in 1828 soon internally bore little resemblance to the original Greenway design. The builders took short cuts which, within a few years, required the sagging roof to be held up by poles and columns, while alarming cracks appeared in walls. Ventilation in summer was almost nonexistent. In winter, when the wind blew from a particular direction, the poorly built fireplaces heating the two courtrooms filled them with choking smoke, making them uninhabitable. When windows were thrown open at the height of summer to admit fresh air to a stifling courtroom, the noise of passing traffic sometimes required proceedings to be temporarily suspended.

While the members of the judiciary who used the building complained bitterly about its shortcomings, the architectural features of the courthouse were the last thing on the minds of the men and women who came here to be tried, or to watch the theatre of court proceedings play out. The Supreme Court's public gallery was frequently packed, especially if a particular case caught public attention. On any given day as many as three hundred spectators could be expected to pass through the courthouse doors.

This autumn morning was one of those days. The gallery was full. The Barker case had created something of a sensation, dealing as it did with the robbery of an honest couple by their own trusted nephew; at least, that was how it was being portrayed in the press. At the forefront of the gallery sat the court reporters of Sydney's leading newspapers. With pencils and notebooks at the ready, and chatting among themselves, journalists were here from the *Sydney Monitor and Commercial Advertiser*, the *Australasian Chronicle*, the *Sydney Gazette and New South Wales Advertiser* and the *Sydney Herald*.

The *Herald*'s man, Charles Kemp, would provide the most comprehensive coverage of the Barker case. Kemp had migrated from England with his family when only a child. Starting out as a carpenter, in 1838 the young man had been employed by the *Herald*'s owner and editor, Frederick Stokes, as his first parliamentary reporter. In between parliamentary sittings, Stokes despatched Kemp to the criminal court. The *Herald*'s always lengthy, often salacious verbatim court reports soon boosted the paper's readership.

Kemp and his fellow court reporters would record every word spoken during the trial, using shorthand. The ancient Romans invented shorthand, only for the skill to be lost after the fall of the Roman Empire. It was reinvented in Britain in 1786 by Samuel Taylor. His book was shorthand's sole teaching aid until Isaac Pitman published his system in 1837. Charles Kemp and fellow journalists had taught themselves the art using either the Taylor or Pitman books. Always with an eye to advancement, less than a year from now twenty-eight-year-old Kemp would go into partnership with the *Herald*'s printer, John Fairfax, to buy the paper from Stokes. Changing its name to the *Sydney Morning Herald*, the partners would quickly turn it into Australia's preeminent newspaper and foundation of the modern Fairfax media empire.

Joe Windred's parents were in the gallery. Joe's mother, forty-three-year-old Sophia, was nursing her baby daughter Mary Ann, who had only been born in January. Sophia had come to this trial determined to see Joe, her eldest son and pride and joy, acquitted of the charge against him. Sophia had been born free in New South Wales. Industrious, eschewing drinking and gambling, she had never had the slightest brush with the law. Sitting uneasily beside her in the Supreme Court gallery was her husband, Joseph Windred senior, who had a more chequered past. Joe senior's experience of courtrooms had been from the point of view of the accused. Born in Kent, England, Joe senior had come out to the colony in 1815 as a thirty-year-old convict. Good behaviour saw him gain a conditional pardon just five years later, and he soon commenced to live with the attractive Sophia. They could not marry, because in 1812 Sophia, when just fifteen, had married the much older Patrick Brady. According to Brady, a one-time convict gardener at Government House, his wife Sophia had been seduced away from him by Joe senior.

In 1822, at Windsor, Sophia had given birth to Joe junior, the first of the couple's eight children. Two years later, Joe senior was again standing trial, charged with stealing a pig in partnership with Sophia's younger brother James Dargin. Both men had been convicted. Joe senior was sent to the Port Macquarie convict station. Dargin served his time in Van Diemen's Land. Sophia had received permission to join 'husband' Joe senior at Port Macquarie, where he worked as an assigned servant, and moved there with the couple's then two sons, three-year-old Joe junior and one-year-old William, so they could all live as a family. Shortly after, Sophia's estranged real husband Patrick Brady had written vindictively to the colonial secretary, complaining that Sophia and Joe senior were not legally married. Ordered to leave Port Macquarie as a consequence, Sophia had pleaded ill health. By 1827, she had returned to Windsor, pregnant with the couple's third son, John.

Joe senior had been released at Port Macquarie in 1828 after his sentence was terminated with another conditional pardon, and he rejoined Sophia and their boys at Windsor. Toiling as a tanner, Joe senior had spent the next twelve years regaining his reputation and rebuilding his family's fortunes, only for the Barker robbery to shatter the Windred family's domestic harmony. To defend Joe junior, Joe had hired one of Sydney's leading barristers, William Foster. A native of Yorkshire, and New South Wales' solicitor general when he first arrived in the colony in 1827, Foster would before long enter the colony's parliament. Forty-six-year-old Foster had years of experience at the bar, together with a name as a sharp lawyer.

Foster was in his place in court now, wearing barrister's wig and gown. Joe junior had not even met his defence attorney. Foster was working purely on what Joe's mother and father had told him, and on police evidence. Beside Foster sat William Alexander Purefoy, who would be defending Robinson, Garven and Cheeke in the same case. One of just two dozen barristers in the colony, and only accredited to the New South Wales bar for the past seven months, the Dublin-born Purefoy had more work than he could handle defending the colony's numerous less affluent accused.

In their box to one side of the courtroom sat the all-male jury. The prosecutor was in his place, too. This was thirty-seven-year-old John Plunkett, Attorney General of New South Wales. Another Irish immigrant, he was a native of Roscommon, a town which infamously had a female executioner when Plunkett was younger. Plunkett habitually prosecuted the criminal cases that came before the Supreme Court. His preparation was meticulous, his court performance wily, and his record of convictions daunting. Plunkett was a notoriously no-nonsense man. Prior to his becoming attorney general, witnesses swearing to tell the truth were required to state whether they were Protestant or Roman Catholic, and, if the latter, to kiss the cross fronting the Bible. Plunkett had dispensed with this in New South Wales, believing that no such act could possibly add to the validity of an oath.

As the clock on the wall ticked over to 10.00 a.m., the clerk of the court stood and called, 'All rise!'

Everyone in court came to their feet, and Sir James Dowling, fifty-two-year-old, London-born Chief Justice of New South Wales, swept into the courtroom wearing black, scarlet and purple and a periwig. Once Dowling had taken his place on the throne-like judgement seat, the remainder of the court resumed their seats. Chief Justice for the past two-and-a-half years, absorbed with detail, a meticulous record-keeper and famously diligent, Sir James was known to sit until 3.00 a.m. in some cases. The previous year, impatient with street noise intruding on his summer sittings, Dowling had demanded that the Governor approve the barricading of King Street. His demand had been rejected.

Dowling nodded, and the names of the first prisoners on the day's docket were called. Up from the cells four young men laboured, with Joe Windred in the lead. Joe's name headed the court list, for, according to the prosecution, he had led the Barker robbery. The stairs from the cells climbed up directly into the 'dock', the elevated wooden box at the centre of the courtroom that held prisoners during their trial. Joe, Garven, Robinson and Cheeke took their seats on the hard bench provided, to sit looking out over the heads of the attorneys and court officers to the judge on the bench.

The charges were now read out. Joseph Windred junior, John Robinson and Andrew Garven were all charged with, on or about the evening of February 18 that year – it was actually the early hours of the morning of February 19 – feloniously breaking into and entering a dwelling house, the property of John Barker, at Windsor, putting the inmates in bodily fear, the accused being armed, and with stealing therefrom £13 and 10 shillings in money, a silver watch, jewellery and sundry items of clothing. John Cheeke was charged with being an accessory after the fact by harbouring the thieves, and with receiving property knowing it to have been stolen. All four accused pleaded 'not guilty'.

Attorney General Plunkett came to his feet. 'If Your Honour pleases, the Crown calls Mrs John Barker.'

Eliza Barker, Joe's aunt, was called into court. Dressed in her Sunday best, she took her place on the witness stand.

The Clerk of the Court held out a Holy Bible to her. 'Take the book in your right hand,' he instructed. And, as she reached out, added, 'Take off your glove, ma'am.'[11]

Eliza removed her glove, held the Bible, and swore to tell the truth, the whole truth and nothing but the truth, so help her God. Plunkett now proceeded to ply her with questions about the night of the crime. In response, she calmly told of how she had gone to bed around 9.00 p.m. that night, only to be awoken around midnight by the sound of bashing on her front door, then narrated in detail how the robbery had unfolded. When asked by Plunkett whether she had recognised any of the members of the gang, she replied, 'They were disguised with black crepe over their faces. I did not recognise any of their voices.'

Plunkett then asked, 'Was the prisoner Windred the only one of the prisoners who was in the habit of visiting your house?' The prosecutor was wasting no time in linking Joe to the scene of the crime.

'Yes,' Eliza answered.

'When did you see Windred next?' It was a cleverly worded question that implied that Eliza had seen Joe on the night of the crime.

But Eliza worded her answer with equal care. 'I saw Joe next morning, about 7.00 a.m. He came on business, from his employer, Mr Cullen.'

'What did you say to Windred?'

'I told him what had occurred on the preceding evening.'

'And what was his reaction to what you told him?'

'He appeared quite embarrassed by my statement, and he said it must have been some of the neighbours' men.'

'Tell the court what was said to you by the robbers just before leaving your premises.'

'Before they left, they said they thought I had more money in the house, or they would not have troubled me.'

'They thought you had more money in the house. Thank you, Mrs Barker. I have no further questions for this witness at this time, Your Honour.' Plunkett turned to the two defence attorneys. 'Your witness.'

As the prosecutor sat back down, Joe's barrister, William Foster, came to his feet, to cross-examine. 'Mrs Barker,' Foster began, 'your nephew Joseph Windred's person is well known to you, is it not?'

'Oh, yes.'

'Would you have recognised Windred, had he been one of the robbers?'

'Oh, yes. Joe has a lame foot, which is perfectly visible. I would have recognised him.'

'But you did not recognise Windred as one of the robbers?'

'I did not. Joe is the son of a very respectable inhabitant of Windsor. Joe is a native of the colony, and he has always borne a very good character.'

'Do you know a person named Nichols in Windsor?'

'I do.'

'Could you say that he was *not* one of the members of the robber party?'

'I could not say that Nichols was *not* one of them. One had a musket. It was in the hands of the man who remained at the door.'

Thanking her, Foster resumed his seat.

Plunkett quickly came to his feet to pose Eliza one last question. 'Equally, Mrs Barker, can you swear to this court that all the prisoners in the dock were *not* the parties who took part in the robbery?'

Unhappily, Eliza shook her head. 'I would not swear that they were not the parties.'[12]

Eliza Barker was excused, and the Barkers' servant Thomas Keane was called to the stand.

'Tell the court your recollections of the night of February 18,' said the prosecutor to Keane.

Keane proceeded to tell his side of the story of the robbery, which agreed in all respects with the testimony of Eliza Barker.

In cross-examination, defence counsel Foster asked Keane, 'Do you know Joseph Windred's voice when you hear it?'

'I do, sir.'

'Did you recognise that voice among those of the robbers?'

'No, sir, I did not.' Then Keane had an afterthought. 'The man with the musket appeared to speak Scotch just before they left.'[13]

'He spoke Scotch?' Foster responded, intrigued and pleased. 'Thank you, Mr Keane.'

The prosecutor now called his ace witness, Henry Nichols. Nichols, in his admissions to police, had incriminated himself in relation to the Barker robbery. At the very least, for failing to inform on Robinson after supposedly hearing his description of the Barker robbery the following night, Nichols had left himself open to the charge of being an accessory after the fact. But Nichols had done a deal with the attorney general: in exchange for turning Queen's Evidence and testifying against the four other accused, Nichols was promised a pardon in relation to his role in the Barker robbery.

In legal parlance, Nichols was testifying in this case as an 'approver', or implicated informer. Like Windred, Robinson, Garven and Cheeke, Nichols had been kept in gaol up to this point, although deliberately segregated from the others. For, Cheeke had implicated him in the burglary of the premises of Samuel Ashcroft the tailor, and Nichols still faced charges in that matter. But, with the judge's approval, Nichols would walk out of the court a free man at the end of this trial if the others were convicted of the Barker robbery.

Nichols came into the courtroom and took the stand, but when the clerk of the court held out the Bible and required him to take the oath, he refused to do so.

An unsurprised Attorney General Plunkett asked him, 'Mr Nichols, you do believe in a future state of rewards and punishments?'

'That I do,' Nichols acknowledged.

'Do you know an Andrew Riley, and an Andrew Burge?' It is unclear who these men were. They were possibly prisoners on remand at Sydney Gaol, or gaolers.

'I do.'

'Did you say, within their hearing, that you neither believed in God or devil?'

'I never did, sir,' Nichols retorted. 'No, sir. Never.'

The judge now intervened. 'Witness, do you deny that an oath is binding?'

'No, sir. I do not deny that.'

'The witness may affirm,' Chief Justice Dowling declared.

So, Nichols took the oath to tell the truth without placing his hand on the Bible and without reference to God.

Prosecutor Plunkett now began his questioning. 'What are you?'

'A shoemaker, sir,' Nichols replied.

'And how long have you been in this colony?'

'I have been nine years in New South Wales, sir. I have been free these last two years.' Nichols was exaggerating both figures by several months.

'Do you know all the prisoners in the dock? And how do you come to know them?'

'I do. Robinson and Garven are shoemakers. They work for the same shop as myself.'

'And what of Windred?'

'Windred is a very great friend of Garven's. He has come several times with Garven to my house.'

'Was there card-playing at your house?'

'There was card-playing there. Windred would not play. But I have seen him with a new pack of cards in his pocket.'

'Tell the court what transpired on the night of the robbery.'

'On the night of the robbery, all the prisoners were at my house. They left about eight o'clock. Later, Garven and Windred called and spoke to Robinson.'

'Robinson was there, at the house?'

'He was. He asked if I was planning to sit up long. When I wanted to know why he asked, he said it was because he was going out of town. I told Robinson I was not going to sit up long.'

'Were Garven and Windred present at the time?'

'No, this was some time after I saw Garven and Windred. Windred had on a shirt over his clothes, and Garven had a blue cap on. Robinson went and spoke to them, and then took a stick . . .'

'This stick?' Plunkett had the wooden cudgel that had been found at the scene of the crime and produced in evidence shown to Nichols.

'That's it. He, Robinson, took the stick from some rubbish below the staircase.'

'What were the other two, Garven and Windred, doing, while this was going on?'

'The other two went and stood on a corner, outside, and before they met again Windred went down a lane and returned with a gun on his shoulder.'

'Windred did?'

'He did, sir.'

In the dock, Joe Windred was shaking his head at this.

'What then?'

'They then all went in the direction of the river – that's the way to Mr Barker's. Cheeke asked me if I knew where they were going, and I told him I did not. Cheeke told me they were going to Mr Barker's.'

'What time did they return?'

'About 3.00 a.m., Robinson returned.'

'Did you ask him where he had been?'

'I did. He said, "Not far." I told Robinson I knew where they had been, at Mr Barker's.'

'Did he acknowledge that he had been there, at Mr Barker's?'

'He did, sir. And he said to me, "If I had known as much before I went as I do now, I would not have gone out there." All they got was thirty shillings, and he showed me his share as four half crowns, which he afterwards lost to John the cook, while playing at cards.' Nichols went on to say that he had next day seen Robinson with a pound note, and Robinson had also shown him the other things he had taken from Barker's. 'Eight or nine days later, Windred and Garven came to my house. Robinson was drunk, and had the things in his hat. Windred seeing the watch, he took it, put it in his pocket, and said he would break it or throw it in the river before Robinson should have it.'

'Why would Windred have done that?'

'It was because Robinson was showing the watch about.'

'What name does Robinson go by among his friends?'

'The others call him Paddy. That was the name he was called by when robbing the house.'

'Did you receive any part of the stolen property?'

'Cheeke gave me a brown handkerchief, to make two vests of. That was part of Mr Barker's property, although I did not know it at the time.'

'Did Windred afterwards offer to restore the watch to Robinson?'

'He did, if Robinson would not show it about.'

'Were the others happy with Robinson's actions?'

'No, they were not. They all went out, but when Cheeke returned he told me that Windred and Garven had taken the things out of Robinson's hat while he was asleep, and that they said that Robinson had cheated them out of £3, and that they would keep the bundle and what was in it, for their share.'

Plunkett showed Nichols another Crown exhibit, a silver watch case. 'Have you seen this watch case before?'

'I saw it tumble out of the bundle, thirteen or fourteen days after the robbery.'

'But you had seen it prior to that?'

'Robinson showed me the watch the night after the robbery.'

'This was when he described how the robbery was carried out?'

'It was, sir.'

'What did he tell you about the robbery?'

'He said that Windred wanted them to turn back. But Robinson had said that he'd be damned if he would turn back after going so far. Robinson also told me how they went first to the back, when the dog attacked them. They then went to the front.'

'Who was it who stood sentry over the inmates of the house, with the gun?'

'Robinson made Windred take the gun and stand sentry over the inmates. Garven held the candle, and Robinson plundered the house.'

'Did you receive "hush money", or receive any share of the plunder?'

'I did not, sir.'

'What of the watch case? Tell the court about that.'

'Cheeke returned the case of the watch to Robinson, and on the night when Cheeke was taken, I saw Robinson throw it into the privy [the lavatory], of which I informed the constables, who thereupon searched and found it.'

'Who offered the watch for sale to Norris, Smith and another man? Was that you?'

'No, sir, that was Robinson.'

'I have no further questions of this witness for the present, Your Honour.' With that, Plunkett handed the witness over to the defence.

William Alexander Purefoy, novice attorney for Robinson, Garven and Cheeke, came to his feet to lead the cross-examination of Nichols.

'You told the attorney general that you never offered the watch for sale to Norris, Smith or another man?' Purefoy began. 'Did you never offer the watch for sale to Joseph Perry, nor to the Mr Thomas who lives at Mumford's boarding house?'

'I never did, sir. I never offered Mr Thomas anything but a handkerchief.'

'Tell me, Nichols, if you were to hear of a robbery, would you inform the authorities of it?'

'I would, sir. If it concerned me.'

'Why is it, then, that you gave no information of the Barker robbery until about a fortnight later?'

'That was when I was apprehended for a burglary at Ashcroft's.'

'And you then sent to the chief constable to say that you could give information about another robbery?'

'No, sir, I never did. When I went to the watch-house, I thought that Cheeke had split on me, so I told the watch-house keeper of Barker's robbery.'

'And informed on the prisoners now sitting in the dock. What opinion do you have of the parties in the dock? Are they your friends? Your enemies?'

'I have no opinion of any of them, sir.'

'You turned approver in this case. What do you expect to get out of your testimony here today?'

'Well, sir, I wish to stand my trial for Ashcroft's robbery. But if the judge . . .' He looked around at the grim-faced chief justice. 'If he would let me take a walk first, I would prefer it.'[14] In other words, Nichols was hoping to be pardoned for both the Barker and Ashcroft robberies.

Purefoy now handed the witness over to William Foster and sat back down. Purefoy's questioning of Nichols revealed a lack of preparation for this case. It was not that Purefoy was an incompetent lawyer. In fact, just three months earlier, after securing the acquittal of an accused rapist, Purefoy had been described by the *Sydney Monitor* as 'an orator and logician, and extremely ingenious in twisting into a cord of little strength a few discrepancies of evidence'.[15] But Purefoy was overloaded with criminal cases, and not all his clients could or would receive his fullest attention. Within several years, Purefoy would take the appointment as New South Wales Commissioner of Insolvent Estates, dealing with the cold hard facts of unpaid debts, a far less testing role. Although, he would not leave criminal law behind entirely, as Joe Windred would one day find.

If Joe was to walk from this courtroom a free man, it would not be as a result of anything William Alexander Purefoy did or said. Joe's defence rested solely on the shoulders of his own barrister. And as William Foster came to his feet, Henry Nichols no doubt thought that he had weathered the storm of cross-examination by Mr Purefoy well, while Foster's first, innocuous question might have had him believing that he, too, would be a pushover.

'Where do you live in Windsor?' Foster asked.

'In Fitzgerald Street, sir.'

But now Foster launched into the attack. 'And is it not correct, Nichols, that at your residence in Fitzgerald Street, Windsor, you conducted an illicit gambling house, receiving money from people who gambled there?'

'No, sir!'

'You never received money from people gambling in your house?'

'No, sir, I did not.'

'You never inveigled young men into your house to play cards?'

'No, sir. I did not.'

'What is the favourite card game played in your house?'

'That would be Five and Twenty, sir. But not for money.'

'What is the name of your sister-in-law?'

'She is Jane Whitehead, sir.'

'Are you acquainted with a Frederick Lahrbush, clerk to Mr George Seymour, tanner and currier of Windsor?'

'I know him, yes.'

'And did Lahrbush give you money so as to procure this Jane Whitehead?'

'Mr Lahrbush never gave me money further than to set me up after I had married Elizabeth Whitehead, elder sister to Jane.'

'Did you not receive twelve shillings a week from Lahrbush in return for permission to visit Jane Whitehead?'

'I never did.'

'Is it not true that you have previously managed to escape a charge of horse stealing in this colony, and also one of sheep stealing?'

'I was acquitted in both cases.'

'You have an interesting accent there. What is your native place?'

This sudden change of tack took Nichols by surprise. He thought carefully before answering. 'I am a native of Ireland.'

'A native of Ireland, are you?'

'Yes, sir.'

'Where were you born and raised?'

'I, er, I was born in Scotland. I meant to say that my parents were natives of Ireland.'

'You were born in Scotland. I see. And your accent is therefore, Scottish.' Foster consulted his notes. 'How long have you been married to Elizabeth Whitehead?'

'We have been married these past eighteen months.'

'Your wife has visited you in gaol?'

'She has. She brought me victuals.'

'Have you also been charged with misrepresentation, for changing leather you offered for sale?'

'Yes.'[16]

'No more questions.'

Nichols was allowed to leave the stand, and his young wife was called next to give evidence. When just five years of age, Elizabeth Whitehead had been placed in the Sydney Orphans School, from which Henry Nichols had plucked her when she was sixteen. Since then, Elizabeth's world had revolved around her husband and saviour, for whom she would do and say just about anything.

'Mrs Nichols,' Attorney General Plunkett began, 'how long have you been married to Henry Nichols?'

'We have been wedded nigh on eighteen months. I had been courted about two months by Henry.'

'And you have a child between you?'

'We do, sir. About four months old now.'

'When did you hear of the robbery at Barker's?'

'The day after, sir.'

'In what circumstances?'

'Through the circumstances of Windred accusing Robinson of keeping back some of the swag.'

'Following the robbery, did Robinson make you a present of a pink silk handkerchief?'

'He did, sir, and he told me to be careful of it. On my husband coming in, I showed it to him, and he told me not to keep it, but to give it back. I also saw other things. There was a silver watch. Robinson challenged John Smith to play cards for it.'

Plunkett now handed the witness over to the defence. William Foster cross-examined.

'Mrs Nichols, did you visit your husband in Windsor Gaol?'

'I did.'

'How frequently?'

'I went there between 10.00 a.m. and 5.00 p.m., once a day, and sometimes twice.'

'How often did you speak to your husband in private about the matter currently before this court, to concert your stories?'

'Never.'

'Never?'

'Never.'

'Frederick Lahrbush pays you twelve shillings a week, for your sister, does he not? For what purpose?'

'He does, for my sister's keep. My sister herself receives two pound a week from him.'

'To what do you apply the twelve shillings?'

'To keep the house.'

Foster now handed the witness over to Purefoy, who asked just a single question.

'Mrs Nichols, John Cheeke, one of the accused, lodges with your husband and yourself. Was he out of the house on the night of the Barker robbery?'

'No, sir, he was not.'

Attorney General Plunkett now re-examined Elizabeth Nichols, and in this additional testimony she revealed a tangled web in relation to her younger sister Jane and Jane's relationship with Frederick Lahrbush, a considerably older man. She testified that the girls' mother had been against Lahrbush having anything to do with Jane Whitehead. And when the mother had attempted to separate the pair, Henry Nichols had struck her, after which Nichols had been bound over by a magistrate on a good behaviour bond to keep the peace. Defence counsel Foster had earlier raised this Lahrbush affair in an attempt to blacken Nichols' already muddied name and to destroy his credibility as a Crown witness. Plunkett was getting in first to limit the damage to his case.

Plunkett put his final question to Nichols' wife: 'Did you see your husband at Sydney Gaol on Tuesday last? And, if so, did you speak to him about this case?'

'I did see him then, sir,' she replied. 'But I never spoke to him about this case.'[17]

The prosecution next called Thomas Wilson, the convict employee of Windsor mill owner John Teale. Wilson testified to seeing John Robinson trying to raise money on a silver watch on the Sunday afternoon following the Barker robbery, claiming that he had gone into the Nichols house merely to light his pipe out of the rain.

Joe Windred's counsel swiftly jumped on the latter claim when he had the opportunity to cross-examine Wilson. 'Have you ever played cards, Wilson?' Foster asked.

'I have, sir. At home in England, and once or twice in this colony.'

'Only once or twice in this colony? I see. You are a convicted felon undergoing a sentence of seven years' transportation. How should this court look upon your honesty?'

'I was sent out here for seven years for my health, sir, not my honesty.' This reply generated laughter and smiles in the gallery and jury box.

'Indeed? Are you familiar with a card game called All Fours?'

'I know it, sir.'

'How often did you play that game at Henry Nichols' house?'

Gambling was illegal in the colony. Were Wilson to admit to playing cards for money, he could expect to be prosecuted for it. 'Never, sir,' he answered.

'Never? I see. Pertaining to your honesty, were you not suspected by your master, Mr John Teale, of robbing him at one time?'

'I was, sir. I turned approver and let my companions in for it.'

'You informed on your accomplices, in return for a pardon?'

'If I had not done, so, sir, they would have let me in for it.'[18]

Wilson was excused, and Thomas Bevan was called by the Crown. A former convict, now with a Ticket of Leave allowing him to live free in the Windsor district, young Bevan was employed as a servant by James Cullen, Joe Windred's uncle. Both Bevan and Joe Windred lived under James Cullen's roof. Bevan testified that on the night of the Barker robbery he had gone to Henry Nichols' house to be measured for a pair of shoes. He said that he had stayed to play All Fours with Nichols, his wife, and John Cheeke. About 10.00 p.m., he said, John Robinson had come in. 'Robinson asked Nichols if he could guess what it cost him for the woman he had been with all evening. Nichols could not guess. Robinson said it had cost him three half crowns, but it would cost him another shilling to get rid of the woman.' This produced more laughter.

Notably, Bevan did not corroborate Nichols' testimony that Garven and Windred had stood on a corner outside while Robinson searched for a wooden club, and this troubled the prosecutor. 'Windred is in the same service as yourself, at Cullen's, is he not?'

'Yes, sir.'

'Did you see Windred on the night of the Barker robbery?'

'Yes, sir. He was present with myself at the Cullen house at tea time. Joe has always been treated as a member of the Cullen family.'

This information, favourable to Joe, would not have pleased Prosecutor Plunkett. 'Did you see Windred and Hogan alias Garven in company that evening?'

'Yes, sir.'

'Where? At the Nichols house?'

'I saw them at the theatre, sir, early in the evening. I thought that Joe went later to Parramatta for his master, Mr Cullen, with cattle, about the time of the robbery,' said Bevan, doing his best to help Joe.

Foster, in cross-examining Bevan, asked, 'Where is the Windsor theatre?'

'In the military barracks, sir. It is open once a fortnight.'

'Is Joseph Windred's family well-off?'

'Joe is known to have a wealthy father, sir. But I never saw Joe flush with cash.'

'The prisoner Windred is trusted by Mr Cullen to convey his stock to market?'

'Oh, yes, sir, he is trusted to convey them.'

'And Mrs Cullen is Windred's aunt, his mother's sister?'

'That's so, sir.'

'Have you ever seen young Windred at Nichols' playing cards?'

'Never, sir. Nichols would invite you to play. He invited me to do so. But Joe never played.'

'What time did you leave the Nichols house on the night of the robbery?'

'The only mark I made of the time was about 11.00. On going home from Nichols', I asked Mr Ridge the publican if the coach had gone in, and he said it had just gone.'

'The Sydney coach leaves Ridges' public house at 11.00 p.m.?'

'That it does, sir,' Bevan acknowledged.[19] Two four-horse English-style stage coaches, the 'Victoria' and the 'Greyhound', started several times a day from the front door of Richard Ridge's pub, the Horse and Jockey Inn on George Street, to make the run from Windsor to Sydney and back. Since the Barker robbery, Ridge had purchased the coaches from the estate of their late previous owner, George Seymour of Parramatta, and he was now operating the coach line himself.

The Crown next called Windsor watch-house keeper John Horan. From him, the court heard that after Henry Nichols had been arrested in connection with the Ashcroft burglary he had told the watch-house keeper that Cheeke, Robinson and Garven were responsible for the Barker robbery, later adding Joe Windred to the list. Horan also told of how Nichols had led constables to the outside lavatories from which he produced items stolen in both robberies, 'in a matter of seconds'.

William Foster, in cross-examining Watch-house Keeper Horan, asked: 'Do you know the accused, Joseph Windred junior?'

'I do, sir.'

'How would you characterise young Joe Windred?'

'Joe is a very quiet, decent young man, as far as he is known to me. And I have known him from when he was a child.'

'How would you describe the friends that Joe Windred normally keeps?'

'To my knowledge, sir, his friends are all respectable people.'[20]

Only now did Prosecutor Plunkett call Joe's uncle, John Barker, one of the victims of the crime, having quite deliberately left him well down his list of witnesses, knowing that he was sympathetic to Joe.

'Mr Barker,' Plunkett asked him once he had taken the stand, 'are you in the habit of keeping money in the house?'

'Sometimes I am,' Barker replied. 'About a month before the robbery, I received £60 for wool.'

'Was your nephew Joseph Windred junior aware that you had sold that wool?'

'Joe had no more opportunity of knowing I had sold the wool than any other person,' said Barker, defending Joe.

When Plunkett showed him the silver watch case tendered in evidence, Barker was unable to identify it as his. The watch itself had not been located.

William Foster eagerly cross-examined. 'Mr Barker, how would you describe the general character of your nephew Joseph Windred junior?'

'His general character is that of honesty and industry.'

'Do you know Henry Nichols?'

'I do not.'

'How long have you known Joseph Windred junior?'
'Ever since he was a child.'
'You trusted him?'
'Oh, yes. A few years ago I trusted Joe to draw money from the bank for me, and to hold it, for some days altogether.'
'Without incident?'
'Without incident.'
'What do you know of the company your nephew keeps?'
'I know nothing of the company he keeps.'[21]

Watchmaker Robert Stewart was next called by the Crown. He was unable to say whether the watch case produced in evidence belonged to the Dublin watch he had repaired for John Barker.

Frederick Lahrbush followed the watchmaker onto the stand. Born in Berlin, a soldier and later a mariner, Lahrbush had been transported from the Cape Colony in South Africa to New South Wales in 1828, later receiving a Ticket of Leave. He told the court that he expected to any day receive his certificate of freedom. Lahrbush testified that John Robinson had attempted to sell him various items, but not a watch, and he could not say with confidence that Eliza Barker's silk shawl presented in evidence had been among those items.

Under cross-examination by Purefoy, Lahrbush admitted that Henry Nichols had been present when he had been offered the items by Robinson. Nichols, he said, was a firm friend of his, and Lahrbush now went to great lengths to protect him, denying any improper relationship involving payment of money to Nichols in return for sharing the company of Jane Whitehead. He said, of Nichols' sister-in-law, 'I have had it in mind to marry her, and I was anxious to see her properly kept. I wanted to help her, as she is a poor girl.'[22]

The Crown now recalled Joe Windred's Aunt Eliza.

'Now, Mrs Barker,' said the attorney general, who was determined to link Joe to the robbery, 'clarify for the court, if you will – your nephew, the prisoner Windred, he was present at your house on the morning of the robbery, was he not?'

'Yes, he was present about half an hour that morning,' Eliza replied, before hurrying to add, 'he called for a horse, for his master, Mr Cullen, and took it away.'[23]

Plunkett now recalled Henry Nichols to the stand.

'Mr Nichols, do you recall, on the morning after the robbery, seeing the prisoner Windred mounted on a horse?'

Nichols replied that he remembered it well, and told of how Joe had come looking for Robinson and followed him about the town, putting questions to him, while still on the horse's back. He also recalled that, after Robinson had left Freeman's public house that morning, he had overheard Garven arguing with him about £3 and 30 shillings. Nichols denied accompanying Robinson when Robinson offered to sell various items to Lahrbush, and denied receiving twelve shillings a week from Lahrbush. After Nichols wove a complicated tale about his dealings with Lahrbush and Jane Whitehead, the Crown closed its case.[24]

6

THE VERDICT

Friday, May 8–Saturday, May 9, 1840. Sydney, New South Wales

THE TRIAL HAD LASTED through luncheon and dinner adjournments. It was well into the evening by the time the defence counsels delivered their closing arguments.

William Foster, for Joe Windred, spoke first. Foster reminded the jury of the evidence they had heard relating to his client and the crime. In particular, he drew their attention to the evidence of Joe Windred's aunt, Mrs Barker, and her servant Thomas Keane. According to Henry Nichols, Joe Windred had been the robber armed with the gun. Both Mrs Barker and Thomas Keane had testified that the robber with the gun had spoken a good deal on the night of the robbery. Both also testified that they knew Joe Windred's voice. Yet, neither had recognised the voice of the robber with the gun as that of Joe Windred. What was more, Mrs Barker had testified that Joe Windred had walked with a limp since childhood, yet neither she nor Keane had seen any of the robbers limping. Not only had Mrs Barker failed to incriminate Joe Windred, both she and her husband, the victims in the case, had gone to pains to characterise Joe as an affectionate nephew and an honest boy they loved and trusted.

As Foster was to point out to the jury, all the testimony incriminating Windred had come from Henry Nichols. It was Nichols who had put Joe at the scene of the robbery, and put the gun in Joe's hands. Nichols had said that, on the night of the robbery, Robinson had come in at 11.00, with Garven and Windred close behind. Thomas Bevan had contradicted that testimony by saying that Robinson had come in about 10.00, and Garven and Windred had not been mentioned. Other than Nichols, nobody put Joe Windred anywhere near the scene of the crime at the time of the robbery. It was clear that Joe had eaten at Cullen's around 5.00, and had attended the theatre with his best friend Garven at 8.00. His only fault was in not being able to produce a witness who could say that he was snugly tucked up in bed at Cullen's at midnight, when the robbery was taking place.

If Joe Windred had not been the man with the gun on the night of the robbery, as he clearly was not, then who was? It had been established that Cheeke was not that third man. Eliza Barker's servant Thomas Keane had told the court that, just as the robber band was departing the Barker house, the third man, the man with the gun, had spoken 'Scotch'. Was it not interesting that Henry Nichols spoke with an accent acquired while growing up in Scotland? Nichols clearly had a role in the robbery. He had admitted to being an accessory after the fact, and there was strong circumstantial evidence to make him the man with the gun on the night, the man in charge. Thomas Bevan had testified that he had last seen Nichols just prior to 11.00. The robbery had begun about midnight. Nichols and his two accomplices could easily have covered the distance on foot from the Nichols house in Windsor to Sefton Cottage in an hour. Yet, the prosecutor had persisted in persecuting innocent young Joe Windred, in Nichols' place, painting him as the betrayer of the trust of his own aunt and uncle.

'Gentlemen of the jury,' Foster concluded, 'I contend that there is not a tittle of evidence that goes to affect my client which has not been successfully impeached. Not a tittle! I would also call your attention to the fact that none of the property produced by the prosecutor has been linked to that stolen from Mr and Mrs Barker. Nor has the prosecutor been able to connect the prisoner in any way with the robbery.' On that basis, he said, the jury could only have one option, that of acquitting his client.[25]

W. A. Purefoy followed Foster with a forensic examination of the evidence against his three clients, pointing out numerous discrepancies in the testimony. It all came back to the approver, Henry Nichols, he said. Without Nichols' testimony, the case fell to pieces. Yet, how reliable a witness was a man who had faced numerous criminal charges, who had been found guilty of assaulting his wife's mother, and who, even though the Crown had agreed to pardon him for any part he had played in the Barker robbery, at this moment faced burglary and fraud charges in other cases soon to come before the court? What sort of a man was this, what colonial Fagin was this approver whom the prosecutor chose to shield, a man who would sell the body of his wife's sister for a few shillings' profit?

'Gentlemen of the jury,' Purefoy wound up, 'I call on you to consider well: Is not the approver in this case the most depraved character that has ever entered a witness-box?'[26]

Now came the turn of the judge to address the jury. Sir James Dowling's summing up lasted several hours. He informed the jury of the fine points of the law as it affected the evidence of approvers, and that of other witnesses. And he went through the evidence tendered against the prisoners, in detail. It was 12.30 in the morning when he concluded by saying, 'Members of the jury, I have pointed out such circumstances as tend to circumstantially connect the prisoners with the crime with which they are charged. I leave it to you to determine whether the approver, Nichols, has been so far corroborated to entitle him to belief. You may now retire to consider your verdict.'[27]

Despite the fact that it was now the early hours of the morning, the judge clearly anticipated that the jury would come to a swift verdict in this case. In some cases lately decided in the Supreme Court, the juries had literally been out for five minutes before returning with their verdict. So, now the jury retired to the jury room, the judge resorted to his chambers, the prisoners were taken back to the courthouse cells, and the exhausted attorneys, court officers and gallery sat and waited.

When, by 2.00 a.m., the jury had not returned, the judge recalled them to the courtroom. As the jury box populated with weary jurors, the prisoners were returned to the dock. Sir James Dowling was in poor health, which would not be improved by the long hours he imposed on himself. Impatient now, he demanded to know whether the jury had agreed on a verdict.

'No, Your Honour,' replied the foreman of the jury. 'And we are not likely to agree.'

'And why not, may I ask?' snorted the judge, indignant that his guidance had apparently been ignored by some jurymen.

'Several of the members of the jury are of the opinion that neither the property nor the prisoners have been so identified as to warrant us in returning a verdict of "guilty", Your Honour.'

Chief Justice Dowling glowered at the foreman. This impasse had several potential solutions. The judge might discharge the jury and order a retrial. But he was obliged to give this jury every opportunity to agree on a verdict before he went down that road. Besides, to Dowling, the verdict was blatantly obvious. And he had a backlog of cases to try. Determined to expedite a verdict in this case, the judge took a drastic step. An authoritarian step. For, he had no intention of discharging this jury before they reached a verdict. 'I must, under these circumstances,' he growled, 'order you to be locked up until you *do* agree.'[28]

The judge sent the stunned jury back to the jury room, appointing two constables to stand guard over the door, then adjourned the sitting until 10.00 that morning.

As 10.00 a.m. Saturday approached, Sophia and Joseph Windred senior joined other members of the public filing back into the courtroom, to take their seats and wait for their son's trial to resume.

Outside the courtroom that morning, a reporter from the *Australasian Chronicle* spoke with a number of people who had sat through the trial the previous day. He would write, in his paper's Tuesday edition, 'Some doubts arose as to whether the prisoner Windred was really present at the robbery, and from the very minute and circumstantial description of the affair by the witness Nichols it was the opinion of many that he was himself more actively engaged in the transaction than he was willing to acknowledge.'[29] Sophia and Joe senior could only hope that the jury would feel the same way.

By 10.00, the judge, opposing counsel, court officers, the four prisoners, and the members of the gallery were back in their places. Sir James now sent a message asking the jury whether they had agreed on a verdict. A reply came back that the jury had still not agreed, nor were they likely to agree. But, the note from the foreman went on to say that the jury wished to ask His Honour a question. So, Dowling sent for the jurors, and they all trooped in and took their seats.

The foreman then put his question. 'We would like to request that Your Honour go over that part of the evidence that refers to the identity of the prisoners as the parties who committed the robbery.'

Dowling was a master of shorthand, and made a point of noting down the testimony given before him. As a result, he was able to read aloud the relevant testimony in this case from his notes, for the benefit of the jury. Once he had done this, the jurors briefly consulted, after which their foreman asked, 'Could we also request that Your Honour also read over the evidence as to the identity of the property?'

Exasperated, the judge read selected passages regarding the stolen property. By 10.30, the readings had been completed. Laying his notes aside, Dowling scowled at the foreman. 'Well?'

Again, the jury briefly engaged in whispered consultation, before the foreman said, 'We shall not trouble Your Honour any further. We have come to a verdict.'[30]

A buzz ran through the gallery. In the dock, Joe Windred tensed. Like the reporter from the *Australasian Chronicle*, he was confident that much doubt had been raised in the minds of most of those in the courtroom the previous day – about Nichols' testimony, and about whether he, Joe, had really been present at the robbery. The jury briefly withdrew, and when they returned a few minutes later the foreman handed the clerk of the court a piece of paper on which he had written the verdict of the jury.

The piece of paper was handed by the clerk to the judge, who, stone-faced, read it, then said, 'The prisoners will rise.'

Joe, Garven, Robinson and Cheeke all came to their feet and faced the judge.

'Members of the jury,' said the clerk in a raised voice. 'In the matter before this court, how say you? Are the prisoners guilty, or not guilty?'

The foreman of the jury cleared his throat. 'We find the prisoner Joseph Windred junior, guilty as charged.'

Many in the gallery let out a gasp of surprise.

'However,' the foreman added, 'we recommend Windred for

mercy, as we believe him to have been entrapped into the crime by Nichols. The prisoners Garven and Robinson we find guilty as charged. The prisoner Cheeke, as to the first charge, we find him not guilty; as to the second charge, that of receiving stolen goods, we find him guilty.'[31]

Chief Justice Dowling thanked and discharged the jury, then adjourned the sitting until Monday, May 18, when he would pass sentence on the four now-convicted felons.

Stunned, Joe tramped back to Sydney Gaol in chains. Everything had pointed to a verdict of not guilty in his case. His conviction was almost entirely the result of Henry Nichols' uncorroborated evidence – often hearsay evidence, at that. What was more, the jury had twice said it was unable to agree on a verdict, showing that some jurymen felt Joe to be innocent. If the judge had not intimidated the jury into reaching a verdict with his threat to keep them locked up until they did so, Joe would have been looking at a fresh trial.

Joe's conviction was all the more surprising considering the fact that the victims in the case, his aunt and uncle, had testified in his favour. This fact did not escape the attention of the court reporter from the *Sydney Monitor*. In its following Thursday's edition, under the headline, 'An Affectionate Nephew', the *Monitor* would point out this glaring discrepancy: 'The most extraordinary part of the matter is that the man and his wife both gave Windred an excellent character as a well-behaved and honest young man.'[32]

Joe was not the first innocent man to be convicted of a crime he did not commit. Nor would he be the last. The best he could hope for was a lenient sentence, with the jury's recommendation for mercy lending weight to that hope. Besides, Joe's mother and father had gone to great lengths to organise a petition which spoke of Joe's previously unblemished character and fine personal qualities, and of his father's now respectable position in the community. This had been handed over to Chief Justice Dowling by attorney Foster, with the expectation that the judge would take it into consideration when deciding the sentence he would hand down to Joe.

Come Monday week, Joe would know his fate.

7

THE SENTENCE

Monday, May 18, 1840. Sydney, New South Wales

THE EARLY MORNING RASP of the turnkey's voice summoned six men from their Sydney Gaol cells. Apart from Joe, Garven, Robinson and Cheeke, two other convicted prisoners were being sent up the street to the Supreme Court this morning to hear their sentences read. All six were chained together for a 'general gaol delivery'.

Both of these other men were named James, and both had been convicted of the same horse-stealing crime. The older man, James Froud, had come out to New South Wales as a convict in 1827, later being granted his freedom. In contrast, the younger man, James Warner, was the son of highly respected Lake Macquarie magistrate Jonathan Warner, a former army lieutenant, now successful farmer, after whom Warner's Bay was named. Young Warner, well-educated and from a prosperous and influential 'Fancy' family, was apparently confident that, despite his horse-stealing conviction, he could escape the full force of the law. For, just as Joe's parents had worked assiduously behind the scenes to provide him with a strong character reference, Warner's parents had provided the chief justice with impressive references for their boy.

While Warner and Froud waited in the courthouse cells for their turn at sentencing, just after 10.00 a.m. Joe, Garven, Robinson and Cheeke were brought into the Supreme Court. Once again, Joe's parents were in the gallery.

Chief Justice Dowling sat with sentencing documents in front of him. 'Windred, Garven and Robinson,' he gravely began, 'you have been convicted of stealing in a dwelling house, and putting the inmates in bodily fear for their lives, all of you being armed at the time. John Cheeke, you have been convicted as an accessory to the crime. I have paid every attention to the recommendation of the jury in favour of the prisoner Windred. It is my belief that he had been entrapped through the machinations of some heartless and designing villains.'

Just as things were sounding positive for Joe, the judge's tone changed.

'But,' Dowling continued gravely, 'Windred committed the robbery upon his own aunt. His own aunt!' Dowling scowled censoriously across the courtroom at Joe before returning his attention to the paperwork. 'A petition presented to me states only that his father has been a respectable tradesman in Windsor, and spoke also of the character of the prisoner. All well and good, but I feel bound to observe that Garven, convicted of the same crime, is at least free from the imputation of having plundered those with whom he is related!'

There was an uneasy shuffling of feet in the gallery.

Dowling resumed, 'I regret that so many youths have been convicted, but I must make an example, to deter others from crimes of a similar nature. Accordingly, I feel bound to give the prisoners a warning for their future guidance.' He proceeded to deliver a sermon on the need to tread the path of honesty and industry. It was a sermon lost on deaf ears. Several of the young men in the dock were beyond redemption, the others were gripped by fear and dread as they awaited their sentences.

Finally, the chief justice read out the sentence of each. 'Joseph Windred junior, you are sentenced to ten years transportation to Van Diemen's Land. Andrew Garven, alias Hogan, you are likewise sentenced to ten years transportation to Van Diemen's Land. John Robinson, you are an incorrigible, and you will spend fifteen years at the Norfolk Island penal establishment. John Cheeke, you are to serve two years in gaol, to be worked in irons. Take them down.'[33]

Joe was in shock. So much for the jury's recommendation that he receive the judge's mercy! The chief justice was certainly not in a merciful mood this particular day. It was as if the judge had taken a personal dislike to Joe, as if a crime perpetrated against an aunt had a special resonance for Sir James Dowling. So much, too, for the petition and character reference presented to the judge on Joe's behalf. It had apparently not altered Dowling's opinion of him one iota.

Joe, Garven, Robinson and Cheeke were kept in the courthouse cells until James Warner and James Froud were also sentenced. All six were then chained together for the return to the city gaol. When Joe inquired how Warner and Froud had fared with the chief justice, he was in for another surprise. Froud had been sentenced to ten years, to be served, like John Robinson, on Norfolk Island. Yet, Warner, convicted of perpetrating the very same crime, had been given just twelve months in Newcastle Gaol by Chief Justice Dowling.

Sir James had said, in handing down Warner's sentence, 'I cannot express how sorry I am to see before me a young man, who, by all accounts, is the son of a gentleman of rank and influence. From a petition which has been presented, signed by many influential gentlemen, I am induced to ameliorate the sentence I should otherwise have been compelled to pass.'

The evidence presented in the Warner–Froud case had shown that Warner was an equal partner in the crime, and probably even its instigator. The jury in this case had been so convinced of the pair's criminality they had been out literally for five minutes before delivering their verdict that both men were guilty, and equally so. Chief Justice Dowling chose to differ, declaring, as he passed sentence: 'It appears that Warner has been merely the tool of a regular, established set of thieves.'[34]

How strange, Joe Windred would have thought, that the same judge had considered that he, Joe, had been similarly 'entrapped through the machinations of some heartless and designing villains', yet had still overlooked the jury's recommendation for mercy to deliver Joe a harsh sentence. And here was Warner with twelve months to serve, close to home and family, while Joe had ten years in faraway Van Diemen's Land to look forward to.

Sir James Dowling had made a blatant distinction between Warner, son of 'a gentleman of rank and influence', and Joe, son of a tradesman. In the years to come, that distinction would be enough to drive young Joe Windred, a man convicted of a crime he did not commit, to seek to make himself a man of rank and influence. For now, there was the small matter of serving and surviving a ten-year sentence in the dreaded penal colony of Van Diemen's Land, the future Tasmania. In July, Joe would be taken from Sydney Gaol to Circular Quay, and there be loaded in chains aboard the brig *Abercrombie* for the voyage to Van Diemen's Land. Andrew Garven, alias Hogan, would join Joe for the voyage, likewise in chains. But Joe wanted nothing more to do with the Irish thief who had contributed to his loss of freedom.

8

JOE'S BIG FIGHT

Monday, December 30, 1844. Outside Richmond, New South Wales

THE SUN HAD BARELY risen when the roads to the location outside Richmond set down for the last heavyweight fight of the year were clogged with traffic. One of the contestants was the celebrated Ben Mortimer, Richmond's local hero and unbeaten champion. The other, a veritable unknown, was billed as both Young Windred and the Windsor Tanner. Joe Windred junior, only back from Van Diemen's Land a matter of months, was ready to claim more than his share of rank and influence, using his fists. Without a wealthy gentleman for a father, Joe had chosen to enter the arena where winners were, and are, hailed as gods by their fellow Australians – the sporting arena.

Joe's ten-year sentence had been terminated after just four years with a free pardon signed on May 11 by James Bicheno, Colonial Secretary of Van Diemen's Land. Joe had soon found his way back home to Windsor, returning a very different young man, physically and emotionally, from the one convicted in 1840. The first six months of his sentence had been spent in chains in a road gang. It had been relentlessly physical work, and the discipline had been strict. Just the same, Joe managed to sneak out of his hut one night, apparently to meet a young lady. Caught out of his quarters, he was sentenced to a month's hard labour in a quarry gang, breaking rocks. He was only in trouble on one other occasion during his sentence, in December 1842 spending six hours in the stocks for insubordination. Joe had subsequently applied himself to his work, impressing his keepers sufficiently for them to recommend him for a pardon in the autumn of 1844.

Joe's four years in Van Diemen's Land had toughened him up. No longer a naive youth, he was now a twenty-two-year-old adult. Never again would he give his trust easily. Handsome of face, he had grown to stand over six feet tall. Chain-gang work had developed his shoulders and biceps so that he was a powerful-looking though lean figure of eleven stone seven pounds (72.6 kilograms), with not an ounce of fat on his body.

On his return to Windsor, Joe had hoped to regain employment with his uncle James Cullen. But, despite the fact that the Barkers and Joe's parents were all convinced that Joe had been innocent of the 1840 robbery, Cullen wouldn't have a convicted felon under his roof. So, Joe's father took him into his tannery business, training him to tan hides. Joe senior was doing well; well enough to move out of rented premises in 1842 while Joe was in Van Diemen's Land and into a cottage built with his own hands in Windsor, at 29 North Street – a street named after the 'beak', or police magistrate, who had committed Joe junior for trial in 1840. Joe senior was proud of his cottage, with its sandstock bricks on a sandstone foundation and boasting handsome sandstone lintels and sills. This, Joe senior declared, would do him for the rest of his days.

But Joe junior wanted more than a tanner's stinking, dirty existence. Not for him his father's stained hands and permanent perfume of ammonia. Not for him a simple cottage beside the flood-prone Hawkesbury. Impatient to make up four lost years and prove his worth, Joe was determined to make a name for himself, to blot out the humiliations he had experienced because of lying, thieving Henry Nichols – who was currently serving a fourteen-year sentence for the Ashcroft burglary, which was some satisfaction to young Joe.

Joe's return to Windsor coincided with a blossoming of the pugilistic art in New South Wales. Strictly speaking, prize fighting and wagering money on any form of sport were illegal. But policemen and magistrates were not only turning a blind eye to professional boxing, some 'blues and beaks', as they were known colloquially, were to be seen in the big crowds that attended the fights in and around Sydney.

Windsor had given boxing a number of talented competitors in earlier decades. Joe's Uncle Tom Dargin, who had died just the previous year, had been one of them. When Joe's maternal grandfather Thomas Dargin senior was running Windsor's Red Lion Inn, Uncle Tom had competed in rollicking but illegal bare-knuckle bouts on the premises, being briefly jailed in 1821 as a result of one such bout. It was no doubt pointed out to young Joe that he had developed the build for boxing while in Van Diemen's Land, and that big purses of £50 a bout and more were on offer for those who stepped into the ring and came out victorious.

Joe had needed little convincing. He had gone into training with a Windsor local, old George Cupitt from Derbyshire, another who had shown talent with his fists when young. Cupitt's pugilistic protégés included his own son, the Windsor-born George junior. As Joe devoted every spare moment to training after toiling in the tannery, friends and family pitched in to put up the £50 he would need to lay down a challenge to a professional. Ben Mortimer was happy to accept the challenge from the novice and put down his £50, winner take all, for a bout following the year's Christmas festivities.

An excited journalist from *Bell's Life in Sydney and Sporting Reviewer* came along to report on the Mortimer–Windred fight. His paper actively encouraged professional fighting – but not the illegal gambling that accompanied it – and published lengthy reports of the better bouts. 'The various roads leading to the action were completely lined with pedestrians and vehicles, to witness what they fully expected to be a downright good mill,' the *Bell's Life* man would exuberantly report of this event. 'From the swell in his natty rig and rum trotter to the old Hawkesbury settler in his humble drag or mounted on his old favourite.'[35]

A boxing ring had been set up in a field, with the ground cleared, corner posts pounded into the earth the regulation twenty-four feet apart, and ropes strung from post to post. 'The situation where the ring was pitched was truly picturesque and delightful,' reported *Bell's Life*, 'commanding one uninterrupted view of the highly cultivated and fertile districts of Richmond and the Kurrajong, with the Blue

Mountains in the distance.'[36] No seating was provided. The hundreds of audience members stood around the ring. And no admission was charged. Profit for the organisers would come from wagers laid on the fight.

The experienced Mortimer was firm favourite, although Joe was well fancied by the large band of supporters who accompanied him from Windsor, among them Joe's father and younger brothers William, John (known as Jack), Henry and Charles. Joe's mother, Sophia, wasn't here. Apart from the fact that women never attended boxing matches in these times, Sophia seems not to have approved of her boy taking up this damaging sport. Ever since Joe's wrongful conviction for the Barker robbery, Sophia and Joe senior had become increasingly estranged. It's possible that Sophia blamed her husband's criminal background for her eldest boy's conviction. And, while Joe had been in Van Diemen's Land, too, his ten-year-old brother, Richard, had died, creating further strain between his parents. Even though young Joe would do just about anything to please his mother, he was determined to make a name for himself in the ring.

Joe and his opponent Mortimer both arrived for their bout equipped with the required boxing rig of the day. This comprised tight-fitting calico knee-breeches that were tied at the knee with blue ribbon, and shoes that were soft and light. Plus, importantly, mufflers, lightly padded leather boxing mitts, which, according to *Bell's Life in Sydney*, were buckled at the wrist. There were still brawling bare-knuckle fights in Australia's back blocks, but the organisers of the professional boxing circuit that had recently developed around Sydney, Parramatta, Richmond and Windsor considered their sport civilised, as the use of boxing gloves was intended to show. On the other hand, the fact that prize fights were not limited in their duration, that some bouts lasted for hours and ran over more than a hundred bloody rounds, was used by the sport's detractors as proof that prize fighting was far from civilised.

For today's contest, the organisers provided the necessary 'officials' – a referee, a timekeeper and marshals, men with long sticks whose job it was to keep the ring clear of interlopers. Each man came to the match with several 'seconds'. Joe's seconds were his trainer George Cupitt and Frank Norris, an up-and-coming fighter just a year older than Joe who was also trained by Cupitt.

Before the early morning fight began, a coin was tossed to decide the choice of red or blue corner. Where an outdoor ring was set up east–west, the man coming out of the east corner had the advantage of the rising sun behind him, which could hamper his opponent's vision. But, where it was north–south, as it was today, there was no advantage to either man. Once the toss decided corners, the combatants tied large handkerchiefs in the colour of their corner around their waists.

To the cheers and applause of the animated crowd, Joe climbed into the ring at 8.10 a.m., followed by Cupitt and Norris. Stripped to the waist, Joe looked impressively muscular and fit. A deafening roar greeted Mortimer when, not long after, he and his seconds made their entry. Wearing a white shirt tucked into his breeches, Mortimer, shorter and bulkier than Joe, had a weight advantage. To counter this, Joe had the reach advantage. In the crowd, turf accountants were offering keen odds on Mortimer winning. Young Windred, despite his powerful frame, had been seen limping slightly as he arrived on the scene, convincing many that he would simply provide Mortimer with sparring practice before succumbing to a knockout blow. Although, uncertain of the stamina of the Windsor boy, no one was prepared to predict the round in which Mortimer would triumph.

The combatants met in the middle of the ring, where the referee reminded them of the rules. These were a colonial combination of the eighteenth-century Broughton Rules and the London Prize Rules of 1839 – this was some years prior to the Queensberry Rules. The combatants were not permitted to hit or grasp below the waist. Nor were they allowed to hit a man while he was down, or to kick, gouge, butt or bite. With no time limit to the contest, a winner would be decided when one or other of the contestants could not, or would not, continue the fight. Joe and Mortimer came to centre-ring and shook gloved hands.

'All out!' called the marshals, shepherding the seconds from the ring, before making their own departure. Joe stood facing Mortimer, mitts raised, his stance balanced, and looking coolly into his opponent's eyes.

'Box!' called the referee.

The pair began to circle the ring, offering feints, looking for an opening. It quickly became apparent that Joe's lame foot was no impediment. He was perfectly balanced, and surprisingly agile. Blows began to connect. Mortimer swung a left which collected Joe's right eye. Joe countered with a left which snapped Mortimer's head back. The crowd roared. Mortimer, surprised by the power of Joe's blow, pulled him into a clinch, then wrestled him to the ground. Under the rules, a round ended when one or both boxers went down.

Both men returned to their corners, their seconds hurrying through the ropes to join them. In Joe's corner, Frank Norris dropped to one knee so that the upper part of his other leg projected, flat, like a seat. Joe sat on Norris' leg while old George Cupitt stood fanning his face with a towel and offering advice on how to avoid Mortimer's left in future.

The timekeeper, consulting his fob watch, yelled, 'Time!'

Joe rose up. His seconds slipped through the ropes. Hostilities resumed. This round lasted much longer than the first, with a lengthy exchange of blows. The counterblows had most effect, with Joe several times hitting Mortimer on the face. But, according to the reporter from *Bell's Life*, Mortimer's face was so tough that not even paint would stick to it. In contrast, Mortimer planted a right on Joe's left eye, causing a cut which bled profusely. The pair traded punch for punch. Mortimer dragged Joe into a clinch, then wrenched him off his feet, sending Windsor's hope tumbling to the ground and ending the round. In his corner, Cupitt applied ointment to staunch the blood from Joe's cut eye, and urged his boxer not to let his opponent open it up again. Easier said than done.

A long, even third round ended with Mortimer hitting Joe a blow to the temple which floored him, after which Joe staggered back to his corner. As Cupitt dowsed Joe's face with a bucket of water, the bookmakers were yelling their latest odds, offering £5 to £3 against Joe. But, in the fourth round, Joe turned the tables, scoring freely to the head with the left hand before knocking Mortimer down for the first time.

Round five began with Mortimer, whose pride had been hurt by the knockdown, charging Joe and letting go with a wheeling right. Joe merely stepped out of his way. After several ineffectual rallies, Joe hit Mortimer squarely on the jaw. The punch staggered Mortimer, who again pulled Joe into a clinch. In the wrestle that followed, both men fell, with Joe on top. The *Bell's Life* reporter went to Mortimer's corner at the end of this round. Studying the champion, the newspaperman saw no blood, but Mortimer's face was swelling up.

With round six, Mortimer again began by letting go powerful rights and lefts. But Joe produced new tactics, dodging, weaving and rocking back out of range, so that each punch missed its mark. In turn, Joe planted two heavy blows in the ribs that made Mortimer grimace. A long exchange followed, before Mortimer went down, apparently to get a rest. Round seven was more even, with heavy hits exchanged as the pair stood toe-to-toe. George Cupitt was yelling for Joe to move, but, too late. Joe took a blow to the jaw which knocked him off balance. But, as he fell, Joe let rip with a punch to the side which was so powerful it drove Mortimer through the ropes. The crowd roared, and the *Bell's Life* reporter began to think that Joe might just pull off the fight.

Round eight saw Mortimer come out swinging once more. His haymaking right missed, as did three desperate-looking lefts. Joe countered with a right below the ribcage which momentarily doubled Mortimer up. Straightening, the champion glared at Joe, then rushed him. Joe nimbly side-stepped, hitting Mortimer a glancing blow to the head as he passed, which grounded him.

Between rounds, the bookmakers were offering new odds: '£5 to £3 on a win by Windred.'

With the ninth round, Joe fended off a right with his left arm, then hit Mortimer in the lower body once more, having learned that this was his weak spot. In obvious pain, Mortimer pulled Joe to him, and both fell heavily against a neutral post. Mortimer was slow coming to his feet, and had to be led to his corner by the referee. *Bell's Life* reported, 'On being led to the second's knee, Mortimer was much distressed.'

Joe's friends and family members were hoping Mortimer wouldn't come out for another round, but he would not surrender. Out he came, though wheezing. 'The superior length, strength and science of the young tanner was quite apparent,' said *Bell's Life*, but Mortimer had more courage than sense. A left to the face staggered him. A right to the body buckled him. Charging Joe like a wounded bull, Mortimer drove them both to the ground, with Joe underneath.

'£10 to £5 on the tanner,' called the odds-makers.

The next round was brief, with Mortimer missing with rights and lefts as Joe danced out of range. In return, three jabs struck Mortimer on the face. Closing in, Joe dropped his opponent to the ground. Still Mortimer came back for more, opening round twelve with his characteristic rush. As Joe side-stepped, he caught Mortimer with a hook to the left eye. He then rounded on his opponent and slugged him repeatedly in the left side. Mortimer dropped to his knees at Joe's feet.

'Mortimer appears very weak, although he comes to the scratch very manfully,' remarked the newspaperman to those around him as round thirteen got underway.

This was another punishing round for the champion. Joe planted seven successive hits on Mortimer's body. The *Bell's Life* reporter reckoned the impact could be heard fifty yards away. A chorus of groans rose up from Mortimer's pained supporters. A rush at Joe resulted in another crashing blow to Mortimer's left eye. Mortimer saved himself by yet again wrestling Joe to the ground.

It was no longer a fight, it was a massacre. Why didn't Mortimer give in? Out he staggered for round fourteen. For his trouble, he received three more blows to the left side, followed by a right to the jaw and a left just above the left eye. Joe closed in. A left to the head, immediately followed by a right uppercut which, if it had connected, would have sent Mortimer into orbit. Just the same, the left to the head was enough to finish the job. Mortimer again greeted the ground.

As the referee was leading the wobbly Mortimer back to his corner, Mortimer turned to him with glazed eyes, and said, weakly, 'Enough.'

The referee went to Joe's corner, took his right arm, and lifted it into the air. The crowd roared its approval. It was over. In a battle lasting twenty-five minutes, Young Joe Windred, the tanner from Windsor, had tanned the champion's hide. Joe, bloodied and sore, was the new champion of the district, after just one outing.

Joe was driven in a procession of vehicles back to Windsor, to a party at his father's house that would flow to local pubs and the homes of friends. The celebrations lasted well into the next day. The reporter from *Bell's Life* joined in, and became so drunk that when he awoke with a throbbing head on Tuesday, he realised he'd missed his paper's deadline for his fight report; it would run a week later.[37]

Courtesy of *Bell's Life*, the victory of Young Joe Windred over feted champion Mortimer made Joe an instant celebrity in his home district, and noted throughout New South Wales. Joe would set his sights on climbing to the top of the boxing tree and becoming a New South Wales identity. As for Ben Mortimer, he would continue to seek challengers, but he would never be allowed to forget the day he received a thrashing at the hands of the new star of the local ring.

Saturday, October 11, 1845. Parramatta, New South Wales

A large crowd of expectant men and boys filled the Long Room at the rear of Parramatta's White Hart Inn, on the Windsor Road. Parramatta, the district's first and largest town, sat midway between Windsor and Sydney.

Earlier in the year, Cooks River boxer Bill Sparkes had defeated Bill Davis at Lane Cove to secure the belt of Middleweight Champion of Australia. Now, the White Hart was staging a benefit for twenty-five-year-old Sparkes, 'the Patriot of the Australian Prize Ring', as *Bell's Life* called him.[38] This was to involve exhibition bouts by the champion plus several genuine bouts with stakes of £25 and £50 a man. An indoor ring had been erected in the Long Room for the day's events, with regulation posts and ropes. And now boxing fans from as far afield as Windsor and the city crowded in to see the best in the business ply their pugilistic profession.

Young Joe Windred, unbeaten in the ring over the past ten months, and rated one of the most scientific boxers in the colony's new crop, was among the fighters invited to perform at the Sparkes benefit. As part of the engagement, Joe, like the other boxers, was required to go several exhibition rounds with Sparkes. He was under strict instructions not to hurt the champ, and to go down on one knee every now and then to end a round. Sparkes was under no such instructions, and enjoyed himself pummelling most of his opponents. To Sparkes' annoyance, he rarely laid a glove on Joe in their contest.

Late in the day came Joe's featured fight. His opponent was Jack Hand. An older, experienced, out-of-town brawler of fourteen stone (90 kilograms), Hand had a weight advantage of more than seventeen kilograms over Joe. Hand's followers reckoned he was 'as strong as an elephant'. But Joe and his trainer, wily old George Cupitt, knew that science could overcome strength any day. The Windred–Hand fight only lasted three short rounds. 'So dexterous was the young-un,' *Bell's Life* would write of Joe, 'and such a proficient in the art that, notwithstanding the main strength of the countryman, who rushed at him like a mad bull, he succeeded in flooring him three times in succession.'[39]

Hand didn't get up following the third knockdown. The elephant was slain. Joe won the bout, the prize money and the admiration of the audience.

9

THE LOVE OF JOE'S LIFE

Friday, January 22, 1847. Sydney, New South Wales

IT WOULD HAVE BEEN the oddest feeling for Joe, walking down Lower George Street past the now levelled site of Sydney Gaol. Seven years before, he had been incarcerated here. Now, the gaol, like his innocence, had gone. As Joe turned into sloping Brown Bear Lane, Circular Quay and the wharf where he had boarded the *Abercrombie* in chains for the voyage to Van Diemen's Land were at his back. It was one of life's ironies that, had he not gone to Van Diemen's Land and slaved in chain gangs, Joe may not have developed the physique for boxing or the passion to prove himself.

Up Brown Bear Lane he strode, surrounded by his high-spirited brothers and friends from Windsor. In his hand, Joe carried a portmanteau containing the tools of his trade – calico boxing breeches, boxing shoes and gloves. Members of an expectant crowd milling outside the Fives Courts applauded him, shook his hand and clapped him on the back as he made his way inside. The site of the day's bouts was the home of the gentlemanly sport of Fives, or handball, developed at English private schools Eton and Rugby. In Britain, Fives courts had also become a place where amateur boxers trained. Today, Sydney's indoor Fives Courts were being used as the venue for a professional boxing event.

Joe's boxing career had hit an obstacle the previous June, when his trainer George Cupitt unexpectedly passed away. Joe subsequently became his own trainer and manager, and remained undefeated through 1846. He was also training others, including another fighter with a disability, Deaf Bob. The previous December, Joe had pitted Deaf Bob against Bill White in a £25 a side contest near Wilberforce, outside Windsor. The gruelling three-hour fight lasted 134 rounds before Bob was knocked out.

Today's Sydney event was a benefit for Isaac Gorrick, alias 'Bungarribee Jack', another well-known New South Wales fighter, one who had given Bill Sparkes a run for his money in the past. And Young Joe Windred was on the card. Joe was still not able to rely on prize fighting for his living, as a boxer or trainer. Unlike other boxers, who made and lost large sums with the bookmakers, Joe refused to bet on himself, or on anyone else. The only way he would make more money from his fights was to fight more often, and for higher stakes.

Here at the Fives Courts, the promoters weighed Joe in at eleven stone ten pounds, then loudly repeated the challenge that was printed on the handbills advertising the event. 'Young Joe Windred will take on any man in the colony, for £100 a side!'[40]

But Joe's reputation as a 'scientific' fighter, combined with his unbeaten record and the high stake money, frightened off challengers. Joe had hoped to attract the likes of his Windsor sparring partner Frank Norris, but even Norris found the stake too high. So, Joe had to be satisfied with going a few perfunctory rounds with Bungarribee Jack. But there was no profit in exhibition matches, unless the benefit was staged for you. After the event, patrons flooded out to drink to the health of their favourites at the nearby pubs, the Brown Bear and the Black Dog. Surrounded by brothers, friends and fans, Joe celebrated the night away, discussing the finer points of boxing, and wondering how he might profit from this prize-fighting game enough to give up the filthy tanner's trade.

After dragging himself from his pub bed at the crack of dawn next day, Joe breakfasted with his hosts, then he and his brothers walked out into the morning's summer heat. In front of them spread Circular Quay, with the sun sparkling on the harbour waters. As always, the port of Sydney was alive with activity.

Joe and his brothers set off up George Street for the pub which served as the city starting point for Richard Ridge's morning coach to Windsor. They were retracing the path Joe had trod in chains close to seven years before. As they walked, Joe would have paid no attention to the *Royal Saxon*, a barque of 511 tons just then coming into Circular Quay. Only in future years would Joe realise what an incredible role coincidence played in his existence. And, as coincidence would have it, two passengers aboard the *Royal Saxon* that day as Joe walked away from Circular Quay were fated to change his life.

There were only fourteen passengers aboard the *Royal Saxon* when she sailed from Calcutta, India the previous November 22. Nine, including two British Army officers, were in first-class cabins. The remaining five passengers sailed in steerage, their swaying hammocks slung between decks. Two of those steerage passengers were prisoners of the Crown, in chains, on their way to servitude in Australia. But they were not the pair who would soon be impacting on Joe Windred's future. The travellers in question were twenty-two-year-old Mrs Mary Anne Walwyn (pronounced Wallin) and her three-year-old daughter, Isabel.

For young Mrs Walwyn, nee Douglass, this was her second arrival in New South Wales, and under very different circumstances from the first. She had been born into a poor Newcastle-upon-Tyne family in the north-east of England. At thirteen, Mary Anne Douglass had been convicted in Lancashire of petty theft, and transported to New South Wales on a seven-year sentence. Arriving aboard the convict ship *Henry Wellesley* in 1837, Mary Anne had been assigned as a servant to a family at Windsor. Also arriving in New South Wales in 1837, as a guard aboard a different convict ship, was twenty-seven-year-old Private James Walwyn, a native of Alton, Staffordshire. Walwyn's regiment, the 80th Foot, the Staffordshire Volunteers, had been transferred to Australia, and for the voyage out from Britain the unit was broken up into detachments which guarded the prisoners aboard convict transports.

The 80th Regiment's headquarters in New South Wales was established at Windsor, with a garrison building in Bridge Street, just around the corner from George Street. Several large houses in the town were also rented as billets for officers and men. James Walwyn, promoted to corporal and then quartermaster sergeant, was based in Windsor on the headquarters staff. The regiment's presence in Windsor was a significant boost to the local economy, and Quartermaster Sergeant Walwyn in particular became well-known to local businesspeople. It was his job to buy the Garrison's provisions, be it grain from John Teale's Endeavour Mill or meat from James Cullen's butchery.

Joe Windred, while working for his uncle James Cullen, would have come to know Walwyn when he shod horses for the 80th Regiment's officers and senior non-commissioned officers. Joe probably also ran across Walwyn at the fortnightly theatre sessions held at the garrison, which Joe regularly attended with his then mate Andy Garven. Another Windsor resident came to know Sergeant Walwyn even more intimately; pretty Mary Douglass was courted by Walwyn. To a teenage convict girl a long way from home and loved ones, Walwyn's smart red uniform, and the way that locals bowed and scraped to him to secure the army's business, were attractive. Walwyn was a big red-coated fish in the small local pond, and he offered Mary an escape from her lonely existence as an assigned servant.

In 1841, while Joe Windred was off in Van Diemen's Land serving his Barker robbery sentence, the 80th Regiment had relocated its headquarters to Parramatta, closer to Sydney. This removal of the regimental HQ from Windsor hit local businesses hard. James Cullen, for one, was forced to open his home up as a public house, a pub, to try to make up for the loss of business. There were already sixteen pubs in Windsor, so competition for the shrunken market was keen.

The army's relocation also impacted on relationships built up between members of the 80th Regiment and Windsorites. Now that they had been parted, Sergeant Walwyn proposed marriage to Mary Douglass. And she accepted. In 1842, eighteen-year-old Mary was granted her freedom and married thirty-two-year-old Walwyn at St John's Church of England in Parramatta, thereafter setting up home with her husband in the town. The following year, Mary gave birth to their first child, Isabella Jane Walwyn, who would always be known as Isabel.

In the autumn of 1844, just as Mary realised she was again expecting a child, the 80th Regiment was ordered to transfer to India. Ships carrying men of the 80th began departing Sydney in June. Sergeant Walwyn, the pregnant Mary, and one-year-old Isabel were among the first to depart. It was a difficult voyage – two of the ships carrying the regiment's men were wrecked on the way to Calcutta. Mary was close to giving birth when her ship finally docked in late October. Transferred to the military hospital at Calcutta's Fort William, Mary delivered a son, James Frederick, within days.

Fort William had been the site, ninety years before this, of the infamous Black Hole of Calcutta incident – when British prisoners died at the hands of their Indian captors. Capable of housing 10,000 people, the massive complex became temporary home to the men of the 80th Regiment and their families as the British Government built up its forces for a planned push into the Punjab, which was under Sikh rule. In January 1845, the regiment relocated inland to Agra. Before year's end, the 80th Foot was one of a number of units of the British Army and British East India Company engaged in the bloody, five-month-long First Sikh War. Quartermaster Sergeant Walwyn survived this war, but his marriage did not. Neither did his son. Some time prior to November 1846, baby James Frederick Walwyn died, and Mary separated from her husband. Taking infant Isabel with her, and with just enough money to pay for steerage fares to Sydney, she set off back to Australia.

Mary had friends in Windsor from her years there. In hopes of finding work at Windsor, on the afternoon of this January day Mary came down the gangway of the *Royal Saxon* with little Isabel and landed at Circular Quay. They, and their baggage, found their way to the same Windsor coach stop that Joe Windred had used earlier in the day. Before long, Mary and Isabel were on Ridge's afternoon coach, following Joe Windred to Windsor, little knowing that their futures would soon combine.

Thursday, May 20, 1847. Windsor, New South Wales

Two hundred people had crammed into the Long Room at Coffey's Hotel, many of them the district's leading farmers and graziers. English boxing champion Isaac 'Ike' Read was staying with his old friend the hotelkeeper, Edward Coffey, who'd decided it would be good for business to stage a few exhibition bouts. So, a morning's entertainment was organised at short notice. No money was on offer for contestants, but it was an opportunity for aspiring champions to go a few rounds with Ike Read or settle a grudge in a bout with a genuine foe.

Joe Windred and his brothers were here. Twenty-four-year-old William was still celebrating his marriage to local girl Sarah Silk two weeks before. Another Windred brother, nineteen-year-old Jack, had come to fight. Jack was down for a bout with Joe's sparring partner, twenty-six-year-old Frank Norris from Cornwallis, north-west of Windsor. Ever since old George Cupitt's death, Jack had helped Joe with his training. Two months prior to this Ike Read event, Jack had himself stepped into the ring, with Joe as his second. Reporting on Jack's first bout, which he won, *Bell's Life* had declared, 'Windred is somewhat lighter [than his opponent], and although a novice appears a great favourite with his friends, who fancy he will astonish the nerves of his opponents.'[41]

The Ike Read event offered Jack the opportunity to settle a grudge with Frank Norris. So, now, Joe was his little brother's trainer, while Norris had George Cupitt junior in his corner. The *Bell's Life* boxing reporter was in the crowd. With characteristic colour he described Jack Windred and Frank Norris as 'two young aspirants for fistic fame, one or other of whom, we should not be surprised, one future day, to see contending for the honour of the Australian belt'. Norris weighed just a pound short of thirteen stone (82 kilograms). Jack was much lighter. Their bout was long, and inconclusive, with *Bell's Life* disappointed when it ended with a handshake.[42]

Wednesday, October 27, 1847. Windsor, New South Wales

The Long Room at Windsor's Cricketer's Arms Inn was almost bulging at the seams. The big crowd, made up of locals and many members of the Fancy – men of money, influence and rank who had made the trip from as far afield as Parramatta and the city – had come to see Bill Sparkes, who had recently returned from a championship fight in England that became part of boxing legend.

While Sparkes was star of the show at the Cricketer's Arms, Joe and Jack Windred were also taking part. Not only had they teamed up as trainers, the brothers were now working together in their regular employment, as butchers. With Joe having become a local celebrity, the brothers' uncle James Cullen had changed his attitude to him, and agreed to teach him the butchering trade, alongside Jack. Butchering was still tough, physical work, but it was good for Joe's fitness. Most importantly, it allowed him to give up the stinking tanning trade. Joe had a new incentive for escaping the tanning factory and looking more presentable. Joe's fancy had been taken by a recent arrival in Windsor. In fact, Joe had fallen in love. And the object of his heart's desires was Mary Walwyn.

Mary was a married woman, but made no secret of the fact that she had separated from her husband. Joe walked out with her and little Isabel, sometimes taking them to Sunday lunch at Windsor's Sir John Barleycorn Inn on George Street – Joe's brother William now held the licence to the inn, and the boys' mother, Sophia, was helping William run it. Beer ran in the blood of Sophia's family. Her father, William's late grandfather Thomas Dargin, had run several Windsor pubs. Thomas senior's son Thomas and daughter-in-law Mary had run Windsor's Red Lion, Green Dragon and White Swan, with Thomas junior brewing his own beer. Sophia had worked in the family pubs, gaining an intimate knowledge of the trade.

Invariably, pugilism would have come up over Sunday lunch in the Windred parlour. While Mary Walwyn was probably not much impressed with his reputation as a boxer, Joe saw pugilism as his future. It was something at which he excelled. And another opportunity to be seen in the ring with the famous Bill Sparkes was not to be turned down. In September, when Sparkes arrived back in Sydney from England, he'd been welcomed by a massive, adoring crowd at Circular Quay. He'd returned vanquished, but the hero nonetheless.

In May, Sparkes had stepped into the ring at Richmond, Surrey, to fight English middleweight champion Ned Langham. By the sixty-third round, Bill had the better of Langham, but, in a tussle during that round, the Australian's arm was broken. Rather than give in, Bill had fought on for another four rounds using just one fist, until his manager had thrown his hat into the ring to end the bout, and Bill's agony. Although the Australian had been defeated, Bill's courage had so impressed his English audience that, before Bill set sail back to Australia, a group of English gentlemen had presented him with an inscribed silver cup in recognition of his 'manly' performance.

Bill Sparkes' broken arm had mended, and this Windsor benefit at the Cricketer's Arms was designed to improve his finances and show him off to his many fans. Sparkes' younger brother Tom, himself a capable fighter who fought under the name Sprig of Myrtle, also took part in the exhibition. Young Joe Windred, with brother Jack in his corner, went a few exhibition rounds with the champion, just as he had back in January, before he prepared for a more serious contest.

Joe's most anticipated bout was against Robert Lock. It was another exhibition, with no prize money resting on its outcome, but Joe's opponent came with big expectations. Just eighteen years old, Young Lock, as he was billed, was the same height as Joe, and weighed thirteen stone. This was just Lock's second fight. He had won his first with ease, although against an unskilled brawler.

Englishman George Pickering, since February the new editor of *Bell's Life in Sydney and Sporting Reviewer*, would say of the Lock–Windred bout, 'So eager were the members of the Fancy to witness this first exhibition of Lock with an able tactician, that a breathless silence prevailed.'[43] Lock proved a clever fighter, matching every punch that Joe threw, and recognising every feint. Joe was happy to shake hands at the termination of the long contest they put in together.

Following the exhibition, George Pickering said to young Lock, 'With a few months training under the skilled generalship of Sparkes or Gorrick, you would indeed become a troublesome customer for the championship of your native land.'[44]

After overhearing this, Joe took Lock aside, and offered to become his trainer. Lock agreed to come under the wing of Joe and Jack Windred, in preparation for a big fight before the year was out.

Wednesday, December 1, 1847. Outside Richmond, New South Wales

As dawn broke, a crowd of close to seven hundred was assembling around a boxing ring set up in a field, beside a lagoon near Farlow's Hotel. Some who had come some distance had slept at the hotel. Others had spent the night camped out beside the ring, to secure the best vantage points.

The boxers for the 'mill' were Young Lock and Frank Norris.

Both weighed much the same. Lock was taller, Norris the more robust in appearance. At 7.35 a.m., the pair climbed into the ring, with Norris looking odd in trousers and bare feet – a friend had gone off with the bag containing his boxing rig. The pair's seconds followed them through the ropes. Norris was now trained by the famous Bill Sparkes and George Cupitt junior. But Young Lock was not attended by Joe and Jack Windred. Not long before the fight, after weeks of intense training by the Windred brothers, Lock had dumped them and joined the stable of established trainers Thompson and Cable.

The first round of the Lock–Norris contest lasted thirteen minutes. Early in the second round, Norris collected the teenager with a left to the side of the head which dazed Lock. The youngster put up a feeble fight after that, and was knocked down and out in the fifth round. Said the omnipresent *Bell's Life*, 'Lock was brought out [trained] by the Windreds, and though "licked" apparently with much ease, gave indication of having had every justice done him in his training.'[45]

Lock's defeat would have been poetic justice to Joe Windred, who had been betrayed again by another young man he thought a friend, although Andrew Garven's betrayal had had much more impact on his life. Like Garven, Robert Lock had failed to profit from his deed.

10

THE CRASH

Wednesday, February 7, 1849. Outside Penrith, New South Wales

AT 6.00 A.M., PENRITH POLICE constables Dennis Marney and Charles Stewart mounted up and rode out of town. Both were wearing plain clothes. For three hours, the pair scoured the countryside. Only they and their chief constable back in Penrith knew who they were looking for. As 9.00 a.m. approached, the two policemen were ten kilometres outside Penrith when they came on a vast collection of vehicles and tethered horses on the land of a farmer named Richey. Beyond, a crowd numbering upward of three hundred men was assembling around a boxing ring. Dismounting, the two policemen separated, and mingled with the boxing fans.

Through 1848 and into the summer of 1849, pressed by the clergy, the government of New South Wales had been making a concerted effort to stamp out prize fighting and its accompanying gambling. Uniformed police had turned up at every advertised event. Lookouts were always posted by the organisers, with eyes peeled for 'beaks and blues', and they were able to alert boxers and bookmakers before magistrates or police intervened. The police found boxing rings, they found rapidly dispersing crowds, but they found no fights in progress. Still, the police campaign disrupted the established and thriving professional boxing circuit, forcing publicans and other fight promoters to abandon the usual pugilistic haunts and find new locations. These had to be many and varied, and neither posters nor the press could give advance warning of fights, as that would only tip off the police.

Now, it depended on word of mouth for news of an impending boxing contest to spread. This Penrith fight had been carefully organised with security in mind, but the police had still come to hear of it. With previous attempts to catch participants in the act having failed, this time the chief constable of Penrith was trying a new, stealthy approach. He sent his constables to this event in plain clothes and with orders not to disrupt the fighting.

Today's bout was between two promising youngsters, Richard 'Gosh' Sherringham and William 'Bill' Dawes junior. Both had fine trainers, with Isaac Gorrick and William Chaulker for Sherringham, while Dawes was trained by Young Joe Windred and Tom Sparkes, Bill Sparkes' younger brother. Joe himself had not fought in a while. It seems that neither Joe's mother nor Mary Walwyn approved of him fighting, so teaming up with young Sparkes to train others was his way of compromising. As Constables Marney and Stewart watched from the crowd, the fighters and their seconds climbed through the ropes and clustered at centre-ring with the referee. It was already a hot day, with the sun beating down from a clear blue antipodean sky, and, expecting a long contest under that sun, both fighters were wearing tight white shirts as protection against sunburn.

Outside the ring, bookmaker Abraham Myers was loudly calling odds. 'Five to three on Sherringham.'

At the same time, Bill Dawes' father, William Dawes senior, countered with odds of his own: 'Five to three on Dawes.'

The boxers shook hands. Thomas Lovett, one of the event's marshals, shepherded the seconds from the ring with his marshalling pole. With a roar from the crowd, the fight got underway. Rounds came and went. It was so hot that, between rounds, men stood at the corners holding umbrellas above the heads of the boxers as they sat on their trainers' knees. Young Dawes was plucky, but he was not following his trainers' instructions well and was getting the worst of the affair, being felled to close rounds nine, ten and eleven. At the end of round eleven, almost thirty minutes into the fight, Dawes could not get up, and Joe Windred had to go and carry him back to his corner. Once there, Tom Sparkes threw water in the youngster's face to revive him, then fanned him with a towel.

'Time!' called the timekeeper.

On wobbly legs, Dawes went to centre-ring to meet his opponent. The round began and Sherringham soon hit Dawes with several telling blows.

'Gosh has got it!' bellowed someone close to Constable Stewart.

Dawes sagged to the ground, and didn't move. A great animalistic cheer went up.

'Sherringham has won it!' crowed Gorrick, stepping into the ring to congratulate his man.

'It's not fair!' one disappointed patron cried. 'Dawes went down without a blow.'[46]

The bookmakers settled up with their clients, and the crowd chaired Sherringham to a vehicle, which would convey him to the nearest pub for victory celebrations. As Joe Windred and Tom Sparkes carried their defeated boxer to a gig, Constables Marney and Stewart mounted up, and rode back to Penrith. Once back at the Penrith Police Office, the pair compiled a list of fourteen names, handing it to their chief constable. Joseph Windred's was the last name on the list.

Thursday, May 17, 1849. Parramatta, New South Wales

Nine defendants stood in the dock as the Parramatta Quarter Sessions began. Joe Windred was one of those defendants. As were Tom Sparkes, Thomas Chaulker, Abraham Myers, Thomas Lovett, William Dawes senior and Richard Sherringham. Five of the men sought in connection with this affair, including Isaac Gorrick, could not be found. 'The court was crowded in every part throughout the trial,' reported the *Sydney Morning Herald*, for public interest in this legal disruption to the fight game was intense.[47]

The authorities were using a novel approach to those who engaged in prize fighting. They would consider a prize fight a common brawl, with the defeated man the victim and all other leading participants his assailants. Said the presiding magistrate, 'You are brought before this bench charged with assault and battery, on the person of William Dawes junior, on February 7 last. How do you plead?'

Joe and all the other defendants pleaded not guilty to assaulting young Bill Dawes. A defence counsel retained by the fight's promoters now rose to represent all those charged. Coincidence, which was to haunt Joe Windred's life, now raised its head – the attorney employed to represent Joe and the other members of the boxing fraternity before the bench was none other than William Alexander Purefoy. The very same barrister had unsuccessfully defended Joe's co-accused, Garven, Robinson and Cheeke, in the Barker robbery trial almost exactly nine years before.

The two constables who had attended the Dawes–Sherringham fight in plain clothes were called by the Crown to give evidence. Marney testified first. After describing the preparations for the fight, he went on, 'I saw Dawes and Sherringham fight, and strike each other about the face. When each party fell, that is what I call a "round". Sparkes and Windred were for Dawes. I saw Windred pick up Dawes. He wiped his face. Sherringham went to the corner with Gorrick, and Bedder was inside the rope and held a parasol over Dawes. Lovett held a parasol over Sherringham. I saw Dawes knocked down by Sherringham.'

'You saw Dawes knocked down by Sherringham,' Crown Prosecutor John Moore Dillon repeated, before, almost tongue in cheek, asking, 'Did there appear to be a disagreement between Sherringham and Dawes?'

This brought a hearty laugh from the gallery.

'I saw no disagreement,' Constable Marney responded, straight-faced, 'but they fought half an hour. They hit away at each other.'[48]

Constable Stewart said much the same as his colleague, adding, 'Dawes most frequently fell. They fell a dozen times.'[49]

The jury needed little time to confer. They returned to announce they had found all the defendants guilty. The magistrate levied a fine of fifty shillings, or a month's gaol, on each defendant. Joe Windred and his colleagues paid their fines and were discharged. Editor George Pickering, in his next edition of *Bell's Life*, would rail about 'this extraordinary humbug' of a trial.[50] But the Parramatta court case virtually spelled the end of professionally organised prize fights in Australia for years to come. It frightened off the Fancy, and their money. There would be the occasional hastily arranged fight for a purse, but continued police vigilance meant that the professional boxing circuit was dead, and with it, Joe Windred's dreams of a career based around the ring. Joe's quest for respectability had reached a dead end.

Despondently, Joe hitched a ride with Cornwallis farmer John Hoskisson, who, following the Parramatta trial, was going on into Sydney to attend the annual Homebush Races. Joe enjoyed all forms of sport. The previous year, he'd captained a rowing boat's crew in the Hawkesbury Regatta, coming second. Another of his loves was horseracing. Horses had been raced in the Windsor district annually since 1832, at Killarney, near McGrath Hill. Joe Windred senior had taken his boys to these races, and in 1834 had entered a pony, Pieman, in one race. Since 1839, sweepstake races had been held at Windsor itself, with Richard Ridge of the Horse and Jockey prominent in their organisation. Now, as Joe headed for the Homebush Races with John Hoskisson, in the farmer's two-wheeled gig, the thought of changing career path from boxing trainer to racehorse trainer may well have been exercising his mind.

Friday, May 18, 1849. Outside Windsor, New South Wales

Joe and John Hoskisson had enjoyed two afternoons at the Homebush Races and were on their way home in Hoskisson's gig. It was early evening. They were on a country road between Rouse Hill and Windsor, and Joe was taking a turn at the reins. The road here had recently been macadamised, with the gravel compacted. Without warning, Hoskisson's horse slipped on the smooth surface, and fell, flipping the gig over.

As both Joe and his forty-nine-year-old travelling companion were ejected into the air, Joe's instinct was to keep hold of the reins. The *Sydney Morning Herald* would report that Joe 'was dragged beneath the gig, one wheel passing over his back and loins, the other over back of neck and head'. Although Hoskisson suffered 'severe contusions', he was in a better state than Joe. When Ridge's Windsor-bound coach happened along a little later, the driver found Hoskisson in the middle of the road, nursing Joe. Gingerly, Joe was lifted into the coach, which took both accident victims into Windsor and a local doctor.

The *Herald* would report on the condition of the pair a week later: 'They are now doing well, considering the severe nature of their injuries.'[51]

11

THE LURE OF GOLD

Saturday, July 21, 1849. Windsor, New South Wales

THE FRONT BAR OF the Australian Inn on the corner of George and New streets was filled with its usual noisy Saturday evening crowd. Only recently, Joe Windred's brother William had taken over the lease of the Australian from landlord George Freeman, moving up the road from the smaller John Barleycorn, the inn that had established William in the public house business.

As an advertisement in the latest edition of *Bell's Life in Sydney* declared, William Windred wished 'most respectfully to inform his numerous circle of friends and customers, in consequence of the confined limits of his old establishment not affording sufficient accommodation for their reception, he has taken that commodious and well-known establishment the Australian Inn'.[52] William had invested in renovations to the inn's bedrooms, and improvements to the bar's stock of wines and spirits, and his loyal clientele had followed him.

William's celebrated and popular elder brother Joe Windred was here, still sore as he recovered from his accident in Hoskisson's gig. All who knew Joe marvelled at the fact that he had not been killed in the crash, and no one doubted the fact that he kept himself so physically fit was aiding his recovery. As usual, many a patron wanted to talk to Joe about boxing, and to lament the fact that the blues and beaks had closed down the prize-fight circuit that had given so much entertainment to so many.

Alternative entertainment was difficult to find. Some in the bar were thinking about going in to Sydney to see the latest attraction at the Royal City Theatre, Mr Quin, 'the Australian Tight Rope Dancer'. Quin advertised that he would 'leap over six soldiers with fixed bayonets, leap over two chairs, through a hoop of daggers, over a garter eight feet from the rope, over two five-barred gates, and conclude with dancing with the clown on his shoulders'.[53] But, for all their novelty, Mr Quin's antics did not compare to a boxing contest featuring a Windred or a Sparkes.

There was another topic of conversation currently on the lips of many in Windsor, just as it was on the lips of many throughout the Australian colonies. Late the previous year, word had reached Australia's shores of a massive gold find in California, on the west coast of North America. According to reports, it was possible to simply pick up gold from the ground, and men were making their fortunes there. Scores of ships were sailing from Sydney and Hobart Town in Van Diemen's Land for San Francisco, taking thousands of Australian gold-seekers with them. In the United States, it would become a mark of honour for men to say that they had arrived in California in 1849. They became known as 'the Forty-Niners'. But not all were Americans. A third of California's gold-seekers would arrive from Australia.

Windsor greengrocer John Gough was one of those now thinking seriously of joining the rush, selling up and heading for California to make his fortune. Forty-nine-year-old Gough, who lived not far from Joe Windred, had come out to New South Wales in 1825 as a twenty-three-year-old convict. A native of Huntingdon, Cambridgeshire, Gough had received a life sentence at the Devon Assizes for housebreaking, and was assigned as a servant to a Hunter River farmer. After six years of good behaviour, Gough had received a Ticket of Leave, and in 1833 married local girl Elicia Bahan. The couple had settled in Windsor, where Gough opened his grocery store in rented premises. Business had been good between 1837 and 1841 while the 80th Regiment was headquartered at Windsor, but, since the regiment's relocation to Parramatta, life had been a financial struggle for the Goughs. A struggle made all the worse by the fact that the population of New South Wales was in decline because of the numbers now heading for California.

Only months before this, on May 1, Gough had received a Conditional Pardon from the Governor of New South Wales, Sir Charles Fitzroy. This permitted Gough to travel anywhere in the world apart from Britain and Ireland, and this new freedom had set the greengrocer to thinking, and dreaming. As Gough now told Joe Windred, a man could do worse than digging for gold in California. Unlike some men who dreamed of California gold over a pint of beer or porter in the bar at the Australian Inn, John Gough was in earnest. Over the next few months, he would put together a party of Windsor residents to make the expedition to America.

One member of that party would be twenty-nine-year-old Thomas Burdue, an English migrant who had settled in Windsor with his young family only a few years before. Joe Windred didn't know Tom Burdue well, but Joe's ladylove, Mary Walwyn, seems to have known Burdue and his attractive wife, Elen, more intimately, because they had common roots. Like Mary, Tom and Elen Burdue were natives of Northumberland, living for many years at Slaley just outside Newcastle-upon-Tyne – the city where Mary was born. Newcastle was also where Tom Burdue had worked in the early 1840s.

For Joe, all the talk of making a fortune as a gold-seeker was unsettling now that his dream of fame and fortune from a boxing career had been dashed.

Wednesday, November 14, 1849. Sydney, New South Wales

As the 589-ton barque *Victoria* ploughed through the waters of Sydney Harbour with her bucking bow pointing toward the heads and the open sea beyond, she was low in the water. Her hold was full of cargo, and between her crowded decks 276 passengers had slung their hammocks. The *Victoria* was on her way to San Francisco, carrying the aspirations of men and women lured by the glitter of Californian gold. Among those passengers were John Gough and his wife, Elicia, from Windsor, and three others who also had until recently been residents of Windsor – James Smith, Joseph Wright and Thomas Burdue.

There were a number of wives and young children accompanying husbands and fathers on their California adventure, but Wright was leaving his wife behind in Windsor and Burdue was leaving Elen and three young children in Sydney. Both Burdue and Wright had plans to send for their families once they were settled in California, but there was another reason for Elen to wait behind. She was pregnant with the Burdues' fourth child. The plan was for her to have the child in Sydney then set off to join Tom in California, once he was settled and she and the newborn were fit to travel.

Out into the Tasman Sea sailed the *Victoria*, before setting a north-easterly course that would take it across the Pacific to California. As they sailed away, neither Tom Burdue nor John Gough had any idea that their futures were inexorably linked with that of another Windsor resident, Joe Windred, or that before eighteen months had passed they would all be sharing the same nightmare.

12

TO CALIFORNIA

Thursday, February 14, 1850. Windsor, New South Wales

THE DAY'S ISSUE OF the *Sydney Morning Herald* printed, in the letters column, correspondence from Sydney resident John Longfield. The *Herald* had recently published a report that five out of eight members of Longfield's gold-digging party had perished from starvation in California's Sierra Nevada Mountains. Now, while not disputing that fact, Longfield countered that he had still come out of the venture a winner: 'In one day, I got $900 worth of gold.' That was the equivalent of £233.[54] The newspaper's editor remarked that, having recently seen Longfield in Sydney after his return from California, he felt he did not look at all well, and 'did not do any good for himself during his trip'. Longfield, a ship's master by profession, would not only recover his health, he would soon be captaining the vessel *Balmoral* on a voyage back to San Francisco.

As usual, the front page of the *Herald* was a mass of advertisements, in particular columns filled with ads for vessels seeking passengers for their next voyages. London was a popular destination, but by far the largest number of advertisements touted ships bound for San Francisco. One advertisement in particular caught Joe Windred's eye. It was for the ship *Una*. 'Passengers for the Gold Country are invited to come on board and inspect her unrivalled accommodations,' it said. It was an invitation that Joe was about to take up.

Sunday, February 17, 1850. Sydney, New South Wales

As Joe walked along the harbour-front, he might have marvelled at how much Circular Quay had changed since he'd boarded the *Abercrombie* here almost a decade earlier, for the voyage to Van Diemen's Land. Now, the Quay was dominated by a handsome sandstone Georgian building of two storeys, with large windows and a colonnaded front: Sydney's new custom house. Replacing a cramped old custom house in the Rocks, the new building had been erected in 1845 to show off the harbour city's growing prosperity. The collector of customs, Colonel John Gibbes, had proudly watched his new headquarters go up from his waterfront home just across the harbour at Kirribilli. Then called Wotonga House, Gibbes' home would later be renamed Admiralty House and become the Sydney residence of Australia's governors-general.

Tied up directly in front of the new Custom House was the object of Joe Windred's quest. The three-masted, 773-ton *Una* was, up to this time, the largest vessel sailing for California from Sydney. The smallest were several cutters of just thirty-four tons. Arriving in Sydney the previous November, just eight days after the *Victoria* sailed for California carrying John Gough, Tom Burdue and their gold-seeking party away to America, the *Una* had put in a four-month voyage from Southampton, England with a cargo of general freight and 313 free immigrants. By the end of December, the ship's master and owner, Captain William Henry Causzer, had been advertising for cargo and passengers for Bombay in India, and Ceylon (today's Sri Lanka).

But, early in the new year, Causzer's Sydney agents offered him freight for California ordered by San Francisco merchant Thomas Armstrong. Causzer altered his plans, accepting the Armstrong consignment, and by January 14 the *Una* was advertising for passengers to California. The *Una* had been delayed in Sydney until now because, on the way out to Australia, thirteen of Captain Causzer's crewmen had mutinied when Causzer prevented them from mixing with the single female immigrants aboard. Causzer had been forced to run his ship with a pistol in his belt and with several passengers augmenting his depleted crew. Since the ship's arrival in Sydney, Causzer had been giving evidence at the mutineers' subsequent trial.

Joe, walking up the *Una*'s gangway with rising excitement, was met by Captain Causzer, who gladly gave him the guided tour of the ship advertised in the press. 'This splendid and admirably appointed ship offers an opportunity for passengers which rarely occurs,' waxed Joe's guide as they trod the freshly washed deck side-by-side, 'being fitted with the latest ventilators and having eight feet between decks.' When they reached the stern, Causzer showed off the best quarters on board, saying, 'The after part of the 'tween decks is fitted up for a superior class of passengers, with enclosed berths, at a small advance on the steerage passage.'[55]

Not only, the captain boasted, was the *Una* the largest, best-equipped ship yet to sail for California from these shores, with the most generous provisions for her passengers, she would also be sailing with a surgeon, William Tredwen, for the comfort and safety of all. When Joe departed the ship, he was fully sold on a sea voyage and a taste of adventure in far-off America. In his mind, a plan was forming. A plan that would kill two birds with one stone. The acquisition of a rapid fortune was small price to pay for a little hard labour at the gold diggings. Joe was young and fit, and fully recovered from the previous May's carriage accident. And he had never been afraid of hard work. Then there was the matter of Mary Anne Walwyn, the love of his life.

In any other circumstances, Joe would have proposed marriage to Mary by this time. But Mary was already married to Quartermaster Sergeant Walwyn, the British soldier across the sea in India. As much as Mary assured Joe that to all intents and purposes her marriage was over, it was still legal, and binding, as far as Church and State were concerned. There was one other option. It occurred to Joe that if he and Mary were to sail to California together, they could go as man and wife. Neither ships' captains nor Water Police asked to see the marriage certificates of departing passengers. Joe knew that Mary loved him, and wanted to be with him. But would she agree to such a scheme?

Friday, April 5, 1850. Sydney, New South Wales

The captain of the *Una* had received his port clearance papers on April 3, and this morning's press ran an advertisement from Sheppard and Alger, the *Una*'s Sydney agents: 'All intermediate and steerage passengers must be on board this morning at 10 o'clock punctually.'[56]

Among the passengers boarding the *Una* were 'Mr and Mrs Joseph Windred'. Mary had agreed to Joe's crazy scheme, and Joe had sold everything he owned to finance this trip. They were going to California to find gold, and, as far as the *Una*'s passenger manifest was concerned, they were husband and wife. In fact, Mary would be Mary Windred for the rest of her days.

She had no fear of long sea voyages. As a thirteen-year-old, she had lived through the hell of a passage by convict ship from one side of the world to the other. That harrowing experience had toughened her up, and had made her more recent journey in steerage from India to Australia with her infant daughter, Isabel, less of a trial.

But, what of little Isabel now? Many parents travelling on the *Una* were taking their young children with them to California, but not Mary. Isabel, who was approaching her seventh birthday, was staying behind, in the care of Joe's mother, Sophia. Isabel had already become like a sister to Sophia's only daughter, ten-year-old Mary Ann, so she would be in good company while her mother was away in California. The vast majority of gold-seekers leaving Australia's shores had plans to return once they had made their fortunes. And Mary, who was to prove to be a methodical, well-organised young woman, is likely to have extracted a promise and a time limit from Joe – that they spend a year in California, after which they would return to Australia, come what may.

On the three-month journey across the Pacific, with Mary missing her own daughter, she and Joe would make friends with several couples with children aboard the *Una*. Among their fellow travellers were Englishman William Handcock and his wife, Elizabeth. Originally from Manchester, stocky, ambitious Handcock had brought his new bride to Australia in 1841, settling at Port Phillip, Victoria. Since then, Elizabeth had given birth to five children, with the youngest, John, being born in Sydney on November 21. Not only was Elizabeth Handcock now nursing four-month-old John, once she was into this trip she would discover that she was pregnant yet again, with morning sickness combining with seasickness to make her voyage a misery.

With great excitement, and not a little apprehension, Joe, Mary and the *Una*'s other passengers studied the busy port around them as their vessel prepared to get underway with the next outgoing tide.

Tied up at Circular Quay right beside the *Una* was the 900-ton *John Munn*. With the gold-rush exodus from New South Wales now at its height, the *John Munn* was advertising for passengers for California in the morning's Sydney papers, as were the barques *Laura* and *Swallow*, and the brig *Potentia*.

Like the *Una*, those vessels were just as interested in freight for California as they were in passengers. San Francisco was now a boom town, with the gold rush turning it from a sleepy Spanish village into a metropolis with an insatiable demand for all the requisites for commerce and development. The *Una* herself was sailing to San Francisco with a prefabricated wooden house in her hold, plus 20,000 Sydney house-bricks and 5000 roof tiles, 150 tons of coal, eighty tons of iron, plus casks of beer, porter, flour, sugar, bran, lime, pickles and medicinal drugs, as well as bales of hay, and a piano.

That night, for the first time, Joe and Mary sat down to dinner aboard ship with their 210 fellow passengers, as husband and wife. In the early morning hours, the vessel would ease away from her berth with the tide, and by next morning she would be 'in the stream', lying out in the harbour awaiting favourable winds. The following day, April 7, the *Una* would clear Sydney's heads, and begin the 6700 nautical mile journey to California, where Joe Windred would face the greatest trial of his life.

13

WELCOME TO CALIFORNIA

Thursday, July 4, 1850. San Francisco, California

IT WAS A HOT mid-summer's day when the *Una* dropped anchor in San Francisco Bay, joining 620 other vessels in the crowded port. Through the maze of masts and yardarms, Joe and Mary Anne Windred could see a town of mostly wooden buildings spreading back from the water and up the hillsides beyond.

It would take Captain Causzer some time to secure a berth to unload, and he was permitting his passengers to continue to live aboard the *Una* for the next ten days, so that they could get their bearings, make their plans, and buy what they needed before they set off on the next leg of their journey into gold country. That gold country began hundreds of kilometres inland, at the foot of the forbidding Sierra Nevada Mountains, the place where Sydneysider John Longfield had lost five of his seven companions and found $900 worth of gold in a day.

After thirteen weeks at sea, the *Una*'s passengers were keen to land and look around, and the *Una*'s boats were kept busy all this day ferrying them to shore. The San Francisco that Joe and Mary found when they stepped ashore was a frontier town in every sense. White settlement here dated back to 1776, when the Spanish erected a military fort, the Presidio, and friars of the Franciscan Order established the Mission Dolores. In 1847, there were only seventy-nine buildings in the town originally known as Yerba Buena. By the following January, when gold was first found in the Sierras, the future San Francisco had a population of only a few hundred. Now, little more than two years later, over 30,000 people clustered here beside the picturesque bay. It was a far cry from Sydney, itself a city just sixty-two years old yet boasting handsome brick and stone edifices. A few old Spanish adobe mud-brick buildings had survived here, but many people were living in tents. Some miners who were down on their luck slung hammocks in the open. Until only as recently as two months prior to the arrival of Joe and Mary, almost every building in the city had been built from timber.

Wandering San Francisco's streets as tourists, Joe and Mary took in extraordinary sights such as ships propped up beside busy streets. Three, the *General Harrison* on Clay Street and the *Apollo* on Sacramento and *Georgian* on Jackson, had undergone conversion from ship to shop. The old *Niantic*, at the corner of Clay and Sansome, had a building added above its upper deck, creating the Niantic Hotel. Joe and Mary also saw numerous city blocks that had been ravaged by major fires on May 4 and June 14. Three hundred buildings had been destroyed in the first blaze, which had begun in a hotel and gambling house. Another three hundred buildings had been lost in the June fire, which had started in a bakery. In September, local publisher Charles Kimball would say that, in San Francisco, 'whole streets are built up in a week and whole squares swept away in an hour'.[57]

Reconstruction already begun in the wake of the fires would be boosted by the arrival this month of building materials brought by the *Una* and other ships. Just as the *Una* would contribute its prefabricated house and load of bricks and tiles to July's rebuilding, numerous vessels would unload hundreds of thousands of house-bricks, roof tiles and shingles, as well as complete doors, windows and sashes, and barrels of mortar by the thousands. On July 30, the barque *Agincourt* would arrive from Adelaide, South Australia, and in addition to disgorging 111 passengers, she would unload seven prefabricated houses, 18,750 house-bricks and 1500 feet of pine.

On city lots left blackened and desolate by the fires, Joe and Mary saw piles of filthy chequered men's shirts. They were told that when miners came into town from the diggings they spent their money on a good meal and cigars, a bath, a whore and a few new shirts. Rarely washing on the diggings, miners who came into San Francisco would discard their filthy old shirts in the street and put on new ones. There was little market for white shirts in San Francisco; they showed the dirt. Chequered shirts disguising the perspiration and filth they accumulated had become the uniform of California miners.

On every downtown block, the newcomers passed saloons and gambling joints which ran from dawn to dusk, seven days a week. There were hotels and boarding houses galore, thriving restaurants, even a bowling alley. The new arrivals noted how few women and children they saw. In San Francisco, men outnumbered women twenty to one, and there were few family groups here. It was rare to come across anyone aged above thirty, and exceptional for men in their forties or fifties to be seen. Gold-seeking, it was clear, was a young man's game. And every newcomer soon learned to beware young pickpockets whenever a crowd gathered.

As Joe and Mary walked the neat grid of San Francisco streets laid out by a French surveyor in the 1830s, they found that the city had divided itself into ethnic areas. French immigrants populated Merchant Street. Germans and Dutch lined Montgomery Street. Chinese lived on Broadway. On the slopes of Telegraph Hill, 'Little Chile' teemed with Chileans and Mexicans. Next to Little Chile, north of Broadway and all the way to Clark's Point, extended thickly populated Sydney Valley. Later called the Barbary Coast, in 1850 this district was filled with thousands of people from Australia.

One estimate put forty-two per cent of the people living in San Francisco at this time as having come from Australia. By the census of 1852, 11,000 of the 35,000 residents of San Francisco would be officially listed as from Australia – and by 1852 many 'Australians' had left the city as a result of the events that would blow up in 1851 involving Joe Windred. It was estimated that across California at this time, 30,000 of the 100,000 residents were from Australia.[58] The congregation of 'Australians' at San Francisco was not entirely a matter of choice for antipodean immigrants. Californian authorities had imposed a mining tax of $20 a month on all miners other than United States citizens. This was supposedly aimed at keeping Mexicans and Chinese off the diggings, but it had the effect of driving many Australian, British and Irish gold-seekers into the towns in search of work, and a large number had congregated in the one San Francisco valley.

Dubbed Sydney Valley, and Sydney Town, the majority of its inhabitants had come to California from, or via, Sydney. Joe and Mary now learned that Americans referred to all who had come to California from Australia as Australians, no matter where they hailed from originally. And, as Edward Buffum, an American newspaperman in San Francisco at the time, was to explain, 'All the immigrants from Australia were classed under the general title of the "Sydney Ducks", and were regarded with great suspicion.'[59] The title Sydney Ducks was apparently coined because many who landed in San Francisco from Sydney came wearing lightweight summer suits made from 'duck' cloth, or cotton.

'The prejudice in San Francisco at that time against all persons who had come to California from Australia was very strong,' said Buffum. Everyone in Australia, it was assumed by many Americans, was a convict. Like other parts of the city, Sydney Town was full of overflowing boarding houses, taverns, brothels and gambling joints, all of which operated legally and openly under California law. But the convict slur attached to Britain's Australian colonies meant that every crime in San Francisco came to be attributed to people from Australia. 'Some very bad men had undoubtedly arrived from there,' Buffum commented, 'and much of the crime committed in the state can legitimately be charged upon them.' But Buffum was one of the few Americans in San Francisco to also concede that some Australian immigrants were 'very respectable people'.[60]

Because of the crimes of a few Sydney Ducks, the brush of prejudice had painted all Australians the same criminal colour. As history shows, in every community at one time or another, outsiders become the scapegoats for resident dissatisfaction. And there were now many dissatisfied young Americans in San Francisco, men who had failed to realise their dream of overnight wealth after being lured here by gold-rush glorification in the East.

To American residents of San Francisco, the proof of the criminality of all Sydney Ducks lay in the fact that whenever the latest of innumerable fires broke out in the highly flammable city, they never broke out in Sydney Town. This, according to American businessmen, could only mean that the fires had been set by Sydney Ducks. In contrast, one local judge lay the blame for these fires at the feet of greedy, mostly American local shopkeepers intent on claiming insurance money.[61] Yet, the views of the more affluent American businessmen of San Francisco, and the newspapers they supported, led American public opinion, and that opinion was anti-Australian. As each fire razed a few more blocks, Americans would angrily declare, 'The Sydney Ducks are cackling.'[62]

The discovery of this prejudice in San Francisco against people from Australia came as a shock to new arrivals from Sydney such as Joe and Mary. It spurred their efforts to depart the city and make their way to the gold diggings as soon as possible. But, where precisely should they go? There were numerous diggings on the Sacramento, Feather, Yuba and American rivers, the latter being where the first gold had been discovered in 1848, sparking the rush. Hoping for reliable advice from people they knew, the newcomers asked in Sydney Town for news of the members of the Gough party that had set off from Windsor the previous November. To their surprise, they learned that John and Elicia Gough were in business in San Francisco, and they sought them out.

Rather than go inland to the diggings, John Gough, now fifty, had become convinced that he was too old for mining, and, instead, he and his wife had taken a lease on a two-storey wooden house in Happy Valley, a predominantly American district three blocks west of the sleazy bounds of Sydney Town. The lower rooms of this house they turned into a restaurant, the Panama House. And, with a San Francisco Police station house nearby at the corner of First and Mission streets, the Goughs were able to rent one of their upper rooms to a pair of the city's then tiny complement of just fifty-eight policemen. Since the couple's arrival in San Francisco, Elicia had given birth to a child, John junior.

As Joe and Mary lunched with the Goughs, they plied them with questions about the gold diggings and the other members of the party the Goughs had led from Windsor – Wright, Smith and Burdue.

'Wright died,' Gough replied, matter-of-factly. 'Wright's wife is here.' Joseph Wright had sent for his wife not long after arriving in California. 'James Smith is at the mines. I don't know where; don't correspond with him.'[63]

When Joe and Mary inquired after Tom Burdue, Gough replied that he had kept in touch with him, and that Burdue came down from the diggings to San Francisco occasionally. Gough showed them his letter book, in which he recorded all his incoming and outgoing correspondence. Here, the Windreds saw a contact address that Burdue had written: 'Thomas Burdue, City of Auburn, Dry Diggings, to be found at the German baker's there. Write to the care of Mr Gwynn, storekeeper.'[64]

On asking where Auburn was, Joe learned that it was a mining camp in the Sierra Nevada foothills, sitting between the North Fork and Middle Fork on the American River, with the town of Sacramento below it and Lake Tahoe above. Joe and Mary decided to make Auburn their destination, hoping to meet up with fellow Windsorite Burdue there. With Burdue's advice, they would decide where to stake a claim. First, they would have to buy a tent, mining tools, pack mules, then ride a river steamer up the Sacramento River as far as it would take them, before setting off along the rough trail to Auburn.

That afternoon, as Joe and Mary passed through San Francisco's Portsmouth Square, known colloquially as the Plaza, they saw Americans in party mood. Volunteer members of the city's Protection Fire Company Number 2, wearing their new fireman's uniform for the first time, were erecting a thirty-four-metre flagpole, the Liberty Pole, from which would fly a giant United States flag. California was currently a US territory, won from Mexico in the Mexican–American War. But the expectation was that the US Congress would soon admit the territory to the Union as its thirty-first state. In fact, word of that admission in September would reach San Francisco by sea in October. And today was July 4, US Independence Day.

A large crowd had gathered in the Plaza to watch proceedings, and, once the Liberty Pole was up, a patriotic oration was delivered by twenty-nine-year-old Reverend William Taylor. The most senior Wesleyan minister in San Francisco, Taylor was accustomed to speaking in the Plaza. Since arriving from Virginia the previous year, he had set himself the task of converting California's legions of miners to Christian ways. Finding that Sunday was no day of rest in unsaintly San Francisco, this town where gold was god, Taylor conducted regular outdoor services during the week, in the Plaza and on Market Street wharf.

Taylor had a commanding voice. He himself said that it could be heard by half the town, while his wife, Isabel, possessed a sweet hymn-singing voice. Between them, they often attracted 1500 worshippers.

But street sermonising was not the limit of Taylor's pastoral activities. He had also attempted to convince local businesspeople not to open their stores on Sundays and instead observe it as 'the Lord's day'. He was having little luck, for Sunday was the biggest trading day of the week, when many miners went looking for provisions for the coming seven days, or amused themselves by getting drunk and brawling.

Little knowing that within seven months the Reverend Taylor would come into their lives at a crucial moment, Joe and Mary Windred took in the minister's Independence Day speech, then moved on. By evening, Independence Day celebrations extended across the city. For the new arrivals, it was almost as if a party was being held to welcome them. That night, the Dramatic Museum, a new theatre, opened on California Street. This was the brainchild of actor James Everard, who specialised in playing female roles. Among his first night audience would have been Joe Windred, who had displayed a passion for the theatre back in Windsor, and his 'wife' Mary.

Back aboard the *Una* later that evening, Joe and Mary would have shared stories and observations with their fellow passengers. There was no doubt that this first day in San Francisco had been an eye-opener for them all. Within days, the excitement of arrival would give way to pragmatism among some of Joe and Mary's fellow passengers. William Handcock, for one, decided against going to the goldfields. Hearing lurid tales in San Francisco of lawlessness, privation and death in the mining camps, and, told that free grants of hundreds of acres were being offered to new settlers, further up the west coast, in the Oregon Territory, Handcock opted to find a vessel that would take his family there. The Handcocks would sail to Oregon and be among the first settlers in what would become the town of Elkton. There, in December, Elizabeth Handcock would give birth to her latest child, another boy.[65]

But Joe and Mary Windred had not come to America to be settlers. They had come to find gold and make a fast fortune before returning to New South Wales and little Isabel, to start a new life there as a family. When, on July 14, as the last of the *Una*'s passengers disembarked, and Captain Causzer asked his San Francisco agents to find him freight and passengers to Panama, now one of the busiest ports in the Americas due to the California gold rush, Joe and Mary were on their way to the goldfields, in search of Tom Burdue.

14

THE GOLD COUNTRY

Thursday, August 1, 1850. Auburn, California

TWO HUNDRED AND FIFTY metres up in the foothills of the Sierra Nevada Mountains, Joe and Mary reached the diggings in the Auburn Ravine. The first 200 kilometre leg of their journey inland from San Francisco had been aboard a Sacramento river steamer to the riverside town of Sacramento City, a 'vast encampment of tents and rude cabins' boasting a population of 10,000 and serving as 'the commercial emporium for the northern miners'.[66]

This steamboat ride alone cost $30 apiece, plus more for loaded mules. Ministers of religion were permitted to travel free on the river steamers, and a story was doing the rounds about a miner who attempted to board a river steamer, with his mules, without paying. When the master, a Captain Gelson, demanded he pay, the man tried to avoid coughing up by claiming to be a preacher. 'What?' the steamboat skipper had responded, 'Are your mules preachers too?'[67]

Then it was onto another, smaller boat, for the trip upriver to Marysville, just above where the Yuba and Feather rivers met. From there, miners continued their journey into the mountains by stagecoach, horse or mule, or on foot, to reach the many riverside mining camps that had sprung up over the past two years.

Joe and Mary, accustomed to the regularity and sense of permanence of the Windsor township back in New South Wales, found

Auburn less an organised settlement than a sorry and scattered camp of tents and a few log huts and stores clinging to the hillside beside the winding North Yuba River.

The place was also known as Wood's Dry Diggings, for John S. Wood, the American miner who had first struck gold here just a year earlier, and for the fact that Auburn's gold was primarily extracted from banks of dry river shale which stood well above river level. Fifteen hundred miners were hard at work throughout the steep-sided ravine, digging, sifting and making the occasional small gold find.

It was the height of summer when Joe and Mary reached Auburn, where the temperature regularly went into the high 30s Celsius through July and August. There was only a handful of women in Auburn, and very few of those physically mined gold. In the dry heat, the male miners were working in just pants and shirts, usually open at the neck and folded back to the elbows. 'No one ever thought of putting on a coat, waistcoat, or even a neckerchief,' one Australian miner wrote home.[68] For a religious woman, such a sight would have been horrifying. But very few of the women who ventured into these mining camps could afford to be fussy about the mores of the day.

There were only one or two clearly delineated streets at Auburn camp. One was Court Street, home to a rough courthouse built from logs. Another, Commercial Street, which sloped up a hillside, contained a few stores. Otherwise, rough foot tracks wound along the slopes. Following the contact details left by Tom Burdue with John Gough, Joe and Mary went to the store run by William Gwynn. Established on a rise above the diggings by Gwynn and a partner in 1849, this had been the first store at Auburn. Gwynn was able to confirm that he knew Tom Burdue, that he held mail for him, and that Tom boarded with the camp's German baker. But Tom no longer worked a claim here. He was well, and he travelled a great deal. Apart from that, the new arrivals were unable to learn much about Tom, or how he was making a living.

With no one interested in advising them on how or where to launch their mining career, Joe and Mary took pot luck, found a stretch of promising shale up a gulch through which a creek ran down to the main river, and staked their claim. Apart from the foreign miners tax, mining in California was not formally regulated. By mutual agreement among diggers, individual claims could be of a set dimension. Often, it was a ten-metre frontage of a gold-bearing river, and running as far back from the river as the miner liked. Joe and Mary set up their tent, and began digging.

The process was simple. If operating in pairs, one member of a mining team brought a bucket of earth and shale to where the other operated a wooden cradle, which the operator rocked to sift specks of gold from the load. Husband and wife mining teams were rare throughout California, and in the few that did exist it was mostly the women who had the job of hauling the earth-laden buckets, while their men operated the cradle. Only the more gentlemanly miners did the heavy lifting and let their wives sift for gold. And Joe Windred was a gentleman. The object of their quest was shiny yellow specks of dust. Large nuggets were rarely unearthed here. An Auburn miner might collect nine or ten dollars worth of gold dust a day.

Forty-Niner Sheldon Shufelt from New York State wrote home to tell his brother that life here was all about 'stealing, swearing, drinking, gambling, and murdering'. In June, that murdering had included Sheriff Echols of Auburn, who was shot down by two brothers. While the dangers were many, the rewards for miners were few. Said Shufelt, 'Very many that come here meet with bad success, and thousands will leave their bones here.' Shufelt estimated that half the miners never made enough to take them back to where they came from.[69] He himself planned to return home, but, like so many, would not live to see his family again. Fever would claim him in Panama in 1852, while he was returning to New York State.

One miner who went into San Francisco to let his hair down during this period told Reverend William Taylor, 'Every six months has found me either broke or doing so well I could not leave.'[70]

Joe and Mary, having made a pact to stick it out for at least a year, settled down to profit from their time here, despite the conditions. In this lawless camp, having seen how their neighbours lived, and died, Joe and Mary decided that, as a woman was less likely to be robbed than a man, from now on Mary would look after their valuables, especially their gold finds.

Sunday, August 25, 1850. Auburn, California

Tom Burdue at last put in an appearance, riding in from mining camps higher up in the hills. Hearing from storekeeper Gwynn that friends of his had arrived at the diggings, Tom was a welcome visitor to the Windred tent. Thirty years old, and shorter than Joe by several inches, Tom was long-faced, with dark eyes and lengthy, wavy, dark hair that was giving way to a growing bald patch toward the back of his head. Since being in the diggings, Tom had grown a beard, as many miners did. That beard was thick and dark, and put ten years on him. Those who knew Tom would describe him as now looking a lot like the images of Jesus Christ that they saw in church statues.

The son of a Northumberland farmer with a leased property of over 200 acres which employed half-a-dozen farmhands and several house servants, Tom had received a good education in England. But, when he was twenty-one, he had impregnated one of his father's housemaids: Elen. At just the age of sixteen, Elen had given birth to their first child, a son they named Thomas junior. The couple had married, and over the next few years added two daughters to their growing brood. Leaving the farm, Tom for several years worked as a 'fitter', or salesman, for one of Newcastle's large coal companies, before going to sea. During the subsequent years as a mariner, Tom had lost part of a finger in a maritime accident. And, like many a sailor, he had added a tattoo to his physiology, having a ring tattooed around his ring finger.

As Tom supped with Joe and Mary, he told them a little of what he had been doing since arriving in the gold country. He had first come up to Auburn, but finding so many diggers here had moved on higher into the hills, to Foster's Bar, a mining camp 580 metres up, on the west bank of the North Yuba River. In winter, it rarely snowed at Auburn, but up at Foster's Bar the snow was so thick it blocked the trails, while the river and surrounding creeks froze over. Only five hundred of the most hardy miners existed up there at Foster's Bar. When Tom first arrived, the snow and ice of the winter of 1849–50 was melting. A flat-bottomed iron boat serving as a ferry was then the only means of reaching the Foster's Bar camp, with the ferryman and the boat's English owner, a man named Stuart, between them making a tidy profit from the short but necessary transit of the icy North Yuba.

Up there competition for gold was not as intense as at the diggings lower down, so Tom had staked a claim. But the miners tax and antagonism from American miners had soon seen him give up mining at Foster's Bar. Basing himself down at Auburn, Tom had come to lead a peripatetic existence, rambling through the wilds from one mining camp to another. Quiet, sober and independent, Tom was cagey about how he was actually making ends meet, but he had plenty of gold in his saddlebags. He in fact described himself as 'comparatively affluent'.[71]

Pleased to see people from home for the first time in many months, Tom plied Joe and Mary with questions about his wife, Elen, and his children. Having seen Elen only as recently as late March, when they were preparing to board the *Una*, the couple could not give Tom an up-to-date report on her condition. Elen had still been pregnant when the Windreds departed. All being well, she would have given birth by this time.

With friends in the diggings now, Tom decided that it was time to send for Elen and his children, and made plans to travel down to San Francisco in September to make the necessary arrangements for his family to cross the Pacific to join him.

Saturday, September 14, 1850. San Francisco, California

Dining with John and Elicia Gough at their Panama House restaurant, Tom Burdue felt the ground sway beneath his feet. The earth tremor was short and sharp, and Burdue's hosts seemed unperturbed. The Goughs had become accustomed to San Francisco's little earthquakes, which were a regular event, and this latest tremor passed with nary a blink. Most of the city's residents, a number of them drunk and insensible to Mother Nature's little display, likewise paid no heed. The people of San Francisco, reasoning that the tremors never did much damage, assured newcomers that the regular rumblings were to be tolerated rather than feared. Fifty-six years from now, in 1906, the city would be famously levelled by a major quake and resultant fire, with great loss of life.

When Tom parted company from his hosts at the Panama House, he left a bag containing five pounds (2.3 kilograms) of gold dust with John Gough, asking him to keep it safe until Elen arrived in San Francisco with the children. The arrangement was that Gough would hand the gold over to Elen when she landed in the city, so that she could finance her inland journey to join Tom at the diggings.

While on this excursion to San Francisco, Burdue found a ship that was sailing to Sydney, and paid the master to have a letter to Elen included in its mails. In that letter, Tom told Elen of the arrangements he had made, and urged her to pack up at once and bring the children to join him. If Elen acted with despatch, and allowing time for his letter to cross the Pacific in one direction and his family to transit it in the other, they should arrive in San Francisco sometime in February.

Three days later, when Tom was on his way back to Auburn, yet another fire would erupt in San Francisco. The fourth major fire in a year, breaking out in the Philadelphia House, a hotel on Jackson Street, it would destroy one hundred and fifty buildings. And once again the Sydney Ducks would be accused of arson.

Monday, November 25, 1850. Sacramento, California

James 'English Jim' Stuart slipped a key in the lock, and opened the door to Sacramento's City Jail, from the inside. This jail and the town's police office were located in the hulk of an old demasted ship, the *La Grange*, which lay tied up to a jetty at the river end of the town's H Street. Stuart, a former New South Wales convict, was about to make a daring escape.

Stuart's felonious exploits went back to his teenage years in England. He was to claim that he had been born at the English seaside town of Brighton on March 3, 1819, and that he was arrested at fifteen and transported to New South Wales at sixteen with a life sentence for forgery. But, there is no record of a teenaged James Stuart or Stewart being sent to New South Wales or Van Diemen's Land for forgery. Stuart also claimed that he gained a conditional pardon in 1840 and spent the next six years in Adelaide, departing from there in 1846 for South America.

Stuart arrived at San Francisco from Panama in 1849, as a crewman aboard the side-wheel ocean steamer SS *Tennessee*. Like thousands of other seamen, he jumped ship to join the gold rush, along with fellow New South Wales ex-convict James Briggs, alias 'Jemmy-from-Town', who Stuart helped stow away aboard the *Tennessee*. In California, Stuart would use a variety of pseudonyms. One name he used was Stevens, and he had a cousin named Stevens who worked at the Mission Dolores bakery, outside San Francisco. So, this may have been English Jim's real surname. Even so, no teenager named Stevens or Stephens was transported to the Australian colonies for forgery. It's likely that English Jim's true history will never be known.

In April 1849, Stuart had settled at the Foster's Bar diggings, initially working for the Bock Mining Company. After several months, Stuart staked his own claim, and, to get around the foreign miners tax, paid several Americans including a John Sullivan to work the claim for him. English Jim also set up a vegetable garden and a trading post at the house where he lived, took a share in a boarding house that was under construction, and invested $400 in a flat-bottomed iron boat. This was the same iron boat that had ferried Tom Burdue across the North Yuba River to Foster's Bar following that winter's snow-melt. But English Jim, being English Jim, was frequently in trouble at Foster's Bar for one reason or another, and was brought up in front of Justice of the Peace Oliver P. Stidger, who had opened one of the first stores at Foster's Bar. Stidger fined Stuart on numerous occasions.

But, according to English Jim, he was a law-abiding citizen who'd experienced a run of bad luck. First, several mining companies set up in business in Foster's Bar to extract vast quantities of gold from the North Yuba by channelling the river through their earthworks. It sounded a promising idea, and Jim invested $300 in the Missouri Company. By the summer, all the companies had failed, and English Jim lost his investment. After the company left the diggings, English Jim scoured their premises for some way of recouping his loss. Finding a chest full of clothes, he took those items that fitted him. That summer, too, Edward Gifford built a toll bridge across the North Yuba River, putting English Jim's iron boat out of business. Stuart gave his boat away, and running out of money, failed to complete his boarding house.

In a sour mood, English Jim had sat down one night at the residence of a Captain Dodge to play a hand or two of French monte. Stuart considered himself a sharp card player, but he lost $200. Convinced that Dodge had cheated, and observing him place a large wooden chest in a tent, after dark next day Stuart stole the chest. Inside, he found $4600, which he kept. In September, Stuart was arrested; not for the theft of this chest, but for earlier taking the clothes from the other chest, the one belonging to the mining company. Then, something he said alerted the Foster's Bar sheriff to Stuart's part in the second robbery, and he was also charged with that. After returning all but $150 of the $4600, having spent the rest, Stuart had been freed on bail. Deciding to bolt, he had walked five kilometres before stealing a horse and riding it to Sacramento, where he sold it.

Using the name James Campbell, Stuart had stayed two weeks in Sacramento. There, he'd been involved in several robberies with Sydney Ducks, including a raid on a brig in the river which only yielded him $170. Coming down to San Francisco on the paddle-steamer *New World* with several new cronies, he'd earned a share from the robbery of a Spanish passenger aboard.

In San Francisco, Stuart had tried unsuccessfully to rob a store of its safe, then led three Ducks one night in boarding and robbing the ship *James Caskie* as it lay at anchor in San Francisco Bay. Expecting a haul of thousands of dollars, they had tied up the crew, but had only subdued the skipper after a gunfight. The captain's wife had even come at Stuart with a sword. He had disarmed her, and after she begged him not to take a gold watch given to her by her mother, and not to kill her husband, English Jim had promised not to do either. He had kept his word. But the total return of $190 from the *James Caskie* robbery would not make English Jim a rich man.

The *Caskie* job had made things too hot for English Jim in San Francisco, so after just a week there he had returned to Sacramento, where he bought a house cheap from a newly-made widow and operated it as a boarding house, still doing the occasional robbery on the side. While breaking into a house at a Sacramento lumber yard with an accomplice named Smith, Stuart had disturbed the owner, who had begun blazing away with a revolver. Smith had fallen down dead, while a bullet had gone through Stuart's hat, perilously close to his head. Rather than test the gunman's marksmanship further, English Jim had raised his hands and surrendered.

Brought before City Recorder B. F. Washington, Stuart was committed for trial, but while in a cell aboard the *La Grange* he'd been visited by a police constable from Auburn. Two brothers by the name of William and Samuel Stewart had murdered Sheriff Echols in June, and both had subsequently escaped from custody. Thinking that this prisoner Stuart was one of those Stewart brothers, the constable had come to take him back. Three hours later, two more constables arrived at the jail. One was from Foster's Bar, and he identified Stuart as the man who had robbed and murdered a Charles E. Moore in Yuba County. This Moore would be incorrectly described in later histories as the former sheriff of Yuba County. Moore had not been a sheriff. Those writers would confuse Moore with Auburn's murdered Sheriff Echols.

Stuart denied both accusations, and, on legal technicalities, his wily young Sacramento lawyer Frank Pixley twice prevented the serving of warrants for his arrest for these murders. After Stuart handed all his gold dust over to Pixley, the keys to both the jail door and the fetters around his ankles had been secretly passed to him by one of the town deputies. At night, Sacramento's city marshal and his two deputies went home, leaving the jail's occupants to their own devices. Now, in the darkness, English Jim Stuart strode quickly but quietly from the H Street Jetty and disappeared into the night. He would walk halfway to Stockton before stealing a horse, to continue his escape and resume a criminal career that would cement his place as the most wanted man in California.

Before three months had passed, the paths of English Jim Stuart, Joe Windred and Tom Burdue would cross, in the most astonishing, and, for Joe and Tom, most terrifying, of ways.

15

THE JANSEN JOB

Monday, February 17, 1851. San Francisco, California

ENGLISH JIM WAS RUNNING out of money. After his November escape from the county jail at Sacramento, he had come directly to San Francisco, to hide out in the metropolis. There, he boarded at a house near Clark's Point owned by another Sydney man, John Edwards. Though unaware that his new lodger had escaped from jail in Sacramento, Edwards was himself not averse to taking part in the occasional robbery, and would soon be recruited by Stuart. Wearing a Mexican serape, or poncho, growing a beard to avoid recognition, and rarely going out during daylight hours for the same reason, English Jim had been taken at night by Edwards to the Port Phillip House, a boarding house and bar on the corner of Jackson and Gould streets operated by two Sydney Ducks, Edward 'Teddy' McCormack and Sam Whitaker – Whitaker would soon be forced to give up his share of this business, as restitution to an American prize fighter he had swindled.

Stuart and Whitaker had much in common, and immediately hit it off. Around the same age, both liked the better things in life, both had an eye for the easy dollar, and both had been convicts in New South Wales. Whitaker, five feet six inches tall (168 centimetres) and a dapper dresser, was a native of Manchester, England. He had served sixteen years of a life sentence before earning a conditional pardon at Parramatta in February 1849. It wasn't long before he left Australia's shores, landing in San Francisco in August of the same year. Whitaker had quickly thrived here with fingers in many pies, most of them illegal.

Stuart and Whitaker had teamed up, but their joint criminal exploits only amounted to a catalogue of farcical failures. After removing the glass from the window of Flet's Butchery on Broadway, Stuart, Whitaker, John Edwards and another Duck, George Adams, had been forced to leave the butcher's safe in the street after it proved too heavy to carry. Next, an elaborate break-in at a warehouse on Minturn's Wharf went horribly awry when, just as four members of the enlarged gang were preparing to lower a safe through a hole in the floor to a waiting rowboat below, green young lookout Bob McKenzie had given the wrong signal, and, thinking the police were onto them, the others had jumped into the water and swum for their lives. Shortly after the failed Minturn job, Stuart had aborted a planned theft of $30,000 worth of diamonds from a jeweller's store when he decided that, with five people sleeping in the building, it was too risky.

Tonight, the target was the Macondray and Company store on the corner of Sansome and Pine streets, just a few blocks from the waterfront. For a month, San Francisco's elected port warden Thomas Belcher Kay had been paying particular attention to the layout of Macondray's store, and to the comings and goings of staff and money. Englishman Belcher Kay, unbeknownst to the electors of San Francisco, had served time in Van Diemen's Land, sailing to California from Hobart Town. He was in league with Whitaker and Stuart, casing most of their robberies and serving as a lookout on some of their jobs.

Belcher Kay had reported to Whitaker and Stuart: 'There are three safes, and a vault with lots of money – as much as you can take away in a boat.'[72]

Salivating at the thought of a big haul, Stuart and Whitaker had organised a rowboat, then brought together another large gang. In the moonlight, they arrived outside Macondray's store. A problem immediately raised its head. Belcher Kay had observed the store during the day. He had not bothered to see what the situation was at night, when any robbery requiring anonymity for the perpetrators would have to be staged. And as the gang assembled outside Macondray's they saw lights burning in rooms above the store, with men coming and going. A question to one of these men informed Stuart that eleven lodgers slept above the Macondray and Company store.

'Eleven men in the building?' said one of the gang members, shaking his head. 'Count me out, Jim. I'm giving it up as a bad job.'[73] Shoving his hands in his pockets, he quickly walked away.

Most of the others followed suit, leaving Stuart and Whitaker looking at each other. Stuart, increasingly frustrated and desperate for money, urged Whitaker to find him another job, and fast.

Wednesday, February 19, 1851. San Francisco, California

Joe and Mary Windred and Tom Burdue had come down to San Francisco from the diggings at Auburn in hope of news of Tom's wife and children. At Gough's restaurant they found no tidings of an arrival by Elen Burdue, so the three travellers took rooms at a boarding house nearby. If Elen did not make an appearance within the next few days, the trio would catch a boat back up to Sacramento and return to Auburn.

By early evening on the 19th, Joe, Mary and Tom were back at the Panama House for a meal with John and Elicia Gough and several other Australian friends. The identities of all who dined with Joe, Mary and Tom this evening are not recorded, but one was Captain Robert Patterson, a sea captain who had been master of a vessel trading between Launceston and Hobart Town and who now ran a tavern at Pacific Wharf. Another diner was George Cooper Turner, a recent arrival from New South Wales.

Joe's New South Wales boxing colleague Bungarribee Jack – Isaac Gorrick – had scooted off to California after the Sherringham–Dawes fight prosecution of 1849, and was living in San Francisco at this time. It's possible Gorrick was one of those who joined the dinner party. Later events point to other diners that night including James W. Whiting and his wife, Agnes. Whiting, who lived in a Sansome Street boarding house, would later confirm he knew Tom Burdue, apparently befriending him in San Francisco over the past year, having only come to California himself in 1850 from Van Diemen's Land.

As the 'Australians' enjoyed a good meal and hearty company at the Panama House, several blocks away, a crime was in motion. A crime that would change all their lives. At the Port Phillip House, English Jim Stuart, Sam Whitaker and an accomplice, fifty-year-old John 'Old Jack' Morgan, a man with a convict background in Australia and who sometimes used the name Morris in California, were preparing for a 'job'. Old Jack Morgan was bearded, short and stout, weighing close to a hundred kilograms. Leaving the Port Phillip House, the trio now hurried out into the night and met five other waiting Ducks. It was approaching 8.00 p.m. when the eight-man gang made its way through the evening chill to the Jansen and Company dry-goods store on Montgomery Street.

The night before, Whitaker, under pressure from English Jim to quickly find them another robbery target, had shared an idea with Stuart. City merchant Charles Jansen, senior partner of Jansen and Company, lived in first-floor rooms right next door to the Port Phillip House, and had come in for scrutiny from Whitaker some time back. Whitaker had told Stuart of an attempt he had made to relieve Jansen of a shipment of gold being sent from Jansen's old premises to the new shop on Montgomery Street. The wagon carrying the gold had been rigged to break down en route, but the breakdown had failed to eventuate. According to Whitaker, Jansen regularly kept $10,000 to $15,000 in the safe in his store. Much of it, he said, was in English gold sovereigns which he sold to miners returning to Australia and wishing to convert their American dollars and gold dust. Jansen habitually worked late, and alone, in his store.

Across town at the Panama House, as the parlour clock chimed 8.00 p.m., Tom Burdue bade his dining companions goodnight and set off to get a good night's rest before departing for the mountains next day. Not long after, Joe and Mary Windred did the same. As Joe went to bed, it would never have entered his head to remember that, eleven years before, to the day, in the early hours of February 19, 1840, the Barker robbery had taken place at Windsor. After all, he had no cause to recall that traumatic event. He soon would have.

From the wooden sidewalk, Stuart, Whitaker and Morgan looked in through the Jansen and Company store window, and saw the light of a candle in the back office. There, Charles Jansen was working on his accounts. English Jim's plan was for Old Jack to go into the store and distract Jansen. Stuart would then slip in and go forward with the robbery, while Whitaker stood lookout at the door. As Whitaker had discovered when watching the store over the previous few evenings, Jansen left the store's glass front doors unlocked while he continued to work.

Now, at eight o'clock, Morgan entered the store. Outside, Stuart and Whitaker peered through the window glass to try to make out what was happening inside, as their five remaining cohorts lingered close by, on watch for patrolling constables. But, as seconds turned to minutes, there was no sign of Jansen emerging from his back office, nor of Morgan making any move.

'What is taking him so long?' Stuart growled impatiently. 'We'll get no money out of this!'[74]

It seemed that Old Jack had lost his courage. Stuart opened the front doors, and entered the store. Moving like a prowling panther, he slid along behind the counter which ran up one side of the store. Stuart had gone half its length when Jansen, spotting Morgan through his open door, finally appeared from the back office, carrying a candle. Jansen would later recollect that the first man he saw wore a grey coat and a dark, broad-brimmed hat with a low crown.

'What is it you want here?' Jansen warily asked Morgan.

'Blankets,' Old Jack replied. 'I'd like to look at some blankets.'

Jansen, happy to end the day with one more sale, set his candle down on the counter then went to reach up to shelves stacked with blankets. Now from the corner of his eye he spied another man, wearing a cloak and a hat with a high, pointed crown, coming up on him behind the counter. This was Jim Stuart. Turning to Stuart, Jansen said, 'And what can I do for you?'

'I want blankets too, Mr Jansen,' said Stuart, in his friendliest voice.

Turning his back on Stuart, the storekeeper again reached for the blankets.

'Now!' Morgan urged.

From beneath his cloak, Stuart produced a slung-shot, a weapon with a wooden handle to which was attached a chain connected to a metal ball. Raising this, Stuart struck the storekeeper on the back of the head. Jansen let out a cry then collapsed to the floor.

'Take care of him while I look after the money,' Stuart instructed Morgan.[75]

Going to the store's cash drawer, Stuart removed a heavy canvas bag. The bag jingled richly with the sound of coin on coin. Deciding not to worry about Jansen's safe, and calling Morgan to follow him, Stuart headed for the door. Morgan quickly complied. Outside, the pair joined the waiting Whitaker. Then, multiplied by the five who had loitered nearby, the gang hurried away. Along streets lit by gas lamps and bright moonlight the eight men walked, to the Clark's Point house of John Edwards. There, in Stuart's room, they opened the canvas bag. Stuart counted out $1568 in gold coin. The night's haul was much less than English Jim had been hoping for, but it put him in profit for the time being. Retaining half the spoils as leader, he divided the remainder into equal portions of $96. Two of those portions would go to friendly San Francisco police officers.

The gang members then walked to the Hogan House on Sansome Street. This was a boarding house run by pert thirty-five-year-old Mary Ann Hogan. Mrs Hogan had been born in England and immigrated with her parents to New South Wales as a two-year-old, growing up in Sydney and there marrying publican Michael Hogan, a former convict. In October, 1849, the Hogans, and their small son, had sailed from Sydney for California. In San Francisco, Michael Hogan had set up in business as a merchant, but unwise property speculations had cleaned him out. He and Mary Ann had then rented the Sansome Street premises, opening them as a boarding house.

With Mr Hogan frequently away on business, most often in Oregon, his regular absences had allowed Mary Ann to enjoy the company of other men. Two Hogan House 'Australian' boarders, James W. Whiting and Joseph Hetherington, frequently saw Sam Whitaker in bed with Mrs Hogan. But Mary Ann Hogan also wore a locket around her neck containing a daguerreotype, an early form of photograph, of English Jim Stuart. Although Mary Ann Hogan had shared her favours around, she and Whitaker now lived as husband and wife, with Mary Ann's legal husband now domiciled elsewhere.

Whitaker, Stuart and Morgan spent the next three hours in the Hogan barroom with Mary Ann, celebrating their night's work. The band hoped the Jansen affair would pass relatively unnoticed and soon be forgotten. But this robbery would not pass unnoticed. Far from it. While the robbers celebrated on Sansome Street, back at his Montgomery Street store, Charles Jansen had regained consciousness. Pulling himself to his feet, the storekeeper put a hand to the back of his head. He found it covered with his own blood. Slowly, he made his way to the door, supporting himself with a hand on the counter. Managing to open the door, he stepped out onto the threshold, and called for help.

From across the street, Jansen's commercial neighbour Theodore Payne, a real estate agent, came running to his aid. By the time Payne reached him, Jansen had again collapsed, and Payne found him bleeding and unconscious. Jansen's clerks were summoned, and they carried their employer to his residence, next door to the Port Phillip House, which was, unbeknownst to them, a lair of the gang that had carried out the robbery. Jansen's doctor was called. So, too, were the police.

16

A GOLDEN MADNESS

Friday, February 21, 1851. San Francisco, California

IT HAD BEEN A cold, grey day, punctuated by drizzle that oozed in from the Pacific in sheets. The side-wheel riverboat SS *McKim* sat at Central Wharf with smoke curling from its tall, slender smokestack. Lining the rails of the *McKim*'s two passenger decks, hundreds of travellers watched the busy scenes on the dock. The vessel was not due to depart for the journey up the Sacramento River to Sacramento City until late afternoon, and last-minute passengers continued to hurry along damp streets to the dock.

Mary Windred was already aboard the river steamer. She, Joe and Tom had decided to head back to Auburn. While Mary had gone on ahead and boarded with their baggage, Joe had accompanied Tom to the Panama House for one final check for news of Elen Burdue and the Burdue children. Several newly arrived vessels had dropped anchor in the bay that morning, and there was a possibility that the Burdue family was aboard one of them. Finding that there was still no word of Tom's family, the two men set off for the wharf.

It was coming up to 4.00 p.m. when Joe and Tom reached the *McKim* gangway, coat collars up and hats pulled down tight as protection against the weather. Two local police constables were standing at the bottom of the gangway. They were in conversation with a constable from Sacramento who was returning home, but their eyes took in every passenger who passed. The previous morning, Charles Jansen, whose doctor considered him to be in a critical condition, had been visited at his bedside by police, and the victim of Wednesday night's robbery had given descriptions of the two men who had attacked and robbed him. Jansen also told the police that his clerks had checked his cash drawer to find that the thieves had relieved him of $2000 in gold coin, silver coin and gold dust.

In description and total, this loss did not correlate with the $1568 in gold coin that English Jim Stuart had taken from Jansen. But, it was common for San Francisco businesspeople to overstate their losses after robberies and fires, usually with the purpose of increasing their insurance payouts. The previous October, following the raid by English Jim and three cronies, the captain of the *James Caskie* had stated that $900 had been stolen, when the robbers had only escaped with $190. In Jansen's case, his claim of a $2000 loss could have been an error, or he may have deliberately overstated it for insurance purposes. Another possibility was that his clerks, when checking on the loss after Jansen had been taken home, had themselves pilfered an additional $432 in silver coin and gold dust from their employer before reporting a total loss of $2000.

When furnishing the police with a description of his two assailants, Jansen had said both had English accents. Jansen's recollection of the second man was hazy, but the details he provided of the man who hit him immediately led Irish-born Malachi Fallon, San Francisco's city marshal, or chief of police, to declare that the criminal in question had to be none other than the infamous English Jim Stuart.

The news of the Jansen robbery, and the fact that Jansen's doctor did not expect his patient to live, had generated uproar among the town's businesspeople. Claims would soon be aired by leading San Francisco merchants, and repeated by many future historians, that their city was in the grip of a wave of violent crime, involving hundreds of unsolved murders. There had in fact been just two murders in San Francisco over the past two months, and the last robbery with violence, English Jim's attack on the skipper of the *Caskie* out in the bay, had taken place the previous autumn. Of the 741 crimes reported in the city during 1850–51, the vast majority involved disorderly conduct, break-ins or the picking of pockets. Robbery with violence was a rare experience.[76]

Even the *Caskie* affair had excited little interest in the city, because the victim, the vessel's captain, was an outsider. Charles Jansen, on the other hand, was a well-known and well-liked San Franciscan, and, with him expected to die from his wound, his fellow businessmen were fearful that they might be next on the perpetrators' lethal visiting list. As a result, Marshal Fallon had sent his six captains, six sergeants and forty-five constables out with orders to find English Jim and bring him in. The police had been watching the wharves and giving departing passengers the once-over ever since.

As, chatting together, Joe Windred and Tom Burdue went to step onto the *McKim*'s gangway, the policeman from Sacramento frowned Tom's way, then said in a low voice to his San Francisco colleagues that he thought he recognised the shorter of the two men. A policeman reached out, took hold of Tom's arm, and demanded his name.

'Tom Burdue,' Tom replied with surprise.

Tom's companion was also asked his name.

'I'm Joe Windred,' Joe responded.

Now, one of the constables spotted a dark stain on the right elbow of Joe's thick grey winter coat, and remarked that it looked like blood to him. Joe responded that it was not blood, but couldn't remember how it had got there. A crowd quickly gathered to watch as Joe and Tom were taken to one side and searched. There were 'ooh's and 'aah's from the bystanders when the constables took a large amount of gold coin from Tom; it totalled $1700. Joe was not carrying any money; Mary had all their funds.

'James Stuart,' said one of the constables, 'I arrest you for the armed robbery of Charles Jansen.'

'But, I'm not James Stuart,' Tom protested, as the policeman clapped handcuffs on his wrists. 'I'm Thomas Burdue!'

'There is some mistake!' said Joe, as handcuffs were also produced for him. 'I can vouch for the fact that he is not James Stuart.'

The constables were in no mood for discussion. They were convinced that the stain on Joe's elbow was Charles Jansen's dried blood. At this point, Joe had a decision to make. The policemen were only armed with truncheons, and Joe was an experienced boxer packing a proven punch. He could have floored all three constables, and he and Tom might have made their escape. But that would have only made them fugitives. Where would they go? And where would that leave Mary? Deciding it was better to go along with these pedantic constables and clear up this stupid misunderstanding with their more intelligent superiors, Joe did not resist, and allowed his hands to be cuffed. The manacled pair was then led from the wharf and up to Kearny Street and the Police Office at City Hall, three blocks away.[77]

Aboard the *McKim*, the vessel's master, the gentlemanly thirty-three-year-old Captain Charles Brenham, came to Mary Windred and apologetically informed her that her husband had just been arrested and taken away. Swiftly overcoming her shock, Mary had her baggage removed from the boat and left the *McKim* before it sailed, to go in search of Joe.

That evening, Bellini's opera *La Sonnambula* had its opening night at the Adelphi Theatre on Clay Street, performed by the visiting Pellegrini Opera Troupe. It was the first opera ever presented in San Francisco. Yet, for all its colourful melodrama, the Italian opera would not match the gripping real-life drama that would be played out in the city's streets in the coming days.

Saturday, February 22, 1851. San Francisco, California

At 11.00 a.m., on the north side of Portsmouth Square, journalist Edward Gould Buffum was at his desk in the first-floor offices of the *Alta California* newspaper. Twenty-nine years of age, Buffum was at this time the paper's local reporter. Before he had finished at the *Alta California*, he would be its editor. Rhode Island-born, Buffum had left a journalistic post with the *New York Herald* at the 1846 outbreak of the Mexican–American War to volunteer for military service. Commissioned a lieutenant with the 7th Regiment of New York Volunteers, he had subsequently been sent to California with the regiment. Discharged here in 1848, Buffum had joined several other former officers from the 7th New York, including the regiment's commander, Colonel Jonathan D. Stevenson, digging for gold. After six fruitless months in the diggings, Buffum had settled in San Francisco and joined the staff of the *Alta California*.

This Saturday morning, an excited youth came through the paper's door, bearing the news that the two men arrested for the Jansen robbery were to be examined by a magistrate that afternoon. But first, the prisoners were to be shown to the victim, for the purposes of identification. News of the previous afternoon's arrest of 'English Jim Stuart and another Sydney Duck' for the Jansen robbery had appeared in the *Alta California* and the city's four other daily morning papers that a.m., creating great interest and excitement throughout San Francisco.

Buffum was told by his editor, thirty-year-old Edward Gilbert, another former lieutenant with the 7th New York Volunteers, 'Jansen, it appears, has become worse, and it is feared that he will die. It is, therefore, highly important that the men should be confronted with him as speedily as possible, and his testimony taken.'[78]

Buffum was given the task of using his contacts within the police and judiciary to gain access to this confrontation.

Joe and Tom had spent a cold, uncomfortable night in cells beneath San Francisco's City Hall on the corner of Pacific and Kearny streets. Joe was especially cold, as his warm winter coat had been taken from him by the police, as 'evidence'. The pair had been warned by their jailers that nobody had escaped from these cells since new double-acting cam and lever locks had been fitted back in December. Not that the duo planned an escape attempt. Both were determined to clear up the misunderstanding that had led to their arrest, and walk out those cell doors free men.

Now, just before noon, two policemen bundled them out the basement door and into a closed carriage waiting on Kearny Street. The carriage carried them, and their escort, across town to the building where Charles Jansen lived, next to the Port Phillip House. They were taken up a flight of stairs and into an apartment. In a bedroom, Charles Jansen, with pale face and bandaged head, sat propped up in his bed. At the bedside were magistrate Justice Philip W. Shepheard and his clerk, together with a friend of Jansen's and Jansen's doctor. Also present was reporter Edward Buffum, notebook and pencil at the ready. Joe and Tom were made to stand, handcuffed, at the end of the bed, so that Jansen could study them.

'I warn you,' said Jansen's doctor dramatically to magistrate

Shepheard, 'this may be too taxing for my patient. He may be on the point of his grave.'[79]

But Jansen, with a weak voice, announced that he was fit and able to proceed. First, he described the robbery, from his point of view. The magistrate then asked if Jansen recognised either of the men in front of him as participants in that robbery. According to Edward Buffum, Jansen did not answer at first: 'Jansen looked carefully at both of them, scanning thoroughly their features.'

Then, Jansen said, 'I recognise that one, the smaller one.' He pointed to Tom. 'He is the one who felled me with the iron bar.'

'You have identified the man known as James Stuart,' Justice Shepheard confirmed, for the record.

Tom protested that Jansen was in error, and that he was not James Stuart, but the police hushed him.

The magistrate asked the storekeeper, 'Of this you can have no doubt? He is the man who struck you?'

'I have no doubt,' Jansen unhesitatingly replied. 'I am positive he is the man.'

'What of the other man? Do you recognise him at all?'

All eyes turned to Joe Windred. He stood tall, trim and well-groomed, as opposed to short, fat, slovenly Old Jack Morgan, the true accomplice to English Jim's crime.

'As to the other . . .' Jansen hesitated. 'I'm not sure. But, my doubts are light.'

'He was the second robber?' Justice Shepheard pressed.

'I believe so,' said Jansen, adding that the second man had worn a grey coat and black hat, and had been bearded.

Joe was clean-shaven, but his questioners reasoned that he could have shaved off a beard since the robbery. He did wear a black hat. And his coat, with the suspicious stain on the elbow, was grey. Joe now went to protest his innocence, but he too was told to be quiet and informed that he would have the chance to put his side of the story later.

'So, Mr Jansen,' said the magistrate, 'in short, you fully and firmly believe that the two men who committed the crime now stand before you. Is that so?'

Jansen slowly nodded. 'That is so.'[80]

Joe and Tom were promptly removed from Jansen's apartment,

returned to the carriage, and taken to the Plaza, which was beginning to fill with a crowd of many hundreds of young men. There was an old Spanish mud-brick structure not far from the *Alta California* office on the north side of the Plaza. Known as the Adobe Building, it housed various tenants, including Justice Shepheard. Joe and Tom were taken inside, to the magistrate's office. Shepheard and his clerk soon joined them, as did reporter Edward Buffum.

Buffum had walked from Jansen's residence to the magistrate's office. Passing through the now-crowded Plaza to get there, he could sense a threatening atmosphere in the air. Buffum would later say of this moment, 'It was evident that trouble was brewing.' Word had quickly spread that English Jim and another Australian were being brought before a magistrate to face charges for the Jansen robbery. Rumour was rife, and many in the all-male crowd thought the victim of the crime, Jansen, had died. Certainly, Jansen's condition appeared serious, and when Buffum left Jansen's apartment the newspaperman had supposed Jansen's testimony 'to be that of a dying man'.[81]

The men now in the Plaza were mostly members of what *San Francisco Directory* publisher Charles Kimball described as San Francisco's 'floating population'.[82] A mixture of disappointed gold-seekers without gainful employment and miners briefly in the city for a good time, they were, according to police chief Malachi Fallon, 'rough young men with adventurous spirits'. In Fallon's estimation, 'many of them were of the cowboy class, while the worst were deserting whalemen'.[83] In the crowd as Buffum passed through, all the talk was of punishing the Sydney Ducks. Buffum reached the magistrate's office in time to witness the examination of the two prisoners by Justice Shepheard, who, if he felt they had a case to answer, would file a complaint against them. With the magistrate and his clerk at their desks, Tom and Joe were made by their police escorts to stand side-by-side before them.

This whole affair had to be, to Joe, the cruellest of ironies, an insane replay of the Barker robbery eleven years before. Although, this time the roles had been reversed. In both cases he had been wrongly accused of participating in armed robbery. Back in 1840, he had been falsely identified as the affair's leader. This time, his friend Tom was accused of being robber-in-chief. In both cases, wrong identities featured. This time, Joe's mate Tom was being called Jim Stuart, but was not him. Eleven years back, Joe's then best mate had been indicted as Andrew Garven, but was actually Andrew Hogan.

Justice Shepheard looked up at Tom, and asked, coldly, 'Name?'

'Tom Burdue,' Tom replied.

The magistrate instructed his clerk to show the prisoner's name as 'James Stuart, alias Thomas Burdue'. The clerk misspelled Tom's last name as 'Berdue', and so it would be spelled in official documents, newspaper reports and books from that time forward.

Justice Shepheard glared up at Joe. 'Name?'

'Joe Windred,' Joe firmly replied.

'Joseph Windred,' said the magistrate to his clerk, who noted down the name.

In court documents and most American newspaper accounts Joe would be correctly referred to as Joseph Windred, but some newspaper reports and subsequent Californian histories and law books would variously identify him as Robert Windred, William Windred, and Joseph Wildred.

'Where in San Francisco do you reside?' the magistrate next asked Tom.

'I've been in the mines,' Tom replied. 'I only arrived in San Francisco a few days ago, with my chum Joe Windred here. We are chums in the mining camp at Auburn.'

'It's true,' said Joe, backing him up.

'I know nothing of the robbery of Mr Jansen,' Tom went on.

'Nor I,' Joe chimed in.

'Have you ever been known by the name of Stuart?' the irritated Shepheard asked Tom.

'No. Never.'

Since the pair's arrest the previous afternoon, the police had been scouring San Francisco for men who knew English Jim Stuart. Now, in a swift procession, six men were brought in by constables and asked by the magistrate to identify Tom. All swore that Tom was James Stuart. One of these witnesses was an American named John Sullivan, who was working as a boatman on the San Francisco waterfront. This was the same John Sullivan who had been employed by English Jim at Foster's Bar the previous year.

'I have lived with him for months in the same camp,' said Sullivan, indicating Tom. 'I know him well. He had always been known there as Jim Stuart.'

Once the last witness departed, Justice Shepheard said to Tom and Joe, 'This evidence, taken in connection with the testimony of Mr Jansen, leaves no doubt in my mind about the two of you. It is my plain duty to send you before the city recorder, and should he be equally satisfied of your guilt, he will be obliged to commit you to trial.'[84]

This was an era when government and commerce operated six days a week, and the city recorder, Franklin Tilford, was at that moment presiding over a Superior Court session at City Hall. But, for the police, getting their prisoners back to the City Hall building would not be as easy as getting them out of it had been earlier. City Hall was just a block away, but the Plaza outside the Adobe Building, and all surrounding streets, now overflowed with thousands of boisterous young men who were growing impatient for action.

Deciding it was too dangerous to try to take Tom and Joe out the front way, the police opted to smuggle them out the back. The closed carriage was sent to an alley behind the Adobe Building, and Joe, Tom and their guards climbed into it, before being taken on a circuitous back street route which eventually saw the carriage pulling up at the Kearny Street basement door to the cells beneath City Hall.

Reporter Edward Buffum had gone outside into the crowded Plaza, and he was there when word flashed through the throng that the two Sydney Ducks had been spotted just then climbing from a carriage outside City Hall. The crowd, 'moved by one common impulse', said Buffum, 'surged like sea waves through Kearny Street, and reached the courthouse just after the two men had been taken into the Superior Court'.[85] Buffum went with the crowd as it flooded around City Hall. This large corner building of five storeys plus basement had started life as the Graham House Hotel before being purchased by the city in 1850. The building had three ornate balconies around its Kearny Street and Pacific Street frontages, one above the other. These balconies soon filled with a crush of agitated young men, as did Kearny and Pacific streets for as far as the eye could see.

A representative of the mayor of San Francisco who came out onto City Hall's lower balcony called on the crowd to disperse, declaring that the recorder and grand jury would ensure that the men responsible for the Jansen robbery were duly dealt with. But this did not satisfy the crowd, which stood its ground. Soon, another figure appeared on the lower balcony. One of the best-known young men in San Francisco, he raised his hands and called for silence so that he might be heard.

His name was Samuel Brannan, and he was an elder of the Mormon Church. Brother Brannan was just twenty-nine years old, almost the same age as Joe Windred. But Brannan had a lot more money and influence than Joe. He was reputedly California's first millionaire. In 1846, Brannan had led a party of 240 Mormon settlers to California from New York. Arriving by sea after rounding Cape Horn, the Mormons had trebled the size of the Spanish village on San Francisco Bay. Using Mormon funds to set up a trading post upriver at Sutter's Fort, the later Sacramento, supposedly to subsidise the Mormon community, Brannan had kept the profits, for which he was subsequently ejected by his church.

And what profits they had been! It was Brannan who, in the spring of 1848, had run through the streets holding up a glass jar containing pieces of gold purchased from the first American River prospectors, and yelling, 'Gold! Gold!' Brannan's cry had launched the California gold rush. Since then, he had made his fortune by supplying gold-seekers with tools and provisions. He had subsequently bought much San Francisco land and multiplied his profits. Brannan had also been elected to San Francisco's first town council.

Once the shouting had faded away, slight, clean-cut Brannan began to speak, as if from the pulpit. 'I am very much surprised to hear people talk about grand juries, recorders and mayors. I'm tired of such talk. These men are murderers, I say, as well as thieves. I know it, and I will die or see them hung by the neck!' A great roar of approval went up from the crowd. 'I'm opposed to any farce in this business,' Brannan went on. 'We had that eighteen months ago, when we allowed ourselves to be the tools of those judges who sentenced convicts to be sent to the United States. We are the mayor and the recorder, the hangman and the law!'

Yet another great roar erupted from the crowd, for whom a public hanging would be a novel entertainment, a new piece of sport for bored young men.

Brannan, encouraged by the response, continued in the same vein. 'The laws and the courts have never yet hung a man in California, and every morning we are reading fresh accounts of murders and robberies. I want no technicalities! Such things are devised to shield the guilty!'[86] He then urged the young men before him to take the law into their own hands.

With that, baying for blood, the crowd on Pacific Street surged forward and crashed through the courthouse doors. Reporter Edward Buffum was willingly swept forward in the rush, for he was keen to witness, and report on, what transpired. The Superior Court was set up much in the style of an English courtroom. Recorder Tilford sat at a desk at one end of the large room. Joe Windred and Tom Burdue sat in a wooden prisoners' box before him. A wooden railing separated the body of the court from the public gallery.

The mob, as it had now become, surged into the gallery yelling at the top of their voices. Joe and Tom turned from where they sat, and recoiled at the sight of the anonymous hundreds coming for them. According to reporter Buffum, the pair 'trembled like aspen'.[87] (Aspen are a poplar tree variety whose delicate leaves tremble in the slightest breeze.) In any other situation, Joe would have raised his fists and defended himself; but with manacles clamped around his wrists, he was defenceless.

Recorder Tilford jumped to his feet, and, thinking fast, opened a door behind him. Tilford knew that, in the adjacent room, twenty men of the Washington Guard militia were at that moment drilling with their arms. He called for the militia's aid, and their commander, Captain Abraham Bartol, a city alderman, led his part-time soldiers at the rush through the door, with rifles raised and bayonets fixed. Meanwhile, a dozen men at the forefront of the mob's charge had broken down the rail separating the gallery from the body of the courtroom. Rushing to the prisoners' box, they had their hands on Joe and Tom and were in the process of dragging them out. It was at this moment that the militiamen arrived at the run.

Buffum, in the gallery, watched as 'the two frightened wretches' struggled to escape the mob's clutches, then saw the picture quickly change, as the sight of bayonets bearing down on them terrified the insurgents. Mob members let go of Joe and Tom, turned, and fled for the door, crushing into others pushing in behind them. Chasing the now-panicking crowd, militiamen clambered over court tables, 'driving them like sheep', according to Buffum.

In seconds, the courtroom, and then the building, was emptied of intruders. With Recorder Tilford's court left a shambles, he ordered the prisoners returned to their cells below. Joe and Tom were led away, so shaken that they looked 'more dead than alive' in Edward Buffum's view.[88]

More militiamen were summoned by their commander Captain Bartol. Thirty men answered the call. A total of fifty militiamen now lined up along Kearny Street in front of the City Hall basement, guarding and protecting Joe and Tom. The crowd not only remained, but as the afternoon drew into evening it grew even larger, until, by some estimates, it numbered ten thousand men. The vast majority were rowdy young Americans, all shouting for Joe and Tom to be brought out, handed over to them, and hanged on the spot. Some Sydney Ducks were spotted on the crowd's periphery, a few curious, but most looking worried by the calls for the execution of their fellow Ducks. For, who was to say the mob would stop at lynching just two Australians?

One after the other, Sam Brannan and fellow speakers mounted the City Hall balcony and addressed the gathering in passionate tones. Edward Buffum had rejoined the crowd, and made notes of the speeches. 'The story of the robbery was told, over and over again,' he would write. 'The tardy progress of justice [was] complained of, and the probable escape of the prisoners if left to be tried by the instituted authorities.' Extravagant rhetoric prevailed. 'The imagination of the multitude was excited by glowing pictures of San Francisco in flames while murder, robbery and rapine were being committed by the gangs of Sydney Ducks which infested the city. The invariable conclusion of all these speeches was that the prisoners should be immediately brought out and hung.'[89] Yet, even though the mob outnumbered the militia two hundred to one, not even the speakers' incitements could give them the courage to go against the armed men guarding the prisoners.

One later writer of Californian history, who was born six years after these events, would characterise San Francisco in 1851 as a city where every businessman went to work with a pistol in his belt, and slept with the weapon beneath his pillow at night.[90] This description does not match with contemporary accounts. If the men in today's crowd carried pistols, no commentator on the spot mentioned it.

Besides, had these men carried pistols, they would not have let a mere fifty armed militiamen stand in their way. As for Sam Brannan and the other speakers, Buffum was to scornfully say, 'Not a single one of the loud-mouthed orators felt inclined, or manifested the slightest disposition to lead his hearers, to an assault, which, although it might be successful, might also cost him his life.'[91]

Mary Windred was desperate. Late Friday afternoon, after disembarking from the S.S. *McKim*, she had returned to the boarding house where she and Joe had spent the past several nights. How long she would have to stay here, alone, she had no idea. But she was not leaving San Francisco without Joe. Hanging back on the fringe of the mob now, she listened with dread as Americans called for her husband to be brought out and hanged in the street.

During the afternoon, as the harangues continued from the City Hall balcony, Methodist minister William Taylor had stood up in the Plaza at his usual Sunday preaching point in front of the Adobe Building. Apparently, he had originally chosen this location because a large pole with a crossbeam supporting the building's A-frame roof at the Plaza end formed a giant cross. In front of this cross, Taylor now began to deliver a sermon on the preciousness of life, railing against ungodly acts. He soon attracted a crowd of fifteen hundred away from the throng outside City Hall, with Mary Windred among them. Once Taylor had finished speaking and his audience began to drift back to the larger crowd outside City Hall, Mary made her way to the minister.

'Reverend, I am Mary Windred, wife of Joe Windred,' she informed the surprised Taylor. 'You must help Joe and Tom.'

With Mary assuring him that her husband could not have had anything to do with the robbery of Charles Jansen because he had been with her at the time, Taylor agreed that he would go to the prisoners and see what he could do to help them. Leaving Mary at the Plaza, Taylor set off for City Hall. Members of the crowd were standing shoulder to shoulder, but some parted to let the well-known preacher through. 'I, with great difficulty,' Taylor would later say, 'pressed my way through the excited mass.' Reaching a thin line of armed militiamen extending in front of the basement cells, he was able to convince the Washington Guards' Captain Bartol to admit him.

Led to their cells, Taylor joined Joe and Tom, who assured him that they were not who the police claimed they were, and that they had never even heard of English Jim Stuart prior to being arrested by the police at the *McKim* gangway. Taylor promised to do what he could, then went to depart. But the chant outside of 'Hang them! Hang them!' could be clearly heard, and Tom begged the minister not to leave them. Taylor relented, and sat down with the pair. His was the only friendly face they had seen since their arrest. Taylor would write, 'I spent some time with the prisoners, as they were expecting every minute to be dragged out and hung.'[92]

Joe was taking this ordeal better than Tom. His years in convict chains, combined with tough bouts in the boxing ring, had given him endurance and an indomitable will. And he seems to have been born with courage to spare. A member of his family would later say that Joe was 'fearless'.[93] Joe's only difficulty right now was in coming to terms with the false accusation that had been levelled against Tom and himself. Especially when he had gone through a similar traumatic exercise eleven years before. How many tests of character was one man supposed to endure?

While Joe was grateful for the Reverend Taylor's benevolent company, he could see in the minister's eyes, just as he had seen in the eyes of the police, the magistrate, the recorder and militiamen guarding them, the belief that he and Tom were guilty as charged. Taylor would confirm this, when he wrote about these events seven years later. 'In the administration of California lynch law, the thunderbolt of public fury always fell on the head of the guilty man,' he said. In Taylor's view, all men lynched in California were guilty. 'The guilty man,' he went on, 'by the enormity and palpable character of his crime, excited it [the noose]. And then not till his guilt was proved to the satisfaction of the masses comprising the court.'[94] Joe and Tom might have the clergyman's company, but not his sympathy. They were still very much on their own.

The afternoon passed with the minister inside with the prisoners, and with the vast mob still in place outside, like a circumventing army. Come twilight, a freshly printed handbill was distributed through the crowd, whose literate members eagerly read it. Unsigned, the handbill called on all men who valued true justice to assemble here again next day at 2.00 p.m. to settle, once and for all, the issue of the two Sydney Ducks in custody. Prompted by this, after nightfall a number of men departed the scene, but a crowd several hundred strong remained outside City Hall all night to ensure that Burdue and Windred were not permitted to escape.

17

THE KANGAROO COURT

Sunday, February 23, 1851. San Francisco, California

Sunday's weather proved to be mild and pleasant. This, combined with the unfinished business of the Jansen affair, drew an ever-enlarging crowd to the streets outside City Hall as the morning progressed. The *Alta California* was the only paper which published on Sundays, and the latest issue was being voraciously read in the crowd. The paper carried Edward Buffum's detailed account of the previous day's stormy affairs inside and outside City Hall. It also ran a cautionary editorial, penned by Buffum's boss Ed Gilbert, which declared, 'Lynch law is a whirlwind which once set loose may sweep down all peaceable barriers before its angry blast.' But Gilbert's view was in the minority among young Americans in San Francisco.

Along with the legitimate news of Saturday's events, a rumour was circulating through the streets at an early hour. That rumour held that, overnight, a deal had been struck between the authorities and a committee of fourteen businessmen led by Sam Brannan and representing those calling for the lynching of Tom Burdue and Joe Windred. That deal, it was said, was for the two prisoners to be handed over to the mob; not for immediate hanging, but for a trial by what Buffum characterised as a 'lynch court'.[95]

The rumour proved to be true. During the night, the militiamen guarding Tom and Joe had lost their nerve. Only part-time soldiers, they lived and worked alongside their fellow Americans in the city. The friends, relatives and neighbours of those militiamen had worked on them, threatening, cajoling. The militiamen, reasoning that their lives would not be worth living if they continued to guard these Sydney Ducks, prepared to simply walk away. The agreement that Tom and Joe would be put on 'trial' was a compromise secured by police chief Fallon and the city's justices in discussion with Brannan's committee. With Fallon's own men unwilling to put their lives on the line for the two Australians, the police chief and the other legally elected officials of San Francisco now also turned their backs on Burdue and Windred.

Edward Buffum, again in the crowd, estimated that by noon 'nearly all the male population' of San Francisco had assembled outside City Hall and in the streets leading to it.[96] Once more, Sydney Ducks occupied the fringes, anxious to see what became of their compatriots, and equally anxious to gauge the mood in the crowd in case it proved prudent to make themselves scarce. Many Ducks had already left town, just to be on the safe side. For the moment, the crowd was quiet and orderly, with the knowledge that a compromise had been sealed in the night, and in the expectation that the prisoners would soon be handed over to them. Inside the jail, Joe and Tom knew that something was afoot, although they did not know precisely what.

A little before 2.00 p.m., Buffum saw 'a young and well-known lawyer' appear on the courthouse balcony.[97] Six days short of his twenty-seventh birthday, William Tell Coleman had been a wholesale dealer and commission merchant on Sansome Street for the past two years. A native of Kentucky, where his father, the equally colourfully named Napoleon Bonaparte Coleman, had served as a member of the Kentucky state legislature, Coleman was a handsome, clean-cut young man who was well-liked by his fellow Americans in San Francisco.

Although described as a lawyer by reporter Buffum, and he had attended university and possessed pretensions of legal knowledge, Coleman had never practised as a lawyer. It is likely that Coleman had been responsible, at least in part, for having the previous evening's handbill printed and distributed. He had certainly been one of the businessmen who had negotiated with the authorities in the night. Coleman had attended church that morning. Now, once the crowd fell silent, he addressed them.

'We don't want a mob,' he began. 'We will not have a mob. But let us organise as becomes men.' This was met by nods and sober words of agreement in the crowd. 'Let it be done immediately here, as a committee of citizens, and as a court, and coolly maintain the right, and insist upon it.' This brought louder agreement. 'These men can be tried in three hours' time, and the truth known then as clearly as ever it can be. The witnesses are all here. If any delays are allowed, they will be spirited away, as others have been heretofore. And justice cheated, and the high-handed outrages lately so common, will be encouraged, continued and increased!'[98] The crowd roared its support for Coleman's view.

Inside the jail, Joe and Tom could not hear the speech, but they could hear the swelling voices of the crowd, and could hear the tone of threat. To them, the most astonishing thing about their predicament would have been the fact that, prior to this, they had promptly been brought before a magistrate and sent to be committed for trial in the Superior Court by the city recorder, as the law provided. At no stage had the legitimate authorities dragged their feet or even hinted that the two prisoners would not be put on trial. In fact, the recorder had been forced to adjourn Tom and Joe's hearing when the mob burst into his courtroom. If anyone had delayed justice, it had been the mob, and those who incited it. With no legitimate cause for public complaint about the way the two accused had been officially treated to date, Joe and Tom could only conclude that the mob, and more especially their leaders, were merely thirsting to see the pair of them strung up.

'All who are in favour of this motion,' called Coleman, 'that we organise and take this business in our own hands immediately, will signify it by saying "Aye".'

'Aye!!!' was the thunderous response from thousands of voices. Coleman himself would later state, 'There was a unanimous shout and yell.'[99]

Coleman then hurried to the courthouse door, and, with the militia now making no attempt to stop him or his followers, led a surge into the inner hall which served as the courtroom. The debris from the previous day's intrusion still lay where it had fallen; the broken rail, overturned tables and desks. Coleman mounted a chair, and the multitude swelled around him. Only a percentage of the mob could fit into the hall, so the others had to remain outside and await news of developments.

'We should select a good citizen,' Coleman declared from his vantage point, 'one of the best men in the city, to act as judge in this case.'[100]

There was resounding agreement. Whether or not it had been prearranged is not known, but close by Coleman in the crowd stood John F. Spence. Like Coleman a San Francisco merchant of note, Spence operated a store on Leidesdorff Street. Coleman did not know Spence well. He would later say that he supposed, by his accent, that Spence was English. But Spence was of mature age, and no one had any objection to his nomination. Spence's was the only name put forward, and, when the man himself did not object to playing judge in the next act of the Jansen robbery drama, Spence was elected by acclamation.

In swift succession, other 'officers of the court' were nominated and elected on the voices of those in the room. H. R. Bowie and Charles L. Ross were made associate justices, and W. A. Jones clerk of this new 'people's court'. All were local businesspeople. Charles Ross, for example, was a significant landowner in the city and had been San Francisco's postmaster in 1849, before losing that appointment. John E. Townes was elected sheriff for the purpose of the trial, and he selected twenty or so men from the crowd to act as a 'citizen's guard' to keep watch over the prisoners, and these men armed themselves. As Tom and Joe's defence counsel in the planned trial, the crowd elected Matthew Hall McAllister and D. O. Shattuck, practising attorneys both, although neither was present. And to prosecute the case, none other than William Tell Coleman himself was nominated and elected, and he happily accepted the role.

In his speech outside City Hall, Coleman had said that this court could convene within three hours, but no one saw the need to wait even that long. It was agreed the trial would begin less than an hour from now, at 3.00 p.m., right here in this courtroom. Twelve members of the crowd were now selected at random to sit as jurors in the case. At the same time, messengers were sent to find defence attorneys McAllister and Shattuck and inform them that they were required to attend and defend the prisoners.

W. A. Jones, the man appointed clerk of this lynch court, went down to the cells and advised Joe and Tom that they would go on trial for their lives at 3.00. He also asked them to nominate witnesses whom they wished called in their defence. As far as Joe and Tom were concerned, their defence hinged on proving they had been falsely identified as James Stuart and his accomplice, and the fact that they were dining at the Panama House at the time of the Jansen robbery.

Given pen, ink and paper by Jones, Tom wrote a list of the men who had dined with Joe and himself on the evening of the 19th. Jones took the list to 'Judge' Spence, who in turn issued subpoenas for all the named witnesses. With police chief Fallon having surrendered his authority to the mob, at whose beck and call the police now were, Spence summoned several constables, handed them the subpoenas, and instructed the officers to serve them.

Promptly at 3.00, Joe and Tom were brought up from the cells and into the courtroom by their new sentinels, and placed in the prisoners' box. The armed men of the 'citizen's guard' took station around the box and at the courtroom door. The overflowing gallery was full of animated conversation. Outside, the massive crowd would be updated on the trial's progress by a relay of messengers.

One influential later Californian author would say that Windred and Burdue were excluded from the courtroom and were not present, but she confused this trial with subsequent lynch-court proceedings, where the accused were routinely excluded from the trials that decided whether they lived or died.[101] The *Alta California*'s Edward Buffum, who was present in the courtroom for this trial and would write a detailed firsthand account of what took place, not only made it clear that Joe and Tom were in the prisoners' box throughout, but he wrote of their reaction to what transpired around them during the course of the trial.

From his seat in the gallery, Buffum observed the two prisoners as they looked around from the box and surveyed the packed courtroom. According to the reporter, Tom Burdue was trembling with fear. Joe was looking for Mary, or any other friendly face, but found neither. All he saw was a sea of people who had already judged and sentenced him in their heads and hearts. Said Buffum of Joe at this moment as he looked around at the gallery, 'He saw written upon their faces anything but hope for him.'[102]

Joe eyed Coleman, the self-confident young prosecutor, and, at a separate table, the two men who had been selected by the mob to defend the accused. Both attorneys had agreed to act for them, although neither had the opportunity to speak with their clients prior to the trial's commencement. Joe had never met McAllister or Shattuck, and knew nothing about either. Shattuck was a native of Tennessee who had arrived in San Francisco the previous April accompanied by three sons. While two Shattuck sons had high-tailed it to the gold diggings, the father had set up a law office on Clay Street.

Shattuck senior would not play a lead role in determining Joe Windred's fate in the coming hours, but, if Joe could consider himself lucky in any respect when it came to this injustice, he was lucky to have Hall McAllister on his side. Buffum described McAllister as 'an old and conscientious lawyer'.[103] He was old in the context of gold-rush California, at fifty years of age. In the opinion of one later historian, Hall McAllister was rare among lawyers in early California. Rare for his honesty, and his legal ability.[104]

Matthew Hall McAllister had been born at Savannah, Georgia. After attending Princeton University he entered the Georgia State Bar at the age of twenty. In private practice for many years, and United States Attorney for the Southern District of Georgia for seven years, he had also served as Mayor of Savannah and a member of Georgia's state senate. After a failed run as Democrat candidate for Governor of Georgia, by 1850 McAllister had become disillusioned with affairs in his home state and moved to California, setting up in private practice in San Francisco. Of all the people in this courtroom now, McAllister knew by far the most about the law and its administration. But in this unofficial and illegal 'people's court', that knowledge might count for nothing.

'Judge' Spence, sitting at the desk at the head of the courtroom with his two 'associate judges', called the trial to order, and invited Prosecutor Coleman to make an opening address. The courtroom fell silent, and Coleman came to his feet and delivered a short, calm speech to the jury, announcing that he would prove to the jurymen's satisfaction that James Stuart, alias Thomas Burdue, and Joseph Windred were jointly guilty of perpetrating the heinous crimes of armed robbery and attempted murder against the person of Charles Jansen on the night of February 19. Coleman then called his first prosecution witnesses.

To much excitement, Charles Jansen was helped into the courtroom. Many thought the victim of Wednesday night's robbery already dead. But, despite his doctor's grave predictions, Jansen, though bandaged, pale and weak, was making a slow recovery. Taking the witness stand, he placed his hand on clerk Jones' Holy Bible and took the truth-telling oath. Coleman now asked Jansen to describe the robbery in his own words. Jansen proceeded to speak clearly and distinctly, and without falter. When he had finished, Coleman asked him whether he recognised the prisoners in the box.

Jansen turned his gaze to the accused, and nodded. 'Yes.'

'As to the prisoner who calls himself Burdue, the one with the beard . . . ?'

'I quite positively swear that he was the man who hit me,' Jansen replied, impressing Edward Buffum, for one, with his 'evident conviction of the truth'.

'And the prisoner Windred?'

'As to him, I have little doubt that he was the other man who robbed me that night.'[105]

Amid a swell of gallery chatter, Jansen was permitted to depart the stand, without a question from the defence attorneys. At this time, McAllister and Shattuck had no idea that the man with whom Joe Windred was being confused, English Jim's accomplice, Old Jack Morgan, was a good six inches shorter than Joe and more than forty pounds heavier. And, because Jansen testified that his assailant's accomplice had been stationary when he saw him in his store, while it was obvious to all who saw Joe that he walked with a slight but discernible limp, it was pointless for the defence to ask Jansen whether his assailant's accomplice had limped.

Prosecutor Coleman now called one of Jansen's clerks to the stand. That clerk had not been present at the robbery. Although Joe had never seen him before in his life, this man was to deliver telling testimony against him. As Buffum was to say, 'a circumstance had come to light, while Windred was in jail, which told heavily against him'.

With the clerk on the stand, Coleman produced Joe's confiscated grey coat, and showed it to the witness. 'I show you this coat, which was taken from the prisoner Windred. What do you see on the right elbow of the coat?'

'It is a dried clot of what appears to me to be very much like blood,' said the clerk.

Coleman now showed the clerk a brand new folded blanket. 'Do you recognise this item of merchandise?'

'It is a piece of goods that was on the counter in Mr Jansen's store the night of the robbery.'

'Where in the store was this piece of goods located?'

'On a counter, near the door.'

'And what do you see here?' Coleman asked, pointing to a dark red stain on the cloth.

'It looks to me to be blood.'

'Blood? And was this item of goods on a counter near the front door to Mr Jansen's store in just such a position, and at just such a height, that Windred, in escaping the store, might have left the mark upon it as he brushed it with his elbow?'

'It was.'[106]

There was an angry outburst from the gallery, as the audience made Coleman's intended connection, that this was the blood of the victim Charles Jansen on Joe Windred's elbow. To many in the audience, this testimony alone was enough to cook Joe's goose, and to reserve his noose. 'Judge' Spence called for quiet, and, when the gallery had settled, Coleman continued with the prosecution. He next called a string of witnesses, including John Sullivan, who positively and unhesitatingly testified that Tom Burdue was in fact English Jim Stuart.

The case for the prosecution took up two hours of 'court' time. By 5.00 p.m., Coleman had examined his last witness, and the judge turned to Hall McAllister and D. O. Shattuck and invited them to produce witnesses for the defence. McAllister, coming to his feet, held up the subpoenas that constables had earlier been sent out to serve, and which had since been passed to him. McAllister pointed out to Spence that on every subpoena the police had written: 'Could not be found.' Not a single witness for the defence had come forward. Reporter Buffum was to surmise, about the men named on the subpoena list: 'It is altogether probable that, fearful that they too might be compromised by giving testimony on behalf of two such unpopular men, they had left the city to avoid it.'[107]

Defence attorney McAllister now declared with frustration that he had no witnesses to call. As in Australian and British courts at this time, a defence lawyer in a US court did not put his clients on the stand. Neither Joe nor Tom would be given the opportunity to speak for themselves. So, devoid of anyone who would speak for the prisoners, McAllister asked the judge for time to confer with his clients and prepare an argument for their defence. Spence gave him two hours. Adjourning the sitting for supper, Spence ordered both prosecution and defence attorneys to be ready to commence presentation of their final arguments at 7.00 p.m.

Joe and Tom were returned to the cells. It may have been a supper break, but they and the vast crowd outside went hungry. For, the members of the mob did not budge from where they stood – fearful, as some among them declared, that this adjournment might be some trick to disperse them so that the prisoners could be spirited away. Even though the mob had elected its own court officials, no one in the crowd entirely trusted them to do the job expected of them, that of putting a legal gloss on the lynching the mob had come to witness.

Defence counsels McAllister and Shattuck now came to Joe and Tom in the cells. Meeting their clients for the first time, the attorneys posed them a series of questions. According to Buffum, from this interview with Burdue and Windred, McAllister 'seemed evidently convinced of their innocence, and satisfied that in the case of Burdue there was a great error, and that he was neither the man who had aided in the robbery of Jansen's store nor the redoubtable Jim Stuart'. McAllister went away to use what little time was left to him to prepare his plea to the jury. A plea that was now the only thing that stood between Tom and Joe and the lynch mob's rope.

By 7.00, the prisoners had been returned to their box, and the courtroom was once more packed and silent. At the invitation of 'Judge' Spence, William Coleman came to his feet to deliver his final argument for the prosecution. Coleman ran at length through the testimony of the witnesses for the prosecution, and the physical evidence against the accused. He pointed out that Burdue had been positively identified as English Jim Stuart by witness after witness, and that Jansen had not hesitated to identify him as his assailant. As for Windred, he said, the blood on both the elbow of his coat and the item of goods from the store counter positively placed him at the scene of the crime. Coleman concluded by saying that the jury could have no doubts in this case. 'I demand the conviction of the prisoners, with a verdict of "guilty as charged"!'

It was around eight o'clock when Hall McAllister rose to make his plea to the jury. He was a fine speaker, his oratorical skills honed in many a legitimate courtroom over the past three decades, and on the floor of the Georgia state senate. And he was going to make the most of his opportunity to save the lives of his clients. McAllister addressed the court for two hours. 'The old man grew eloquent,' Buffum would write. McAllister spoke about the country's founding fathers' ideals of justice, and of the constitutional right of every man in the United States to a fair trial, no matter where he came from. And, when McAllister finally addressed the case in hand, he made clear the fact that he did not intend to argue that English Jim Stuart and an accomplice did not bash and rob Charles Jansen just four nights earlier.

'Members of the jury, my plea is one for mercy,' McAllister declared. 'Grant us the time to investigate more thoroughly this whole matter. My plea is for an opportunity to be given these men, Burdue and Windred, when the passions of the populace should have subsided, to produce – as I assure you, gentlemen of the jury, we shall and can produce – ample evidence of their innocence.' McAllister's eloquence, and his argument, clearly affected the jury and the gallery, for, said Buffum, 'as he closed, a round of applause greeted his effort'.[108]

Joe and Tom would have been heartened by their attorney's address, and by the way it was received. Perhaps there was hope yet of sanity, and justice, prevailing. It was 10.00 p.m. by the time McAllister sat back down after his marathon. Spence now instructed the jury to retire and consider their verdict. As the twelve jurymen trooped into an adjoining room, and the courtroom door closed behind them, 'Judge' Spence announced that it wouldn't be necessary for the prisoners to be returned to the cells; they could await the jury's verdict in the prisoners' box. Clearly, Spence did not expect the jury to remain out for long.

Now began a nervous wait, for Joe and Tom, for the others in the courtroom, and for the crowd outside City Hall that had remained mostly patient and quiet for the past seven hours.

Only several blocks away from City Hall, the true perpetrators of the Jansen robbery were in a vengeful mood. English Jim Stuart, Sam Whitaker and a number of their cronies had spent much of the day drinking in the barroom at Mary Ann Hogan's Sansome Street boarding house. Through the afternoon and evening they had received reports from friends who had ventured to the perimeter of the crowd to ask for news of the Burdue–Windred trial. One of these messengers may have been James Whiting, who lodged at the Hogan House, or his wife Agnes. Whiting would later state that he was in the Hogan bar to witness what transpired next.

On receiving the latest report, that the jury was now out, English Jim became convinced that Burdue and Windred would be swiftly found guilty and strung up. Both Stuart and Whitaker possessed a surprising pride in their criminal exploits, and a paternal attitude toward their small criminal fraternity. Both went to extraordinary lengths to help friends who had been arrested, from raising their bail to breaking them out of jail, even giving false evidence and bribing witnesses and jurors at their trials. Now, knowing that Burdue and Windred were innocent, both Stuart and Whitaker felt offended by the likelihood that other men would be executed for a 'job' they had carried out.

'I will shoot fifty men rather than see Burdue and Windred hung!' English Jim declared, as his drink and his anger combined.

Most of those in the room roundly agreed. But Sam Whitaker, sitting with his paramour Mary Ann Hogan, reminded his friend that shooting fifty men would draw just a little attention to those doing the shooting. Whitaker, said by one of the Hogan House's boarders, Joseph Hetherington, to be the sharpest and smartest member of the gang, had a better idea. 'If they do hang them,' Whitaker declared, 'we should fire the city!'

A broad grin came over English Jim's face, and his eyes sparkled. 'Fire the city,' he agreed. 'In three or four places at once.'

They had all seen how quickly a fire would spread in this highly flammable metropolis when it sprang from just a single source. A series of fires, ignited in four different parts of the city at the same time, would surely overwhelm any attempt to extinguish them. All present agreed that this was what they would do. If their fellow 'Australians' Burdue and Windred swung, they would torch the city of San Francisco, and wipe it from the face of the earth![109]

Outside City Hall, the time seemed to men in the crowd to drag by, with still no news of a guilty verdict from inside. Eleven o'clock came and went, and then 11.30, without word of the jury's return. Mob impatience began to grow, and as midnight neared, first Sam Brannan and then several others appeared on the City Hall balcony to harangue the crowd, with each urging them to wait no longer, but to settle this matter here and now. It was not up to the twelve men of the jury, the speakers declared; the decision in this matter rested with the vast majority who stood here waiting for justice to be done. At the front of the crowd, there was a sudden rush for the courthouse door, with the intention of seizing Burdue and Windred, dragging them out and hanging them in the street. But the doorway was defended by determined members of the 'citizen's guard' who blocked the way. The assault came to nothing.

Relative calm had only just returned to the crowd when there was another disturbance in the ranks. A woman carrying a baby came pushing her way from the back to the front of the crush, successfully reaching the courthouse door. There, she announced to the 'citizen's guard' sentinels that she was Elen Burdue, wife of Tom Burdue. Edward Buffum was to write, 'Her baby and her woman's weakness were her passports through that assemblage of rough, excited men waiting and hoping for her husband's execution.'[110]

Twenty-seven-year-old Elen had arrived in San Francisco only that afternoon, landing from a ship that had brought her children and herself from Sydney as her husband had been expecting. With those children, eleven-year-old Mary Ann, ten-year-old Catherine, nine-year-old Thomas junior, and her new baby, who was just months old after being born in Sydney following Tom's departure for California, Elen had followed the instructions that Tom had mailed her. On landing, she had gone to the Panama House Restaurant in search of

John Gough and Tom's forwarding address. The streets she passed through were eerily deserted, and when she reached the Panama House she found it closed, with the Goughs nowhere to be seen. Asking around, Elen received the staggering news that her husband was at this moment on trial for his life at City Hall with Joe Windred.

Learning where Mary Windred was staying, Elen had tracked her down. Mary had taken in the Burdue brood, and discussed the precarious situation with the shell-shocked Elen. According to all that Mary had heard, a 'guilty' verdict could be expected at any moment, followed by the swift execution of Joe and Tom. Tom had never even laid eyes on his latest child, and, it seems that, with this in mind, Mary suggested that Elen take that child to the courthouse, so that Tom could see it before he died. Mary would meanwhile look after the older children.

At City Hall, reporter Buffum, sitting in the packed courtroom as the jury's decision was awaited, heard a commotion at the back of the room, and turned to see a woman carrying a baby. She was 'young, and not ill-looking', in Buffum's opinion. No one attempted to stop Elen as she hurried past the public gallery and through the gate on the broken railing that separated gallery and courtroom proper. Both Tom and Joe had looked around at the sound of her entrance. Now Tom watched in disbelief as his wife, appearing like an angel from the heavens, came to the box and handed her baby up to him, telling him that this was their new child. Once she had let go of her infant, Elen collapsed to the floor in front of the box, 'where', said Buffum, 'she lay speechless and sobbing'.[111]

Attorneys McAllister and Shattuck came to Elen. Helping her to her feet, they guided her through the door behind the judges' bench and into the drill hall beyond. A little later they returned. McAllister reached up and gently took the baby from Tom, who now looked even more emotionally shattered than he had before Elen's arrival. Mother and child were reunited in the drill hall. Not only did this occurrence affect Tom and Joe and their lawyers. Edward Buffum, looking around the courtroom, could see that it had a 'softening' effect on many men in the courtroom, who for the first time saw the prisoners as human beings and family men like themselves, not as alien monsters.[112]

This break in affairs was seen by 'Judge' Spence as an opportune moment to send a note to the jury, inquiring how much longer they expected to take before arriving at a verdict. A note of reply from jury foreman R. S. Watson, a Macondray and Company employee, was soon handed to Spence, who read it to himself, then read it aloud to the courtroom: 'We find it impossible to agree upon a verdict.'

A shout of surprise rose up from the gallery, which then filled with conversation. Buffum was looking at the box at this moment. 'A ray of hope shot across the prisoners' faces,' he noted.[113] For Joe, this was an exact repeat of his Sydney trial, when the jury in that case had also informed the judge that they could not agree. Back then, in a legally constituted trial, the judge had ordered the jury to reach a verdict. Now, in this illegal trial, could Joe expect anything better? With his hope tempered by bad memories, he looked to the bench, to see what Spence and his two associates, who had their heads together in conference, would do now.

Word of the jury's message had been immediately relayed outdoors, where it was met with incredulity, and anger – directed at the jury, as well as at the prisoners.

A chant began, about the jury. 'Hang them too! Hang them too!'

Another chant went up, this one referring to Joe and Tom. 'The majority rules. Hang them! The majority decides. Hang them!'[114]

This bloodthirsty cacophony could be heard inside the courtroom, where Tom Burdue suddenly looked fearful once again. The death chants were also heard by the three 'judges'. Spence now called prosecutor William Coleman to his feet. It was Coleman who had convinced the mob to institute this tribunal, and Coleman was now given the task, by Spence, of quieting that same mob. Coleman quickly went out onto the balcony at the corner of Kearny and Pacific streets.

With raised hands, he brought the expectant mob to quiet, before saying to them, 'Gentlemen, having placed this matter in the hands of a court of your own choosing, you are bound in honour to abide by that court's decision.'[115]

It was Coleman's personal popularity rather than his argument that won over his listeners. After urging the mob to await the jury's verdict, and with passions cooled somewhat, he returned to the courtroom. The wait resumed, and at 1.00 a.m. Monday, the jury sent another note to Spence. Again, they advised that they could not agree on a verdict, once more mirroring the Barker trial proceedings. Foreman Watson advised that three of the twelve jurors, including, critically, Watson himself, were not convinced that the prisoners had been identified beyond doubt as the men who had carried out the Jansen robbery. In response, with the courtroom deathly quiet, Spence and his colleagues Bowie and Ross briefly conferred, nodding gravely among themselves. Spence then summoned the jury back into the courtroom.

Would this be a replay of the Barker robbery trial, with Spence ordering the divided jury to deliver a verdict, as Sir James Dowling had done? Once the jurymen had resumed their seats, Spence addressed them. After thanking them for their deliberations, he dismissed them and sent them home. Turning to 'Sheriff' Townes, he instructed him to return the prisoners to their cells. Spence then declared, 'This court is adjourned, to meet at the call of the president of the court.'[116]

It was a stunning reverse for Sam Brannan and all the others who had been itching to celebrate the Sabbath with a hanging. By this time, most members of the mob, inside and outside the court, were tired and hungry after putting in a vigil of thirteen hours or more. The courtroom emptied, and the larger part of the crowd quickly dispersed to their homes. Still, several hundred radical diehards remained outside City Hall, determined to maintain a vigil to prevent the prisoners being spirited away.

Now, several officials stood up before what remained of the crowd and addressed them, urging calm, restraint and recourse to the law. The first was Recorder Tilford. Another was Levi Parsons, judge of the California District Court. Parsons was just twenty-eight years of age. Despite his title and position, many in the crowd did not take him seriously. There were deep mutterings and colourful curses after he said to them: 'Leave the prisoners to the legal courts of the State.'[117]

Seeing that this had not satisfied the crowd, Mayor John W. Geary next took a turn addressing the unhappy gathering. Geary had been elected San Francisco's first mayor just the previous year. Thirty-one years of age, Geary was a mountain of a man, standing a massive six feet six inches tall (198 centimetres) and weighing 118 kilograms. His very size and booming voice commanded attention. Born near

Mount Pleasant, Pennsylvania, and university-educated, Geary had served as lieutenant colonel of a Pennsylvania regiment during the Mexican–American War before coming to California. Here, he had garnered great respect.

Geary first suggested that twelve citizens be selected from among the mob to sit with the examining justice when a properly constituted court duly convened. This idea failed to satisfy many in the depleted crowd, leaving Geary to lose patience with them and say, 'Then I recommend you to retire. I assure you that justice will be done. The prisoners will now have a speedy trial by the regular judicial authorities. I beg you to leave the matter in their hands.'[118]

Geary's words and powerful delivery had an authoritative ring to them. Police chief Malachi Fallon was to say of the young roughs in the mob, 'They needed a strong and experienced hand to keep them in control.'[119] The inadequate Fallon was admitting that he himself was not up to filling that role. He had never before run a police force, and would never do so again following his brief stint as San Francisco's city marshal. Right now, that 'strong and experienced hand' was Mayor Geary, and his address succeeded in sending many of his wearied listeners home. For the moment, the lynching storm passed. But the fallout from this kangaroo court would be lengthy, and lethal to Australians.

While we take it for granted today, there is no record of the term 'kangaroo court' being in use anywhere in the world prior to 1851. Certainly not in Australia. It would not appear in print for the first time until 1853. That was in the US, in reference to an unlawful trial in Texas. The author was Samuel Adams Hammett.[120] A Connecticut native who wrote under the name Philip Paxton, Hammett lived in Texas for many years. He left Texas in 1848, and by 1853 had settled in New York City. It is not impossible that in the interim he spent time in California and witnessed the lynch trial of the two 'Australians', or 'kangaroos'. Or, perhaps Hammett merely remembered the San Francisco newspaper reports of the trial, reports which were reprinted in papers throughout the United States. Either way, a case can be put that this 1851 San Francisco trial of 'kangaroos' Thomas Burdue and Joseph Windred was the inspiration for the term 'kangaroo court'.

Monday, February 24, 1851. San Francisco, California

When the new day dawned, there was still a small crowd in the streets outside San Francisco's City Hall. The editors of the city's papers had heard Mayor Geary's speech to the mob the previous night, and their morning editions contained editorials repeating his plea and endorsing this course of action. Despite this, the *Alta California* did decry the wave of crime which it claimed was sweeping the state, and expressed the hope that the community's elected officials would now accede to the people's concerns and put an end to it.

In support of its strong stand against crime, the morning's *Alta* claimed that five hundred murders had been committed in California over the past few years, with not a single murderer executed by the authorities. The paper offered no source for such a claim, but some future writers would multiply this figure and declare there had been in excess of a thousand murders in San Francisco alone during this period. The facts tell a different story: in San Francisco, for example, through the six months from January to June 1851, nine murders were recorded – down from thirteen during the previous six months – and three during the six months prior to that.[121]

As Monday progressed, it became known throughout the city that a grand jury was sitting to consider the matter of Stuart/Burdue and Windred, and this satisfied most of the radicals, so that only a few knots of stragglers remained outside City Hall through the day. Still, the radical leaders were only biding their time, and reserving their position regarding Burdue and Windred. One of those leaders told *Alta California* reporter Buffum, 'If the judicial authorities fail to punish them, then we will take them in hand and execute them ourselves, without judge or jury!'[122]

That afternoon's San Francisco *Evening Picayune* and the next day's morning papers reported that in the course of Monday the grand jury had found a 'true bill' against Burdue and Windred, who would now stand trial in the criminal court in the coming weeks, and this was accepted by the population. It was a temporary reprieve for Tom and Joe. They were safe from the lynch mob, for now. But, with Sam Brannan and his like threatening to hang the pair if the authorities failed to do so, their prospects were not bright.

18

THE NEW JANSEN TRIAL

Tuesday, February 25, 1851. San Francisco, California

MARY WINDRED WAS NOW permitted to visit Joe and Tom in their cells beneath City Hall, and, with the crowd outside now dispersed, she felt safe to do so. A huge weight of responsibility fell on Mary's shoulders. Not only did she have to provide financial and emotional support for Elen and her children, who were all sharing her boarding house room, she felt that she was the only person on the outside who could do anything to help both their husbands.

Bringing Joe and Tom clean clothes and taking away their dirty clothes to be washed, Mary asked Joe what she must do to help, with the official court case now several weeks away. He told her to talk with Hall McAllister and see if he would again represent the pair. Joe also gave her the task of finding witnesses who would testify that he and Tom had been dining at the Panama House at the time of the Jansen robbery, and who would testify that Tom was not James Stuart. In addition, Tom asked Mary to track down John Gough and retrieve the five pounds of gold dust that Tom had given him the previous September. That gold would pay for the pair's legal representation. Brave Mary hurried away to complete her missions. Calm and collected by nature, she would work through her tasks.

When Mary called on Hall McAllister, and told him that an amount of gold dust was being held for Tom by a friend, McAllister agreed to again represent Tom and Joe – if Mary brought him that gold dust as a retainer against his legal expenses. McAllister also said that he would secure another highly respected local lawyer, Calhoun Benham, to join him at the defence table for the upcoming trial, as he was determined to win freedom for Joe and Tom.

The next parts of Mary's assignment were not as easily accomplished. John Gough was still missing, and he was the key to securing Tom's gold to cover legal expenses. Mary herself had little more than $125 on her. She was also intent on tracking down Captain Patterson, George Turner and James Whiting, the other Sydney Ducks at the dinner party at the Panama House the previous Wednesday evening.

Wednesday, February 26, 1851. San Francisco, California

When Mary answered a knock, she found James Whiting standing outside her boarding house door. Whiting, a twenty-eight-year-old Englishman, had served time in Van Diemen's Land before gaining his certificate of freedom and marrying Agnes Craw at Launceston. There in Launceston in 1850, the eighteen-year-old Agnes had given birth to the couple's first child, James junior. Whiting, his wife and child soon after joined the exodus of thousands who went from Van Diemen's Land to California in 1849 and 1850. Many Van Diemen's Landers in California came to refer to themselves not as Sydney Ducks but as Derwent Ducks – because Hobart Town, their port of departure, was situated on the Derwent River.[123]

Whiting agreed to guide Mary throughout the city in search of trial witnesses, although he himself would not testify. In particular he would take her to places in Sydney Valley where she might meet people who knew either Tom Burdue or the real criminal, English Jim Stuart, and who might testify that one was not the other. Mary was unaware of it, but it seems that Whiting had actually been sent to her by Sam Whitaker. For, one of the first places that Whiting took her was the Hogan House, and there she met both Mary Ann Hogan and Sam Whitaker himself.

The Mary Ann Hogan that Mary Windred found was attractive, well-dressed and well spoken. She looked the last person to have dealings with underworld figures. In fact, William Walker, editor of the San Francisco *Herald*, was to describe Mary Ann Hogan as an 'interesting' woman who was 'quite genteel in appearance'.[124] Mrs Hogan would later claim that she had no idea of Sam Whitaker's criminal activities. Yet, she would admit that she twice sent him to the mines with the hope that he would mend his ways, but Whitaker always returned to her, and to his old pursuits. Mary Ann, who was living with Whitaker as his de facto wife, was sympathetic to Mary's situation, and she now introduced Mary to the mercurial man himself.

At this time, Mary Windred had no idea that Sam Whitaker had been one of English Jim's accomplices in the Jansen robbery, and that Whitaker should be sitting in the county jail in her husband's stead. Whitaker, with a neat goatee beard and dressed as a gentleman, had a calm air of self-confidence about him. When Mary declared to him that her 'husband' Joe was innocent of the crime he was accused of committing, Whitaker produced a smile and said that he knew for a fact that both Joe and Tom were innocent.

'How do you know that?' Mary asked him.

'Because I know who it was that committed the attempt to murder and rob Charles Jansen,' Whitaker replied, matter-of-factly.

'You do?' said Mary, astonished. 'Then, who is it?'

Whitaker shook his head. 'I cannot tell you that. But this I will tell you – should Windred and Burdue be hung for the Jansen robbery, this town will be burned to the ground!'

That was of no help to Mary. She demanded the names of those responsible for the robbery.

Whitaker shook his head. 'My advice to you, Mrs Windred, is to employ a good lawyer to defend your husband. I would recommend George R. Parbutt.' This Parbutt was an American attorney who had only recently set up an office in San Francisco and had represented friends of Whitaker with success.

Mary replied that Mr McAllister had agreed to once again represent Joe and Tom. But she desperately needed to find witnesses who would testify for the pair. Whitaker responded by urging her to come to him again in a few days, assuring her, 'I can obtain all the witnesses you need to prove the innocency of Windred and Burdue.'[125]

Over the next two weeks, Mary Windred would be guided back to the Hogan House a number of times by James Whiting to meet with Whitaker, as she doggedly continued her pursuit of witnesses for her husband's defence.

Monday, March 3, 1851. San Francisco, California

English Jim's temper was being tested to the limit. Although he needed to replenish his funds fast, he had deliberately held off from committing any more robberies while Tom Burdue and Joe Windred were being tried by the mob. Stuart would later claim this lack of criminal activity was motivated by the desire of his friends and himself not to hurt the chances of Windred and Burdue: 'We did not commit any more robberies while the men arrested for striking Jansen were under trial, as we did not wish them hung, as they were innocent.'[126]

In fact, had Stuart and his accomplices carried out fresh robberies during this period and Stuart was again recognised, even though he had shaved off his beard since Tom Burdue's arrest, the lynch mob would have realised that they had the wrong men on trial. So, a robbery or two by Stuart at this time would have been the best thing he could have done to help Tom and Joe. In all likelihood, Stuart quite deliberately lay low in the hope that another man would be convicted in his stead, which would take the heat off him.

But Stuart needed money, and he couldn't hold off for long. Within days of Tom and Joe being restored to the custody of the legitimate authorities, Stuart had resumed his larcenous career. He decided that bank robbing was more his style, and more profitable. For two nights running, Stuart and seven associates, including Sam Whitaker, embarked on bank robberies using inside help, copies of bank keys and the aid of two corrupt San Francisco cops. One planned robbery, at the Beebee, Ludlow and Condon Bank on Montgomery Street, was aborted at the last minute when it was decided there was not enough money on the premises.

The following night, the same gang walked away from Young's Bank next to the famed El Dorado Hotel on Washington Street after it was determined that far too many men were sleeping nearby and the robbers might be caught in the act. On the Sunday night, now deciding that any 'crib' would do, the gang succeeded in stealing a safe from the Emerson and Dunbar auction house on Washington Street. Using special safe-breaking tools and a little gunpowder, they managed to open the safe, to find that it contained just $24.

Now, on the Monday night, the day after the Emerson and Dunbar job, the gang broke into the store of jobbing merchants Gladwin and Whitmore on California Street. Here, they found a small safe on the first floor, which Stuart brought downstairs. They carried this safe between them, huffing and puffing, all the way out to the sand hills that lay between the city and Mission Dolores. There, the gang members huddled around Stuart with greedy anticipation as he knelt in front of the safe with safe-breaking tools in hand. Suddenly, the sound of police whistles pierced the night. Stuart, Whitaker and their mates scattered in all directions, but two members of the gang, Morris Morgan and James 'Jemmy-from-Town' Briggs, were collared by the police and hauled off to the San Francisco Police Office.

Lamenting the fact that he'd been forced to leave behind the safe-cracking tools, which were valued at $500, English Jim returned unhappily to the Hogan House with several other gang members. There, they drowned their sorrows in the bar. The more that Stuart drank, the bolder he became. 'I don't like to see men in the watch-house,' he declared. Drawing himself to his feet, and taking a pistol from his belt and waving it in the air, he said, 'Come on, all of you. We'll rescue Morris and Jemmy from the watch-house by force!'

Sam Whitaker, shaking his head, spoke for all the others. 'No, Jim. We can't do that. I think that by employing Mr Parbutt and other lawyers we'll have Morris and Jemmy cleared.'

The others all agreed. None of them was interested in storming the county jail. In fact, their interest in English Jim's generally unrewarding money-making schemes was fast diminishing. An American in the band, Bill Hughes, had worked for Stuart at Foster's Bar. But this latest farcical exploit, ending in a run-in with the law for no reward, was the last he wanted to do with English Jim.

'I'm going home!' Hughes announced. By 'home' he meant the American East. Hughes there and then took his leave of the gathering, and was never seen again.[127]

Tuesday, March 4, 1851. San Francisco, California

English Jim had decided to get out of town until things quietened down. With the schooner *H. L. Allen* about to sail for Trinidad Bay, in far northern California, Stuart went aboard with a pile of baggage and paid for a passage under the name of Campbell. Apart from seeing if any loot could be had in the north after such a profitless stay in San Francisco, Stuart reasoned that the twenty-seven-day voyage to the remote Trinidad Bay settlement would put 250 miles between the San Francisco Police and himself.

As Stuart sailed away, Sam Whitaker, who remained in San Francisco, living with Mary Ann Hogan still, retained lawyer George Parbutt just as he had proposed to do the previous night. This very afternoon, Parbutt was able to secure the release of Morris Morgan, one of the two men arrested at the sand hills. Briggs was not so lucky; he was committed for trial. Both men had kept their mouths shut after their arrest, and now Briggs, who would plead 'not guilty', continued to protect Stuart, Whitaker and the other gang members as he languished in the City Hall police cells with Joe Windred and Tom Burdue, awaiting trial.

Mary Windred visited Whitaker several times during this period, as she pursued her quest for defence witnesses for the upcoming Burdue–Windred trial, with James Whiting continuing to act as her guide and chaperone. John and Elicia Gough had returned to the Panama House by this time, but like young Whiting both were reluctant to testify that Tom and Joe had dined with them on the night of the Jansen robbery. Gough did hand over Tom Burdue's five-pound bag of gold dust, and Mary took this directly to lawyer Hall McAllister to secure his services. Meanwhile, one potential witness had agreed to testify, but only in return for a 'loan' of $100.

Sunday, March 9, 1851. San Francisco, California

Joe and Tom now found themselves with an unusual fellow prisoner in the cells beneath City Hall, one who had been writing extensively about them. He was the twenty-six-year-old editor of the San Francisco *Herald*, the slight, enigmatic William Walker. At just the age of twelve, boy wonder Walker had started university in his birthplace, Nashville, Tennessee. He had gone on to earn a doctorate in medicine before taking a law degree. After studying in Europe, Walker had settled in New Orleans, where, as editor of the *Crescent*, he had made a name for himself as an anti-corruption crusader. In the wake of the death of his beautiful but deaf fiancée in a New Orleans cholera epidemic, in 1850 Walker had turned his back on his old life and followed an elder brother to California, where he was offered the co-editorship of the *Herald*.

At the *Herald*, Walker had quickly won himself enemies among those he criticised in print. He was still recovering after taking two bullets in the leg in a January 12 duel on Mission Road with a reader who had taken exception to something Walker had written about him. Now, Walker had enraged Judge Levi Parsons, the same district judge who had addressed the crowd following Joe Windred's and Tom Burdue's 'citizen's' trial. After Parsons had been critical, in his court, of the local press, Walker had written a stinging editorial against the judge and the Californian courts, in which he had said, in part: 'If we err not, Judge Parsons was present in many of the scenes before City Hall some ten days ago. He may have observed the deep discontent with which the people listened to him when he counselled them to leave the prisoners, Stuart and Windred, to the legal courts of the state. He may have heard the curses, not suppressed even by his presence, uttered against the courts as now organised and constituted.'[128]

Judge Parsons, incensed by this personal attack, immediately had Walker brought before him, fining him $500 for contempt of court. When Walker refused to recognise Parsons' authority, claiming his constitutional right to free speech, Parsons had consigned him to the same cells as the two prisoners he had just written about in the offending article.

In the Plaza this Sunday afternoon, a crowd of 3000 to 4000 gathered, summoned by Saturday's *Herald* to rally for an 'Indignation Meeting' led by Sam Brannan and the paper's owner John Nugent – a meeting where the community could express its anger at Walker's imprisonment. After Brannan, Nugent and other speakers had stoked their indignation, the crowd swelled around City Hall, demanding Walker's release. Although the editor would not be freed for several weeks, the crowd went home that evening feeling they had sent a message to foolish young Judge Parsons.

They had also sent a message to the state legislature, which, within several months, would consider impeaching Parsons for his high-handed action in Walker's case. Meanwhile, Parsons' immature knee-jerk reaction did nothing to endear him to the citizens of San Francisco, or to engender much faith in the outcome of the important trial over which he was soon to preside: the Burdue–Windred trial.

Friday, March 14, 1851. San Francisco, California

On this day, the California legislature abolished the foreign miners tax that had kept many Australians out of the diggings and forced them to congregate in the built-up areas. The tax had caused more problems than it had cured, and had given rise to much of the petty crime that the citizens of San Francisco in particular were complaining of. The removal of the tax would draw a number of financially struggling Sydney Ducks to the mines, and as such was a crime preventative measure, although it would not have been seen as such by the American residents of San Francisco. To them, the best crime preventative measure would be a severe sentence in the case of master criminal English Jim and his accomplice Joseph Windred, once the Jansen robbery case went to trial before the district court this morning. A sentence that would set an example to all Sydney Duck wrongdoers.

Just before 10.00 a.m., Joe and Tom were led up from the City Hall cells in which they had spent the past three weeks, and into the same courtroom where on February 23 they had experienced the terrifying lynch-mob trial. As before, the gallery was packed. Newspapermen occupied prominent positions. *Herald* editor William Walker was among them, having been released from the cells beneath the courtroom the previous Monday. His close friend, lawyer Edmund Randolph, had secured a writ of habeas corpus from another San Francisco judge to force Walker's release. Walker, a supremely self-confident young man who would lead fifty-seven American mercenaries to Nicaragua four years from now and by force of arms make himself President of Nicaragua, sat, unsmiling, as was his custom.[129] With pencil and paper at the ready, he assessed the scene before him with cold grey eyes.

As Joe and Tom gazed around the courtroom, they saw many familiarly unfriendly faces among the crowded gallery. Mary Windred's was one of the few welcome faces, and one of the even fewer female faces in the court. Hall McAllister was at the defence table. True to his word, the attorney had recruited former district attorney Calhoun Benham to the defence team, and Benham sat beside him now. This time around, the prosecution would not be led by an amateur lawyer. District Attorney George K. Platt was prosecutor, assisted by Charles M. Brosnan, a future Nevada supreme court judge. A legally recruited all-male jury had been sworn in, and now occupied the jury box.

All present came to their feet as the man who would now control Joe and Tom's fate made his courtroom entry. Rash, self-important young Judge Levi Parsons had little experience on the bench, as his run-in with wily William Walker had shown. Parsons, from Gloversville, New York, had been admitted to the New York bar in 1847. After working in private practice for less than two years, Parsons had joined the rush to California, reputedly arriving in San Francisco with just $8.50 in his pocket. After a brief sojourn digging and panning for gold, he had set up a law office in San Francisco and helped found the Whig Party's local organisation. In 1850, Parsons had been appointed to the District Court.

J. E. Addison, Clerk of the District Court, now read the charges against the two accused: 'That in the month of February, in the year of our Lord one thousand eight hundred and fifty-one, Thomas Burdue, alias James Stuart, and Joseph Windred did commit assault on one Charles Jansen, of San Francisco, with a deadly weapon, with intent to kill the said Jansen. And further, they are charged with the crime of burglary.'

Judge Parsons invited District Attorney Platt to launch the prosecution. Platt's case was little different from that presented by William T. Coleman three weeks before. Charles Jansen, astounding many by looking almost fully recovered from the bashing he had received from English Jim, took the stand and once again positively identified Tom Burdue as the man who had struck him. Jansen also identified Joe Windred, with only slight reservation, as his assailant's accomplice on the night. Platt also extracted from Jansen the observation that both his assailants had been wearing dark clothes.

One after the other, a dozen witnesses including John Sullivan, George Mason and George F. Hunt trooped to the stand and positively identified Tom Burdue as James Stuart. Incriminating Joe Windred was not as easy. While Jansen had identified Joe as a participant in the robbery, some doubt hung over that identification. This made Prosecutor Platt all the more determined to nail Joe for the crime. Just as Coleman had done three weeks earlier, Platt introduced Joe's coat and the bloodied store blanket into evidence, and brought one of Jansen's clerks to the stand to testify that it was his employer's blood on the blanket. Platt then played an unexpected card, calling a Frenchman by the name of Eugene Guichard to the stand. Guichard, who lived on Broadway, advertised himself as a chemist.

After establishing Guichard's profession, the prosecutor passed Joe Windred's confiscated grey coat to him, and asked, 'Can you identify the clot upon the elbow of Windred's coat?'

'I can,' came the reply. 'It is blood.'

This testimony produced a ripple of approving gallery comment. *Alta California* reporter Edward Buffum was not entirely convinced of Guichard's credentials, describing him as a 'professed chemist'.[130] Yet, despite the lack of availability of any scientific support of the witness' claim, or for the prosecution's assertion that, if this indeed was blood, it was Charles Jansen's blood, Buffum could see that the vast majority of those in the gallery were keen to see the accused convicted, and so were happy to accept the chemist's evidence as damning and incontrovertible proof of Joe Windred's guilt.

To put the final nail in the proverbial coffin, Platt called to the stand the husband and wife who ran the boarding house where Joe and Tom had been staying on the night of the robbery. Both testified that Tom and Joe wore dark clothes that night, and did not return to the boarding house until late, not a little after 8.00 as the defendants claimed.

Prosecutor Platt, no doubt feeling pleased with himself, now handed the stage over to Hall McAllister for the defence. McAllister called Captain Robert Patterson and George Cooper Turner, who both testified that Tom was not James Stuart, and that Tom and Joe had been dining at the Panama House at the time of the Jansen robbery. District Attorney Platt, in cross-examining Patterson, set out to destroy Tom Burdue's alibi.

'At what time did Burdue leave you?'

'At just about eight o'clock,' Patterson replied.

'At just about eight o'clock,' said Platt, nodding, before remarking, for the benefit of the jury, that Charles Jansen had testified that he had been bashed and robbed at 'just about eight o'clock'.[131] Platt did not ask what time Joe Windred had left the dinner. If he had, he would have been told that Joe and Mary left some time after Burdue, and Joe therefore could not possibly have been at Jansen's store at the time of the robbery. But a clever lawyer never asks a question when he knows the answer is likely to damage his case. And by failing to ask that question, Platt left Joe guilty by association with his friend Burdue in the minds of the jurymen.

When it came time for Hall McAllister to deliver his final address to the jury, he was not able to employ the same argument that he had used at the previous trial. The very thing he had demanded back then, time to prove that his clients were innocent, had since been granted him. Now, he was confined to attempting to leave weighty doubt in the minds of the jury as to the wrongful identification of Burdue and Windred as the culprits, with the hope that the jurors would not vote to convict.

District Attorney Platt, in his final address, declared that all doubt had been removed from the case by the prosecution witnesses, and called for a verdict of 'guilty' and a recommendation for the maximum sentence then provided under Californian law for robbery with violence. After receiving direction from Judge Parsons, the jurors filed from the courtroom to commence their deliberations. This trial had lasted little more than two hours.

The jury did not stay out long. In the afternoon, they returned. Joe and Tom were made to stand. The courtroom was hushed in expectation, as the foreman announced their verdict: 'We find the prisoners, Stuart alias Burdue and Windred, guilty as charged.'

A cheer rose up from the gallery. And the hearts of Joe and Tom sank.

Judge Parsons would duly pronounce sentences on the now-convicted men. On Tom Burdue, as the perpetrator of the bashing of Charles Jansen, he imposed a sentence of fourteen years in the state penitentiary. Joe Windred received a ten-year sentence.

As Joe and Tom were hustled from the courtroom to the cells below, Joe could only reflect with shaking head on the shattering irony of his situation. Eleven years before, as now, he had been convicted of an armed robbery he did not commit, while the true culprit escaped conviction. In both cases, Joe had ended up with a ten-year sentence.

In the early evening, once the San Francisco streets had cleared of the many people who had come out to hear the trial's verdict, a pair of closed carriages drew up outside City Hall. Joe's cell door was opened. He was being taken away first. A warrant had arrived for Tom to stand trial at Marysville, as James Stuart, for the robbery

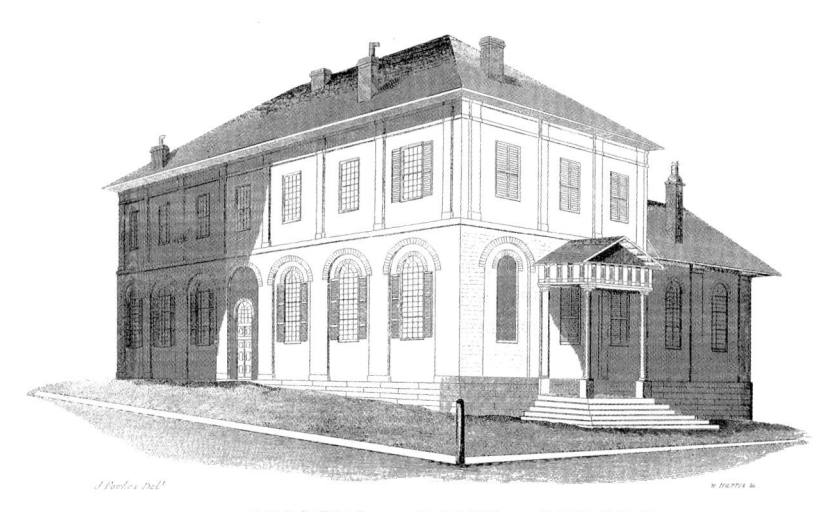

SUPREME COURT SYDNEY.

Sydney Supreme Court, on the corner of Elizabeth and King streets, in the 1840s. Here Joe Windred was tried for armed robbery in 1840. The artist responsible for this sketch was Joseph Fowles, who, little over a decade later, would make a renowned painting of Joe's celebrated racehorse Cooramin. **Illustration from** *Sydney in 1848* **by Joseph Fowles**

Joe and Mary Windred saw this view, at the corner of Clay and Sansome streets, when they landed in San Francisco in July 1850. These structures, including the converted ships such as the Niantic Hotel, were among hundreds destroyed in the massive May 1851 fire said to have been lit to cover Joe's escape from California. **United States Library of Congress**

Sam Brannan, reputedly California's first millionaire, a disgraced young Mormon elder with a wild lust for hangings, who led the mob in attempting to lynch Joe Windred and Tom Burdue, and who helped found the San Francisco Committee of Vigilance. Brannan would die in poverty.

'Sydney Duck' John Jenkins, who had served time in Van Diemen's Land, is lynched by the Committee of Vigilance, led by Sam Brannan, outside the Adobe Building on San Francisco's Plaza. It's likely that Jenkins had been framed for the robbery that resulted in his mob execution.
United States Library of Congress

William Walker, newspaper editor and future president of Nicaragua, backed the San Francisco Committee of Vigilance. Joe Windred shared a jail cell with Walker in San Francisco. **United States Library of Congress**

North side of the Plaza, San Francisco, 1851, with the *Alta California* building second from left, just prior to the devastating May 4–5 city fire which helped cover Joe Windred's escape.
United States Library of Congress

The port of San Francisco from Happy Valley in 1851, about the time Joe Windred escaped. United States Library of Congress

'English Jim' Stuart, master crook and Tom Burdue's double, about to be lynched by the Committee of Vigilance at the end of Market Street Wharf, San Francisco, July 11, 1851.

The Bancroft Library, University of California, Berkeley

Joe and Mary Windred's saviour, Sam Whitaker, is lynched alongside inept thief Bob McKenzie in front of a baying crowd of 15,000, San Francisco, August 24, 1851.

The Bancroft Library, University of California, Berkeley

RACE BETWEEN "SPORTSMAN" AND "COORAMIN," AT HOMEBUSH, 1854.

Racehorse Cooramin is beaten by Sportsman in a Homebush match race in 1854, two years before Joe Windred purchased Cooramin.
National Library of Australia

In 1862, Joe Windred chose to open his new Sportsman's Arms Hotel at the Lambing Flat goldfields, site of the later town of Young, just as the Lambing Flat riots broke out. To Joe's horror, an Australian vigilance committee was formed. National Archives of Australia

A stagecoach leaving Bathurst for Forbes in 1862. Joe Windred was aboard a similar coach also heading to Forbes that same year when it was swept away by a flooded creek, and Joe made valiant efforts to save a female passenger from drowning.

The Commercial Hotel, Byng Street, Orange, which Joe Windred's son-in-law, James Torpy, and stepdaughter, Isabel, were running in 1867, when Joe's love of horseracing delivered him one of his reverses of fortune. Both photos courtesy of the NSW State Library from the Orange & District Historical Society photograph collection

Joe Windred, in 1883, when he was elected Mayor of Orange for the second time. Central West Libraries image collection

and murder of Charles E. Moore in Yuba County the previous December. Tom would shortly be hurried out of San Francisco and lodged in Yuba County Jail at Marysville for that trial, in a case in which the maximum penalty provided by Californian law would be death by hanging.

Through the cell bars, Joe, with manacles on his wrists and fetters around his ankles, shook a glum Tom Burdue by the hand and wished him good luck. Joe and Tom would never see each other again. Taken out to one of the waiting two-horse carriages, Joe was sped, with his police escort, through the night to the waterfront and a waiting boat, where he was handed over to prison officers. At this time, California's state penitentiary was a floating prison, the former 268-ton sailing vessel *Waban*. Stripped of masts, yards and rigging, the *Waban* had been fitted out as a prison hulk, with cells for thirty long-term prisoners and accommodation for several jailers.

Joe was rowed to the *Waban*, which was moored off Angel Island, on the northern side of San Francisco Bay. Some days, the floating jail's inmates rowed ashore to Angel Island, escorted by guards equipped with top hats and truncheons. In a quarry on the western side of the island, the prisoners had to quarry and shape stone. Other days, they were landed on the northern mainland, at Point Quentin, where they lay that stone in the process of constructing a new, permanent state penitentiary. The following year, that new penitentiary, San Quentin, would open and take delivery of its first intake, of sixty-eight prisoners. But, while Joe Windred would help build San Quentin, he would not be among those first inmates.

Monday, April 1, 1851. Trinidad Bay, California

Bob McKenzie, who had proven such an inept thief in San Francisco that English Jim Stuart had thrown him out of his gang, walked into one of the little northern settlement's few saloons. Tall, gangly McKenzie, whose real name was McKinney, had been branded a Sydney Duck in California, yet had never set foot in Australia. When only a small boy, he'd migrated from England to New Orleans with his parents. He was more American than British. New Orleans, like New York, had regular steamship departures to San Francisco via Panama and Nicaragua. McKenzie, like so many others from New

Orleans, had followed that route to California with golden stars in his eyes. And, like some other disappointed gold-seekers, once his fortunes faded, crime had seemed to him an easier route to riches.

McKenzie now saw two men playing cards in a corner of the Trinidad Bay saloon. One was a local constable. McKenzie recognised the other as none other than English Jim. 'Hello, Jim!' said McKenzie, walking up to the card players. 'How is it you're here?'

Stuart glowered over the top of his cards at the youngster. 'You do not know me, sir,' he said, coldly.

'But, Jim . . .'

'You do not know me, sir!' the Englishman snarled.

The cold look in Stuart's eyes sent a shudder down the young man's spine. McKenzie backed off. He avoided the card players after that. Later, after McKenzie departed the saloon, he was walking away when he heard his name called. Turning, he saw Stuart hurrying after him. Stuart, grabbing McKenzie, forced him up against the side of a building.

'What did you think you were doing in there?' Stuart demanded.

'Jim, Jim, I was only being friendly,' McKenzie protested.

'Just keep out of my way, boy!' Stuart warned, before storming back into the saloon.[132]

19

THE PRISON BREAK

Wednesday, April 16, 1851. San Francisco, California

SAN FRANCISCO'S FIRST STEAM-POWERED excavator was noisily at work on First Street as James Whiting led Mary Windred through the city. For the umpteenth time, Mary was on her way to the Hogan boarding house to meet with Sam Whitaker.

This time, Whitaker had a proposition for Mary. He knew someone, he said, who could arrange for Joe Windred's escape from prison, and from California. The cost to engineer Joe's escape would be a mere $400. Whitaker boasted that his friend had arranged numerous other jail breaks, and, to get friends off, had paid witnesses, jurors, prosecutors and judges. Crafting an escape for Joe would be a simple matter for this mystery man, according to Whitaker; $400 was a small price to pay for freedom. This 'friend' was Whitaker himself.

Some later historians would surmise that Whitaker's professional pride had been hurt by the arrest of a guiltless fellow Sydney Duck for a crime that he had committed, and this was why he proposed to help Joe Windred escape. California history professor William Henry Ellison would paint Whitaker more in the mode of a Robin Hood, suggesting that he chose to help Joe to lift the weight of injustice from his shoulders.[133] Then again, Whitaker's motive for engineering an escape may have been merely a cocky desire to prove that he was smarter than the authorities.

Mary Windred, who had already taken out a $100 loan to pay one of the trial witnesses, told Whitaker that she did not have $400. She had tried to access some of the gold dust being held for Tom Burdue by lawyers McAllister and Benham, but the pair had refused to part with any. Their excuse was that they would need all the gold to cover every contingency regarding the cost of Tom's Marysville trial in the forthcoming Moore murder case. After the Marysville trial they would reckon up the costs, and if there was any gold left over, then Mary might be able to access it. Whitaker left Mary to think on his proposal, and to find friends who might lend her $400.

'Where's Whitaker?' the drunken miner demanded, angrily waving a knife. 'I'm going to kill him!' Pushing past Mary Ann Hogan, the miner scoured the Hogan House's barroom, then went into Mrs Hogan's adjoining sitting room. After failing to find Whitaker, the miner departed, swearing to track him down, and kill him.[134]

Until recently, this miner had been a lodger at the Hogan House. One morning, he had awoken to find that he had been relieved of $1500. Since leaving the Hogan House, someone in the know had informed him that it had been Sam Whitaker who'd robbed him. The information was correct. Whitaker and a crony known as Long Charley had teamed up to get the miner drunk, then stolen his money while he slept.

That same afternoon, Captain Andrew McCarthy and Second Sergeant Robert McIntyre of the San Francisco Police Department paid a visit to Mary Ann Hogan. Both policemen had been in league with Whitaker and English Jim in various robberies in the past – Mrs Hogan knew it, and the two corrupt cops knew that she knew it. City elections were coming up in several weeks' time, at which every one of San Francisco's officials had to stand for re-election. Mayor Geary, a Democrat, had announced that he would not be seeking another term. McCarthy and McIntyre, who had been elected on his ticket the previous year, did not fancy the chances of the Democrats' mayoral candidate, Recorder Tilford, against popular Whig Party candidate Charles Brenham, captain of the SS *McKim*. Expecting to lose their jobs within weeks, McCarthy and McIntyre were eager to line their pockets as much as they could while they still could.

'We hear that Whitaker has won $2000,' said McCarthy, referring to the robbing of the miner at the Hogan House.

'Not that much,' Mrs Hogan replied.

'If Whitaker doesn't come to the Police Office and pay us some money,' said McIntyre, 'we will get out a warrant for him.'[135]

That evening, when Whitaker slipped into the Hogan House via the back way, Mary Ann urgently told him about her visitors during the day – the knife-wielding miner looking to slit Sam's throat, and the two policemen looking to shake him down. Whitaker decided that, for the time being, he should change addresses and lay low. That same night he took a room with respectable physician Dr Bernard Lambert at his premises at 248 Montgomery Street.[136] From now on, Mary Ann Hogan would bring messages to Whitaker at the Lambert house, and run his errands, acting as go-between in his various 'business' dealings. Meanwhile, Whitaker himself would remain behind closed doors, with a loaded pistol close handy.

Thursday, April 17, 1851. San Francisco, California

As Mary Windred left her lodgings, she was painfully aware of the unpaid bill she had run up for the Burdue family and herself in their crowded room, and for the cost of washing clothes for them and for Joe and Tom in jail. With what little money she had left, Mary, having promised her landlords that she would pay the bill as soon as funds were released by her husband's attorneys, headed out to buy provisions for Elen Burdue, the Burdue children and herself.

There was considerable excitement in the streets this morning. A miner had been found, bound and dead, floating in the bay near the end of Sacramento Street. The Clark's Point boarding house operated by John Edwards was not far from the scene. This was the same John Edwards who was a friend of English Jim and Sam Whitaker, and who had taken part in various break-ins with them. The miner with the knife never returned to the Hogan House to threaten Sam Whitaker, and the possibility that the floating corpse was that of the very same miner would have exercised the mind of Mary Ann Hogan once she learned of the discovery of the body.

During this morning, Mary Windred was approached and taken aside by Mrs Margaret Walton. She was the wife of William Walton, a wool commission merchant originally from New South Wales. Englishman Walton was in partnership with William Turnbull at 251 Montgomery Street – right across the street from Dr Lambert's surgery, above which Sam Whitaker was now holed up. Both Walton and Turnbull were ex-convicts, having served time in New South Wales before earning their certificates of freedom in the 1840s. Walton had subsequently worked in the Illawarra, apparently on sheep properties, and in 1849 married Margaret Leighton. Within a year, they were on their way to California.

It seems that Margaret Walton urged Mary to do all she could to help Joe get away from California, suggesting that, should Mary make her a 'loan' of $400, her husband would be able to take care of the necessary arrangements. Mary surely knew that Sam Whitaker was behind the approach from the Waltons. As much as she disliked dealing with the criminal fraternity, she must have been beginning to think that anything was better than letting Joe rot in prison for the next ten years. She returned to the Hogan House to discuss the matter with Whitaker. But, according to Mary Ann Hogan, Whitaker had since left town on business.

Mary Windred's mission was not in vain, for Mrs Hogan knew all about her lover's plans for Joe Windred. For $400, Mary was told, a key would be provided to unlock Joe's cell door. Once free of his cell, Joe would have to swim to shore, where he would be met and taken to a secure hiding place. A ship's captain would then be found, one with a minimum of inquisitiveness, a captain planning to soon sail for Sydney. And a fare would be paid, in a false name, for Joe's passage home to New South Wales. Because Mary could be expected to be watched by the police, who would be hoping she would lead them to fugitive Joe following his escape, Mary would not be able to see Joe while he was hiding out. Nor could she accompany him when he sailed for Sydney. Mary could follow him home on another ship a week or two later. Despite these conditions, and feeling she could trust Mary Ann Hogan, Mary agreed to the scheme.

Mary went to John Gough to borrow the $400. When he knew the purpose of the loan, Gough handed over the money, on the understanding that he would be repaid from the Burdue gold being held by McAllister and Benham, following the Marysville murder trial.

Sunday, April 20, 1851. San Francisco Bay, California

The waters of San Francisco Bay can be icy cold in April. With a shiver, Joe Windred looked down from the rail of the prison hulk *Waban* and prepared himself for the shock of the water closing around his body. Taking a deep breath, he launched himself from the side of the ship, and dropped into the bay.

A key to his *Waban* cell had been passed on to Joe via Whitaker crony Thomas Belcher Kay, port warden of San Francisco. In the dead of night, when all was silent aboard the *Waban* but for the snores of prisoners and guards, Joe had used the key to unlock his cell door. Barefoot, and on tiptoe, he had passed the cells of the other, sleeping prisoners and climbed a companionway to the deck. In the moonlight, he had hurried to the rail nearest the distant Angel Island shoreline, and mounted it.

English Jim would later tell the story of another crony, Johnny Griffiths, who had attempted to escape from the *La Grange*, the prison hulk moored at Sacramento. Stuart was away at the time, auctioning off stolen goods to raise $1500 bail to get Griffiths off the *La Grange*. But Griffiths had neither the patience to wait for Stuart's return nor the common sense to think through his escape. With plans to swim to shore, Griffiths one night plunged into the Sacramento River. But aboard the *La Grange* prisoners were kept in leg-irons day and night. Those leg-irons had of course dragged Griffiths down, and he had drowned.

Joe Windred suffered from no such limitation, and, a strong swimmer since learning to swim in the Hawkesbury in childhood, he made short work of the swim to shore. Several later colourful but spectacularly inaccurate Californian historians would say that, in escaping from the state penitentiary, Joe dug his way out – which would have been an interesting proposition considering the fact that the penitentiary was, at this time, a ship afloat in San Francisco Bay.

Around the point on Angel Island, out of sight of the *Waban*, there was a house owned by Daniel Wilder, a friend of Sam Whitaker and English Jim. Apparently at Wilder's house, where English Jim had stayed in the past, Joe was able to change into dry clothes, after which a small boat conveyed him across the bay. That boat was likely to have been manned by either Wilder or James Kitchen. The boat landed Joe just outside San Francisco, where Thomas Belcher Kay was waiting for him with a carriage. Belcher Kay then drove Joe three kilometres to the house of an English doctor friend on Mission Road, near the Mission Dolores, where Joe went into hiding.[137] Sam Whitaker's escape plan for Joe had so far worked to perfection.

The next day, the message was passed to Mary Windred, apparently by Margaret Walton, that Joe had safely made his prison break and was now with friends. How long Joe would have to remain in hiding would depend on how long it took port warden Belcher Kay to find a captain bound for Sydney, one who would ask no questions about his Australian passenger. In the meantime, with the news breaking in the press that Joe had escaped, and with a large reward soon offered by the authorities for information leading to his recapture, Mary would have to take care, knowing that she would now be watched by the police.

Sunday, April 27, 1851. San Francisco, California

It was Joe Windred's twenty-ninth birthday. Hiding near the Mission Dolores, he was a free man, but a lonely fugitive, waiting for news that a passage had been organised for him to Sydney.

This afternoon, the schooner *H. L. Allen* dropped anchor off San Francisco, returning from Trinidad Bay after sailing there two months before. English Jim Stuart was aboard, just as he had been on the vessel's northward voyage. 'I found Trinidad to be a bad place for me,' Stuart was to later say. Several of his old acquaintants had been there. Apart from Bob McKenzie, these had included a fellow nicknamed the Poet, and James 'Dab' Peate. 'I played cards with Dab, and won all his money, about $300,' Stuart would say. Stuart, Dab and the Poet came down to San Francisco together on the *H. L. Allen*, with Stuart paying all their fares. Despite Stuart's generosity, Dab was still smarting after being cleaned out at the card table, and, as they were being rowed ashore he extorted money from Stuart. 'Dab threatened to inform on me if I didn't give him some money.' Reluctantly, Stuart paid up. 'I gave him fifty dollars.'[138]

Stuart landed well armed. Beneath his coat, a revolver sat in his belt and a sheathed fourteen-inch Bowie knife trailed down one leg. Once he was ashore, he parted from his companions and went to the Clark's Point home of long-time friend James Kitchen the boatman, who agreed to let Stuart stay with him. While Kitchen rowed out to the *H. L. Allen* to collect Stuart's baggage, English Jim himself made a beeline for the Hogan House. Mary Ann Hogan was far from pleased to see him. She had learned, to her regret, that wherever English Jim went, trouble was sure to follow.

'Where's Sam?' Stuart asked her.

'Not here,' she said. 'I've secreted him away.'

'Why? What's happened?'

'There's a warrant out for Sam and Long Charley, for robbing one of my lodgers of $1500. I advise you to leave town, Jim. The police are always searching my house these days, looking for Sam.'

'So, where have you secreted him?'

'At the Mission,' she said.[139] She was lying – Mary Ann wanted Stuart to have nothing more to do with her man.

Stuart left the Hogan House in a black mood. That mood soured even more as he was making his way back to James Kitchen's house. Walking along a street, he heard his name called. Turning, he saw Dab Peate, accompanied by a policeman. Instead of running, English Jim sauntered up to the pair.

'What can I do for you?' Stuart asked.

'I want you to accompany me to the recorder's office,' said the constable, 'to answer accusations laid against you.'

As the policeman went to take hold of English Jim's arm, the crook reached beneath his coat and drew the revolver from his belt. Jabbing the gun into the constable's ribs and cocking it, Stuart growled, 'Stand off, or I will shoot you down!'

The constable immediately stood back, fearfully urging Stuart to keep calm. English Jim was as calm as could be. There were two ways he could keep the copper quiet. One was a bullet to the heart. The other alternative was less bloody. Suggesting that they could settle this like businessmen, Stuart reached into his pocket and took out a purse containing $100 in gold coins. Pressing the money onto the policeman, he reckoned that should keep him quiet.[140]

Stuart, flashing his blue-grey eyes threateningly at Dab, backed away with his revolver levelled, then slipped into the passing crowd as he returned the gun to his belt. In moments, he was gone. Mary Ann Hogan was right: this town was no place for Stuart to dally. He would spend that night at Kitchen's, before, bright and early next morning, hiring a horse at a local livery stable, using the name James Carlisle. Jimmy Kitchen had told him about a big job some of their mates had pulled down in Monterey, 190 kilometres to the south – the theft of $13,000 from the government custom house. The robbers had been caught, but not before the loot had been stashed. Lawyer Parbutt was going down to Monterey to represent the prisoners at their trial, and English Jim saw a way of profiting from that trial. Mounted on his rented horse, he would go down to Monterey.

Wednesday, April 30, 1851. San Francisco, California

In the early hours of the morning, Thomas Belcher Kay came to Joe Windred at his Mission Road hiding place and instructed the fugitive to accompany him. In his carriage, Belcher Kay drove Joe into the city via back streets. At the waterfront near Clark's Point, the pair alighted, and Belcher Kay handed Joe over to the waiting Sam Whitaker. Whitaker introduced himself, before they slipped into a back alley and waited in the darkness. Presently, a pair of patrolling policemen strolled by.

Once the officers were long gone, a voice from down by the water whispered hoarsely, 'All clear!'

Shaking Joe by the hand, Whitaker wished him the best of luck, then said there was someone in the next alley who wanted to bid him farewell. Following Whitaker's directions, Joe scuttled through the night to find two women waiting for him. One was Mary Ann Hogan, the other was Joe's Mary. After an embrace and a parting kiss from Mary, Joe followed Mrs Hogan's instructions and hurried to a boat drawn up on the sand. The face of boatman James Kitchen loomed from the gloom, and together the pair pushed the boat out into the water and clambered aboard.[141]

Kitchen rowed Joe out through the maze of ships anchored in the bay, to the trim little 110-ton, San Francisco-registered schooner *Herculean*, which sat almost hidden among the array of much larger vessels cluttering the waters off the city. Kitchen shook Joe's hand and bade him good luck, then the Australian climbed up the side of the schooner and set foot on her deck.

'Mr Johnson?' asked the waiting skipper of the *Herculean*, Captain William Hickens.

Joe's passage had been booked in the name of Johnson.

'Yes,' he acknowledged.

Hickens, an American, welcomed Joe aboard. He didn't ask why Joe chose to board at such an early hour. Nor did he ask why he didn't have any baggage. He merely conducted him to the cabin below.

Thursday, May 1, 1851. San Francisco, California

During the day, the city was shaken by the first of what would be four earth tremors to rock the San Francisco area in May. More serious than most past tremors, this Mayday quake had buildings and street lamps swaying, broke many glass windows and left cracks in new brick walls. Still, no one in San Francisco, other than insurance brokers, blinked an eye.

That evening, Mary Windred put on men's clothing and crammed her hair beneath a man's hat. Then, disguised as a man to evade police attention, and with James Whiting as her guide and escort once more, she ventured out into the city's back streets. Using a circuitous route, they paid a visit to Mary Ann Hogan on Sansome Street. On finding Mrs Hogan, Mary begged her for news of Joe's sailing from San Francisco. But the tidings were not good. The *Herculean* had not completed loading her cargo, and had yet to sail. With so many participants in Joe's escape bid now aware of where he was, every moment he remained at San Francisco had Mary dreading that someone would let something slip about his whereabouts, or, worse, tip off the police in return for the large reward on offer for his recapture.

Every night for the next few nights, Mary Windred would repeat this exercise, slipping out into the night disguised as a man to visit Mary Ann Hogan, always in quest of news of Joe's departure. The news would always be the same – the *Herculean* still lay at anchor in the bay, meaning Joe had not yet made his escape.

Saturday, May 3, 1851. San Francisco, California

Mary Windred had not long returned to the boarding house room she was sharing with Elen Burdue and her four children. She had just completed her latest, fruitless visit to the Hogan House for news of Joe's final escape. Now, she heard fire bells ringing across town. After four major conflagrations over the past twelve months, the people of San Francisco had become increasingly edgy about the possibility of another major blaze breaking out in their fire-prone city. As San Francisco publisher Charles Kimball wrote in 1850, 'We have seen the whole congregation of a religious meeting start from their seats at the ringing of the bells of other churches, supposing it was fire.'[142] But, this Saturday night, the clanging of bells proved to be no false alarm.

At about 11.00 p.m., a fire had ignited in the Baker and Meserve paint and upholstery store on the southern, Clay Street side of Portsmouth Square. The paint and fabric in the store was hugely combustible, and the store was quickly devoured by the blaze. A strong Pacific breeze was blowing in from the west, and this drove the flames down onto neighbouring buildings, and then across Kearny Street. The city's volunteer firemen rushed to fight the blaze, pushing their fire engines to the scene. It would be months before it dawned on the firemen that it was a good idea to hitch horses to their engines, and only then for a street parade.

The fire spread from building to building along Kearny Street to north and south. Not even brick or corrugated iron walls provided protection, for, a great many of the city's buildings were roofed with wooden shingles. These shingles burst into flame long before wooden walls or doors or window frames caught fire, enabling the blaze to leap from rooftop to rooftop on the wind. Eventually, burnt roofs would cave in, to shower flame and cinder on all that lay below. By the time that the fire had finished with these brick structures, most of them less than a year old, many walls were left standing, scorched and gaunt. But they were useless, precarious shells surrounding blackened hearts.

This sprint of flames across the shingles did give occupants below time to evacuate themselves and many of their belongings. The Reverend William Taylor, emerging from the house he had built with his own hands on Jackson Street, watched, helpless and horrified, as the fire spread with terrifying speed. Coming down Jackson Street to Portsmouth Square, Taylor observed that the broad expanse of the Plaza, whose buildings other than those on its blackened southern side had been spared the flames, was filling with piled-up furniture, other household items, suitcases, clothing, shop goods and all the detritus of nineteenth-century human existence.

Sunday, May 4, 1851. San Francisco, California

As midnight came and Saturday became Sunday, the unstoppable flames swept east down the slope toward San Francisco Bay, crossing the commercial thoroughfares of Montgomery and Sansome and many smaller streets and alleys in between. Over the past few wet winters, San Francisco's potholed streets had become so muddy that humans and beasts of burden risked life and limb traversing them, and gullible newcomers were told that entire wagons, complete with teams of horses, had disappeared beneath the mud. To counter this mud problem, the city authorities had recently planked over most of the central streets, not just the sidewalks, with wood. In addition, a wood-paved tollway being built all the way out to Mission Dolores to carry horse-drawn omnibuses was just a month away from completion. This planking of the streets was a welcome measure in winter. But now, as the Reverend William Taylor observed, even the wooden roadways and sidewalks in the affected areas burst into flame, so that the streets of San Francisco literally burned.

Out on San Francisco Bay, like passengers and crew aboard the hundreds of ships in port, Joe Windred watched from the deck of the *Herculean* as the city burned. The waters of the bay reflected the flames, while the sky above glowed orange. That glow in the night sky was seen as far away as Monterey, almost 200 kilometres distant. Joe's main concern was for his wife, Mary, who was ashore in the midst of the growing disaster. Yet, there was not a thing he could do to help her.

In the city itself, Ed Gilbert, editor of the *Alta California*, was a more close-hand but equally helpless witness to the fire's horrific progress. Now, in the early hours of the morning, with the fire continuing to rage unabated, and driven back indoors by the choking smoke, Gilbert sat down at his desk to write an editorial for his Sunday edition. He wrote hoping that, come daylight, his printing press downstairs would still be capable of getting out that edition. So far, the *Alta* office, on the north side of Portsmouth Square, had not been touched by the fire, and unless the wind completely reversed course, it was likely to survive.

Shocked to his core by the disaster, Gilbert wrote his editorial for May 4's issue reflecting on what he had seen outside his office door: 'San Francisco is again in ashes. The smoke and flames are ascending from several squares of our city, as if the God of Destruction had seated himself in our midst . . . Here and there, a brick building stands like a tomb among a nation of graves, yet even they in most cases have nothing but their walls standing.'

This fire changed Gilbert's attitude to lynching. Angry that his city had now been devastated by four major fires in a year, and ready to accept the popular claim that the Sydney Ducks, and not poor fire prevention and inadequate fire-fighting facilities, were to blame, Gilbert would from now on no longer be a very public voice of restraint. Gilbert and other leading men of San Francisco would support the patriotic rush to punish outsiders for their grievous loss. And anyone who looked and sounded like their enemy would suffice.

With the dawn, the *Alta California*'s press was in operation, printing the morning edition. The *Alta* would be the only San Francisco paper to produce an edition for days to come, with the offices of every other newspaper in the city destroyed by the fire. Likewise, many of the firms advertising in the *Alta* no longer had premises from which to sell their wares, if they still had wares to sell.

By 9.00 a.m., the wind had died away and the city's overstretched fire-fighters had finally brought the fire under control. The last flames had been extinguished, but a pall of black smoke hung over the bay area, and the pungent smell of burnt matter filled nostrils. According to contemporary estimates, two thousand buildings over eighteen city blocks had been destroyed, with a total damage bill of around $12 million in 1851 money.

To the east, the march of the ten-hour blaze had been held along much of the length of Battery Street, preventing the flames from reaching the waterfront and the vessels clustered there. The southern limit of the fire had been Pine Street, after the flames had successively crossed Commercial, Sacramento and California streets. The blaze had spread north from Clay Street, too, over Washington and Jackson streets to Pacific, and a little way into Sydney Town beyond Broadway, around Battery and Front streets. Five men had perished when they were trapped in a brick building fitted with closed iron shutters.

Just after 11.00 a.m., singing voices were heard in the Plaza.

Methodist minister William Taylor usually held open-air services in Portsmouth Square on Sundays, and this morning at 11.00 he stood at his usual vantage point outside the Adobe Building, surveying the smoking ruins on two sides of him and the piles of items saved from the fire which littered the Plaza. To the Reverend Taylor's mind, there could be no better time to offer thanks to Heaven, after the salvation of the vast majority of the city's population. He and his wife began to sing a hymn. Taylor's singing and subsequent sermonising drew a congregation of well over a thousand residents this morning, among them Mary Windred, Elen Burdue and the Burdue children. Sitting on a slope above Portsmouth Square, the boarding house where Mary and the Burdues were staying had remained, like the ships on the bay, outside the reach of the blaze, and the women and children had safely seen in the arrival of the new day.

Partly because Sydney Town was so little affected, many future American historians, writing decades after the event, would accuse the Sydney Ducks of igniting this fire. Some would repeat an apocryphal story that a well-known Sydney Duck had been seen running from the paint and upholstery store shortly before it erupted in flame, although no San Francisco newspaper contained any such report during this period. Conversely, Baker and Meserve, owners of the store in question, would claim in the press that the fire had not even started on their premises, no doubt trying to escape blame from fellow shopkeepers for being the source of the expensive disaster.

The following year, James M. Parker, editor of *San Francisco Directory* for 1852–53, would write, in his publication: 'This fire, though by some ascribed to design, is now charged to accident or carelessness.' Nonetheless, some San Franciscans held firm to the belief that the blame should be laid squarely at Sydney Duck feet. And perhaps they were right. Sam Whitaker had previously threatened to fire the city, and in the coming weeks he would apparently claim to have ignited the fire with the aim of covering Joe Windred's escape. Was this fact, or boast? If Whitaker, or a crony, was the incendiary, Whitaker certainly had his fingers burnt – Whitaker's hiding place, Dr Lambert's residence on Montgomery Street, was destroyed in the blaze, as was the Hogan House on Sansome, the boarding house operated by Whitaker's ladylove Mary Ann Hogan.

20

AN ESCAPE, A LYNCHING

Monday, May 5, 1851. San Francisco, California

MONDAY DAWNED WITH SAN Francisco paralysed by the shock and disruption of the devastating fire, which had left thousands looking for shelter, and by the workings of the city's political system. For, this was the day on which the city's newly elected government was due to take office. The Whigs had swept into power. San Francisco had a new mayor, Captain Charles Brenham, who had only stood for office on condition that he could still serve as master of the riverboat *McKim*. Now, the demands of rebuilding the city would tax his ability to effectively do both jobs. Not only did the city have a gaggle of new aldermen, its civic offices were filled with a host of new Whig faces. Police chief Malachi Fallon had lost his job to Robert G. Crozier, and Crozier had a revamped police force under his command.

    San Francisco did rebuild remarkably quickly following the fire. Reconstruction of some buildings began the very next day. But, for the moment, not only were new men taking up all important administrative positions, many of them had lost homes and possessions in the fire and were physically or mentally absent from their posts as they sorted out personal affairs. Sam Whitaker took advantage of the chaos to do a good deed. Since losing his hidey-hole at Dr Lambert's, Whitaker had decided to go down to Monterey to join English Jim in trying to profit from the custom-house robbery trial. Mary Ann

Hogan was remaining in San Francisco, and, supported with funds from Whitaker, would take a lease on a large house at the corner of Green and Dupont streets, where she would quickly open a new boarding house and bar.

That evening, after dark, Mary Windred, at her undamaged lodgings, received an unexpected visit from Mary Ann Hogan.

'Hurry and pack,' Mrs Hogan instructed. 'You are going to join your husband on the *Herculean*.' An anonymous benefactor had paid for Mary's passage to Sydney with Joe. That anonymous benefactor had to be Whitaker, playing the gallant before he too left the city. Mrs Hogan knew for a fact that, at this moment, no police were outside the boarding house on watch for Mary. 'But, be quick,' she added. 'You have just half an hour.'

During the day, Mary had received a note from John Gough of the Panama House. The excuse for the note was that Elicia Gough was again unwell, and her husband asked Mary to pay his ailing wife a visit. He also expressed the hope that Joe would be able to return safely to Australia, and remarked that he and his wife were beginning to think that their future also lay back in New South Wales. But there had been a more pecuniary motive to Gough's letter. Like Elen Burdue, Gough had been corresponding with Tom Burdue at Marysville Jail by letter, and Gough told Tom that he had given his five pounds of gold dust to Mary Windred. Gough seems to have informed Mary in his letter that Tom had written back to say that he had not authorised Gough to dispose of his gold, intimating that he did not trust Mary with it.

Not surprisingly, this infuriated Mary, who had been struggling to look after Tom's wife and children while also trying to find defence witnesses for both Tom and Joe. Besides, she had assumed that Elen Burdue, in her letters to her husband since her arrival in San Francisco, had told Tom that Mary had passed his gold onto McAllister and Benham to secure their services for him and Joe, and that she had borrowed money against it. So, after packing her bags, Mary penned a note in reply to the one from Gough:

San Francisco, May 5, 1851

Mr Gough,
I hope you will not think it strange of me in not coming down to see you before I start. But I have only half an hour to get ready, so

the time is short, and you know how I am situated, and you will not be angry. I shall see you in our own country. I hope, soon. I trust Mrs Gough will get over her trouble soon, and be sure to come back to our own welcome home.

I would tell you more, only the time is short. Should they never let poor Burdue come into this town – should they murder him for another man's crime – I enclose the following bill, to be presented to Mr McAllister, and you will oblige.
M. Windred

Mary went to pen an invoice to Burdue, but had another thought, and, with Mary Ann Hogan at her shoulder and urging her to hurry, she hastily added a P. S. to her note to Gough:

Should Tom come down to him [McAllister], let him do as he likes, only I would [not] like to see him rob me, or his wife either; for Tom knows I borrow[ed] 500 dollars from two parties, and they will look to be paid some time or other. The 500 dollars was on Tom's account, to whom I am responsible for the sum, and would like to pay it.
M. W.[143]

Quickly folding the note, she handed it to Mary Ann, asking her to deliver it to Gough. As Elen Burdue and her children tearfully watched on, Mary pulled on her hat and coat. After a rushed farewell to the Burdue clan, with kisses and caresses, she hurried out the door with a bag containing her and Joe's things in each hand, following on the heels of Mrs Hogan.

Down sloping streets, skirting the ashes of downtown San Francisco, hustled the two women. At Clark's Point, boatman James Kitchen waited, and he loaded Mary's bags into his boat. It seems, from later events, that Mary Ann Hogan now told Mary that the fire of May 3–4 had been no accident, that Sam Whitaker had kept his old promise of setting the city alight, doing it to cover Joe's escape. This may have been an invention, designed to impress and amplify the fugitives' gratitude to their saviour Whitaker, but Mary seems to have taken the claim seriously, as would her husband.

After thanking Mrs Hogan and bidding her farewell with a hug,

Mary climbed into the boat. A quarter moon peeked from behind clouds as Kitchen rowed his lone passenger out through the maze of ships clogging the harbour. Eventually, they slid in alongside the *Herculean*. Hitching her skirt, Mary climbed up the schooner's side to join her husband. Her departure from her lodgings had been so rapid that Joe was not even expecting her. Kitchen handed up the bags, then rowed off into the night.

How pleased Joe was to see Mary can only be imagined. But the couple had to temper their joy. Captain Hickens and their fellow passengers, James Mackay and a Mr Woods, must not be allowed to know that Joe was a prison escapee, and that 'Mr and Mrs Johnson' were desperate to get away from San Francisco without delay.

Tuesday, May 6, 1851. San Francisco, California

Come the morning tide, the schooner still lay at anchor off San Francisco, with Captain Hickens still not yet ready to sail. The Windreds spent an anxious day eyeing every approaching boat, in case it contained police or port officials coming to search the vessel for prison escapee Windred, now that the *Herculean* was preparing to leave port. But the disorganisation in the city in the wake of the latest fire served the couple well, and no one came to search the *Herculean*.

Mary realised that, in her rush the previous evening, she had failed to write the invoice to Tom Burdue that she had intended to enclose with her letter to John Gough. In the cabin of the *Herculean*, she now penned the invoice:

San Francisco, May 6, 1851

Thomas Burdue.
    To Mrs Mary Windred.
Lent money to Mrs Walton .... 400 dollars
Lent money to witness ....100 dollars
Board and Washing....................................125 dollars
_____
625 dollars

At the bottom of the invoice, Mary added a note to attorney Hall McAllister:

Mr McAllister,
Have the kindness to see that Mr Benham pays the money due to me to Mr Gough, and you will oblige your obedient servant,
Mary Windred

Now, too, Mary dashed off another letter to John Gough, to whom she would send the invoice after failing to include it with her last missive:

San Francisco, May 6, 1851

Mr Gough,
Should poor Tom ever be permitted to return to San Francisco, tell him that I never got any of his money. Mr McAllister and Benham still hold it. That I assure him is the case. Tell him that I paid Mr Walton $400 and other expenses I can scarcely recollect. However, I trust he will soon be down and astride his own affairs.
   And by doing so you will oblige yours,
M. Windred[144]

Mary had the letter and invoice taken ashore to John Gough with the last boat to leave the *Herculean*'s side.

Tuesday, May 7, 1851. San Francisco Bay, California

A favourable wind was blowing. In the early morning darkness, the *Herculean* had weighed anchor with the tide, and now she was moving slowly across the bay. Carrying a cargo of general merchandise, a crew of seven and four passengers, the schooner cleared San Francisco's heads and sailed out into the Pacific, setting a southwesterly course for Sydney, Australia.
   No alarm was raised. No vessel gave chase. Joe Windred had succeeded in escaping from California.

Monday, June 9, 1851. San Francisco, California

Joe Windred had made his getaway, but his mate Tom Burdue, imprisoned at Marysville, was still in danger of being hanged. Tom's trial for the murder of Charles Moore was just weeks away. But, another trial was about to change the complexion of legal affairs in California, and to influence Tom's fate.

In San Francisco, rebuilding work was proceeding at breakneck pace in the wake of the May fire, while the price of goods in the city had risen by twenty per cent. Another thing generated by the fire was a sense of righteous indignation. Despite the recent change of city administration, this latest fire, combined with Joe Windred's escape from the state penitentiary, motivated several businessmen to take the law into their own hands.

On Sunday, June 8, an unsigned notice appeared in the *Alta California* calling on all right-minded men to combine to form a Committee of Vigilance for the protection of lives and property. It might as easily have been called the Committee of Vengeance, for vengeance was what the frustrated businessmen of fire-ravaged San Francisco were aching for. The notice called for a meeting to take place the following evening at the rooms above the fire-station house of the California Engine Company, on the corner of Market and Bush streets. Now, on the Monday evening, seven men met and elected office bearers of this Committee of Vigilance, which became the forerunner of, and model for, vigilante movements that would arise across California and then across the United States as a whole in the months and years to come.

As their first president, these San Francisco vigilantes elected Sam Brannan, the disgraced Mormon elder who had led the calls for hangings during the Burdue–Windred trials. Isaac Bluxome junior, a merchant whose San Francisco premises had been burned out in three successive fires, was elected secretary. It was agreed that the Committee of Vigilance would appoint its own chief of police and operate its own volunteer police force. To protect members from the legitimate administrators of law and order in California, all would only be identified publicly by a number rather than by name.

Once office bearers had been elected, the Committee of Vigilance set to work consigning to paper the organisation's written constitution. They were working away, well into the night, when the door suddenly opened and a man was forced into the room at gunpoint. Redheaded, close to six feet tall and powerfully built, he was John Jenkins, a resident of Sydney Town. Jenkins' face was badly bruised;

it had been punched, or pistol whipped. Behind him, with a levelled revolver, came boatman John Sullivan.

The gunman was the same John Sullivan who had worked with English Jim Stuart in and around Foster's Bar the previous year, and who had sworn in two trials that Tom Burdue was English Jim. According to the *Alta California* next day, Sullivan now declared that he and other boatmen had spotted Jenkins rowing away from Central Wharf with a bag, after which shipping agent George Virgin had hurried up and declared that the man had stolen a small safe from his premises on Commercial Street. According to Sullivan, he and other boatmen had given chase, and Jenkins had tossed the bag into the waters of the bay. Sullivan said that, after an almighty tussle, he had overpowered Jenkins, before bringing him to the Committee.

Sam Brannan despatched Sullivan to retrieve the evidence of the alleged crime, the discarded safe. At the same time, Brannan had the fire station's deep-toned bell rung twice every minute. This would become the standard vigilante call to action. The ringing bell soon attracted a crowd which filled the street outside the fire station. Numerous businessmen also joined Committee members upstairs, bringing the number crammed into the room to around eighty, as John Jenkins was made to sit and await Sullivan's return.

Jenkins was acquainted with English Jim Stuart, but had never taken part in the criminal exploits led by Stuart or Whitaker. Jenkins had legitimately prospered as the proprietor of a pub called the Uncle Sam on the San Francisco waterfront. He later changed the pub's name to the Shipman's Arms, and by the spring of 1851 had sold or leased it to a couple from Launceston in Van Diemen's Land by the name of Connolly. Mr Connolly had died shortly after. Jenkins had not previously been accused of any crime in California – unless the accusation levelled against Mrs Connolly of 'comforting herself too promptly with the attentions' of John Jenkins following the death of her husband can be considered a crime.[145]

After a lengthy wait, Jenkins' accuser, Sullivan, laboured through the door bearing a small safe which, when opened, was found to contain just a few dollars. Apparently, the safe was not locked. Sam Brannan, revelling in his newfound power, declared the safe proof that a crime had been committed and announced that the

Committee would try Jenkins for grand larceny, here and now. It was past midnight by the time the Committee of Vigilance's trial got underway. From among their own number the Committee appointed a judge – Sam Brannan – and a jury and prosecutor. No one was appointed to defend the prisoner. Although vehemently denying any wrongdoing in California, under intense questioning Jenkins, a native of London, admitted to serving time in Australia.

The *Alta California* would report, 'He has been known to the police for some months, as a desperate character from the penal colonies, where he passed away many years as a transported convict.'[146] It was later established that Jenkins was transported to Van Diemen's Land. Which of the eleven convicts named John Jenkins sent to Van Diemen's land he was cannot be determined. But he was apparently there in November 1849 when news of the California gold rush prompted Hobart Town merchants such as John T. Waterhouse, Andrew Haig and Captain Edward Gilbert to advertise places aboard chartered ships departing Hobart for San Francisco.[147]

John Sullivan testified that he had witnessed Jenkins dump the safe a little after 9.00 p.m. Were Jenkins allowed to mount a defence, he would surely have asked the 'jury' to consider why he would steal a safe when he was quite well-off after selling/leasing his pub. Was it not strange that the safe's supposed owner, Mr Virgin, had not personally appeared to testify that Jenkins had stolen his property? And, if, as it appeared, the safe had not been locked, would a thief have bothered to carry it off when he could have merely removed the few dollars it contained and walked away?

As it happened, some members of the Committee's jury had their doubts about Jenkins' guilt. After all, just a single witness, Sullivan, had testified against him, and he hadn't witnessed Jenkins actually commit the robbery. What if Sullivan had a grudge against Jenkins? What if Sullivan was jealous of the widowed Mrs Connolly's affection for Jenkins? It is possible Jenkins made just such a claim, but his defence was never committed to paper by the Committee of Vigilance.

Despite swirling doubts and flimsy evidence, the jurors, railroaded by their more aggressive colleagues, declared Jenkins guilty of grand larceny. To the shock of both Jenkins and some members of the Committee, Sam Brannan pronounced sentence: Jenkins was to be hanged, at once. Some present argued that the sentence was overly harsh, and that they should not rush to execute the man.

To this, one of the later arrivals to the Committee's meeting, William H. Howard, impatiently remarked, 'Gentlemen, as I understand it, we came here to hang somebody.'[148]

Still, Committee members were divided. So, Sam Brannan, anxious to string up his victim before the legitimate lawmen of the city could be alerted and intervene to save Jenkins' life, proposed to seek a vote of the citizens gathered outside. Going out onto a sandy bank opposite the fire station, and without identifying himself, Brannan announced that a Sydney Duck thief who had been caught red-handed had been convicted in a trial conducted by the Committee of Vigilance.

'He has been fairly tried, convicted on the strongest evidence, and offered no denial of the robbery,' Brannan went on, his declaration untruthful in every aspect.[149] Announcing that sentence of death had been pronounced against Jenkins, Brannan asked the crowd to vote in favour of immediately carrying out that sentence.

There was a cry of approval from two thirds of those present. After all, there had never before been an execution carried out in San Francisco; this would be a novel entertainment. When Brannan rejoined his Committee colleagues, he informed them that the vast majority of 'the people' had voted in favour of Jenkins' immediate execution, and urged his fellow Committee members to act at once. To minister to the condemned man, Presbyterian clergyman Reverend Flevel S. Mines was sent for. Not unsurprisingly, Mines found Jenkins unrepentant, contradicting Brannan's claim that he had confessed to the crime.

At 2.00 a.m., Jenkins was hustled downstairs and out into the moonlit street. The waiting crowd surged around the party as Jenkins was dragged to the Plaza. According to Sydney men in the crowd, along the way some Americans landed punches on Jenkins, adding to the damage to his face. Committeeman Edgar Wakeman, an out-of-work sea captain with a thick dark beard in the Abraham Lincoln style, produced a coil of rope. The first idea was to hang Jenkins from the Liberty Pole in the centre of the Plaza, but many protested that, as the flagpole flew the Stars and Stripes, that would be an unforgivable sacrilege. Instead, Brannan led the way to the Adobe Building, thirty metres away on the north side of the Plaza, adjacent to his own business premises. The A-framed Adobe Building's thick upright post and crossbeam presented an ideal gibbet.

According to the *Alta California*, Jenkins was calm, and even had a cigar in his mouth.[150] In contrast, Reverend Mines described Jenkins as 'sullen' and 'vindictive', as he apparently loudly, angrily protested that he'd been framed.[151] Women and children were seen on the fringes of the vast throng that filled the Plaza to watch as the long rope was thrown up over the Adobe Building crossbeam. A noose was tied at one end, and a number of eager young men took hold of the other end. Edgar Wakeman, acting as hangman, used a leather belt to circle Jenkins, pinning his arms by his side. He then looped the noose around Jenkins' neck, over his neckerchief.

Sam Brannan wasted no time. 'Pull away!' he called.

It was 2.10 a.m. when John Jenkins was hauled into the air by his neck. According to the *Alta California*, Jenkins was dead in moments. Next day's *Evening Picayune* told a very different story – of a slow, agonising strangulation. As Jenkins struggled, young Americans in the crowd came forward to take turns at the end of the rope and claim a hand in the execution of a Sydney Duck. Suddenly, several policemen and citizens dashed forward to free Jenkins. Committee of Vigilance men roughly pulled them off, and, with drawn pistols, forced them to retreat. Not long after, a second rush was beaten off after friends of Jenkins tried to end his agonies by dragging on his legs and speeding his strangulation.

'At last, drawing up his knees with a convulsive jerk,' said the *Evening Picayune*, 'he expired.' When City Marshal Crozier cut Jenkins down at 6.00 a.m., his corpse was still attracting sightseers. Sydney Duck friends who later that morning viewed his body in the city mortuary hardly recognised his battered face. The *Alta California*, while describing the lynching as 'a tragedy', would add, 'Of the guilt of Jenkins there was no doubt.'[152] No doubt in the minds of mad Sam Brannan and the mob.

A proclamation was shortly issued by the Committee of Vigilance, which said, in part: 'We are determined that no thief, burglar, incendiary, or assassin shall escape punishment, either by the quibbles of the law, the insecurity of prisons [a direct reference to Joe Windred's prison break], the carelessness or corruption of the police, or a laxity of those who pretend to administer justice.'[153] Even though a grand jury subsequently found that Jenkins' execution amounted to murder, and compiled a list of the leading participants, no one was arrested. For, not a single member of the crowd would testify to what they saw, or who they saw doing it. This was the sort of mob lynching that Joe Windred had narrowly escaped back in February. And it would not be the last.

Sunday, June 22, 1851. San Francisco, California

In the middle of this Sunday morning, a fire broke out in a wooden house on Pacific Street, between Stockton and Powell, and quickly spread to surrounding buildings. The Committee of Vigilance was mounting volunteer street patrols to further its stated goal of protecting life and property, yet not even these saved the city from another disaster.

This conflagration was not as extensive as the May 4 fire, but over four hours three hundred buildings on ten city blocks were destroyed. Among the buildings razed was City Hall, where Joe Windred and Tom Burdue had suffered through two trials in the courtroom and spent long weeks in the basement cells. A Sydney Duck, Ben Lewis, would be arrested by the San Francisco Police on suspicion of lighting this fire, only to be released after a judge found the case against him flawed. This would only increase public suspicion of the Ducks and cynicism about the city's legitimate law enforcers.

The Reverend Albert Williams, whose First Presbyterian Church was destroyed in this blaze, said, of the six great fires that had afflicted the city in eighteen months: 'It began to be the confirmed conviction that they were not accidental, but incendiary.'[154]

The fire acted as a stimulant to Committee of Vigilance recruitment, and within a month membership would peak at 719 vigilantes. None of the city's newspaper editors joined up, but all the papers other than the *Morning Post* supported the Committee on their pages. Still, lamented William Walker in the *Herald*, many in the city were 'lukewarm in their support of the Committee', with a number signing up under peer pressure.[155] Captain Robert Patterson, who had testified for Joe Windred and Tom Burdue in March, attempted to join the Committee, but his application was refused. No friend of a Sydney Duck prison escapee or of a convicted thief about to stand trial for murder was welcome in vigilante ranks. He was considered the enemy.

21

TOM BURDUE'S MURDER TRIAL

Saturday, June 28, 1851. Marysville, California

ESCAPEES JOE AND MARY Windred were still at sea aboard the *Herculean* in the South Pacific, and several weeks away from Australia's shores, when their friend Tom Burdue faced his latest test of character, his trial, as English Jim Stuart, for the murder of Charles Moore in Yuba County.

Tom's trial drew a vast crowd to the courtroom at Marysville, seat of Yuba County, 165 kilometres inland from San Francisco. Hall McAllister and Cal Benham had come to Marysville to again represent Tom. Lodging in a local hotel, they spent a week canvassing defence witnesses. District Attorney John O. Goodwin was leading the prosecution, while the district judge was Gordon Newell Mott. Tall, long-faced and as skinny as a beanpole, thirty-eight-year-old Mott was a disappointed Ohio gold-seeker with a law degree who'd recently been elected to the District Court. Tetchy and self-important, Mott would only last a year on the court before being ousted by voters.

Tom Burdue, bearded still, was led into the courtroom. He was a shadow of the quietly confident character that Joe Windred had come to know in California. Cold, damp jail cells in San Francisco and Marysville had damaged Tom's health. Not only had the conditions sapped his physical strength, his inability to prove that he was not English Jim Stuart had drained him mentally. Elen and the children had remained in San Francisco, where they were surviving through the charity of friends like the Goughs. Tom was certain of being convicted yet again, and throughout much of the trial would sit in the prisoners' box cloaked in depression, head bowed or in his hands. To reporter Edward Buffum from the *Alta California*, Tom presented a picture of a 'sad and humble' man.[156]

Tom, referred to as 'James Stewart alias Thomas Berdue', was charged with having robbed and murdered Charles E. Moore the previous December. The crime had taken place on the road to Marysville from Winslow Bar, a small mining camp near Foster's Bar. Moore, riding down to Marysville to stock up on goods for his Winslow Bar store, had been carrying $2000 in gold. Bailed up on the road in broad daylight, he'd been gunned down in cold blood.

Later, English Jim himself would admit to a catalogue of crimes, but would maintain to his last breath that he did not rob or murder Moore. Certainly, highway robbery was not Stuart's usual modus operandi. And, if he did indeed carry out the Moore robbery, it was the one and only time he robbed someone on the road, and the only time he carried out a robbery in daylight. In all probability, Stuart was truly innocent of this crime, but that was not the concern of Hall McAllister and Cal Benham as they prepared Tom Burdue's defence. They had neither the ability nor the need to prove that English Jim Stuart was not responsible for this crime. All they had to prove was that Tom Burdue was not English Jim. And, as McAllister told the jury in his opening address, this would be the basis of Burdue's defence – he was not the man the prosecution claimed him to be, and was therefore innocent of the charges.

District Attorney Goodwin set out to prove just the opposite. After police testimony described the Moore crime itself, Goodwin introduced a dozen witnesses to support his claim that the man in the box was the guilty party. Several said they had known Stuart before he went to Foster's Bar. Most tellingly, John Sullivan and three others testified to having worked with him at Foster's Bar, and to knowing him intimately.

'I have lived for months with Jim Stuart in the same mining camp,' said one witness.

'I have eaten with Jim Stuart at the same table,' said John Sullivan.

'Often?' asked the district attorney.

'Often,' Sullivan agreed. 'I have played cards with him, and slept in the same tent.'

Judge Mott instructed, on more than one occasion: 'The prisoner will stand, so the witness can see him better than when he is sitting.' After Tom had come to his feet and a witness had looked him up and down, the judge would command, 'Turn around.'

Each time, Tom looked at the witness with hollow eyes, turned around, then sank glumly back onto his chair. And each time, the witness announced that they had no doubts whatsoever that Tom was in fact English Jim Stuart.

'Jim Stuart is the same height as the prisoner,' said a typical witness. 'He has curly hair, like Jim. And Jim is slightly bald on the top of his head, like the prisoner. And his actions are the same.'

'Is the prisoner's accent the same as James Stuart's accent?' asked District Attorney Goodwin, after the judge required Tom to speak in his normal voice.

'Yes, his accent is the same,' the witnesses all agreed.[157]

If the real Stuart had been raised in Brighton, Sussex, as he was to claim, his accent would have been markedly different from that of Tom Burdue, a native of Northumberland in the far north of England. But many Americans couldn't distinguish one regional British accent from another.

One prosecution witness now testified, 'Stuart has a stiff middle finger on his right hand, and has an Indian ink tattoo around one finger.'

On hearing this, Judge Mott ordered Tom to come out of the box and show his hands to the jury. When Tom complied, it was immediately obvious to the jury that he had a tattoo around one finger. And, although the middle finger of his right hand was not stiff, the middle finger of his left hand had lost part of its length – in an accident, years before.

Defence counsel Hall McAllister would remark, after the trial, that these physical similarities were seen to be startling to the jury. In his cross-examination, McAllister attempted to sow doubts in the minds of these prosecution witnesses about the certainty of their identification of Burdue as Stuart, but, to McAllister's chagrin, all steadfastly stuck by their testimony and were 'bold and entirely positive', expressing not a single doubt.[158]

The trial was not going well for Tom.

Monday, June 30, 1851. Marysville, California

When proceedings resumed, one prosecution witness in particular was to impress jury and gallery alike. He was the highly respected 'Colonel' James H. Prentiss. An artillery officer in the US Army during the Mexican–American War, Prentiss now owned Five Mile Ranch on the Marysville to Comptonville road, and was the US Government agent to the Juba River Indians. Prentiss testified to having had dealings with James Stuart the previous year. English Jim himself would later recall having a blazing row with Prentiss while digging for gold six kilometres downstream from Foster's Bar in the summer of 1850. So, Prentiss had good reason to remember the real Stuart.

Asked by the prosecutor whether the prisoner in the prisoners' box was James Stuart, Prentiss answered, unhesitatingly, 'Yes.'

Hall McAllister, in cross-examining Prentiss, said, 'Colonel, you have testified that the prisoner is James Stuart. But, could you possibly be mistaken?'

Prentiss shook his head. 'I could not possibly be mistaken.'[159]

Well into the afternoon, these witnesses came and went, identifying Tom as English Jim, and holding firm under cross-examination. The last witness called by DA Goodwin to brand Tom as English Jim was at first glance the least impressive. But hers would turn out to be the most damning testimony of all. Her name has not come down to us, but she was apparently a prostitute from Foster's Bar, for she testified to having slept with James Stuart.

Like all the witnesses before her, she positively identified Tom as English Jim. But she went further, telling the court, 'Jim has a big scar. It runs from below his right ear, along the jaw, and down his neck.'[160]

All eyes in court turned to Tom Burdue. But, with his beard covering his lower face and neck, it was impossible to see whether or not he possessed such a scar. Judge Mott consulted his watch and announced, 'Court will adjourn for the day. But when we come back tomorrow . . .' he looked toward the Sheriff of Marysville, 'I expect to see the prisoner shaved of his beard.'[161]

Tuesday, July 1, 1851. Marysville, California

When Tom was led back into court this morning, sure enough he was clean-faced. His jailers had shaved him as instructed. A gasp went up from the crowd – Tom Burdue clearly possessed a scar that ran from below his right ear, along the line of his jaw, then down his neck.

It was never later established whether or not the real English Jim had such a scar, but it would not be mentioned once the real English Jim returned to the spotlight, suggesting that he did not possess any such scar. It's likely the prostitute had seen Tom Burdue when he first arrived at Foster's Bar in the spring of 1850, when he was clean-shaven, and she had noted how much he and English Jim looked alike. Now, she was trying to help personable rogue Stuart. Whatever her motivation, the prostitute's testimony left Hall McAllister struggling to make up ground.

District Attorney Goodwin's final witness was named Thompson, and he was a fellow prisoner of Tom Burdue's in the Yuba County Jail at Marysville. Goodwin first established that, the previous December, Thompson had been living and mining at the small Slate's Range camp, eleven kilometres from Foster's Bar and higher up in the Sierra Nevada range, in Yuba County.

'Mr Thompson,' DA Goodwin then continued, 'did the prisoner, about the date of the alleged murder in December last, come into the camp at Slate's Range in the said county of Yuba, on horseback?'

'He did,' Thompson replied. 'He seemed to have plenty of money, and was betting with the boys on a string game, which he played very skilfully.'[162]

To complicate matters, this time there was no case of mistaken identity – it genuinely was Tom Burdue who had turned up at Slate's Range and wagered with miners on a game of chance. Had Joe and Mary Windred been present at this trial, Thompson's testimony would have answered their question about what Tom actually did to make a pretty handsome living – since landing from Australia, Tom Burdue had become a successful professional gambler around the mining camps of northern California.

'In the county jail, Mr Thompson,' DA Goodwin next asked, 'did you have a conversation with the prisoner?'

'I did.'

'And in that conversation did he admit that it was him you saw at Slate's Range at the time mentioned?'

'He did.'

Goodwin handed the witness over to the defence, content in the knowledge that he had placed the accused in the vicinity of the crime close to the time that it had been committed. And, if their meeting had been after the fatal robbery, that would explain why the accused was seen to have 'plenty of money'.

When Hall McAllister cross-examined Thompson, he asked, 'While speaking with the prisoner in the county jail, did he say to you that he was Jim Stuart?'

'No. He did not. He denied to me that he was Stuart.'[163]

Now came the defence's turn to present its witnesses. McAllister fired off his best proverbial ammunition from the outset, calling to the stand Judge Oliver Perry Stidger. In 1849, Stidger had come to California from Canton, Ohio, where he still had a son in university. Gravitating to the Foster's Bar camp, Stidger had opened one of three stores there – at this very moment, he was in the process of buying out his two commercial competitors. In June 1850, Stidger had been elected a justice of the peace, and soon after joined the Yuba County Court. He would go on to become a justice of the Court of Sessions and editor of the *Marysville Herald*.

Hall McAllister asked Tom to walk up and down in front of the witness, then to show him his hands just as Goodwin had him show his hands to the jury. Once Tom had returned to the box, McAllister asked the witness, 'Judge Stidger, having had the opportunity to study him, is the prisoner at the bar that same James Stuart you knew at Foster's Bar?'

'I can swear positively that the prisoner at the bar *is not* Jim Stuart,' Stidger replied without hesitation, causing a stir in the gallery.

'A number of witnesses seem to have confused this man with Jim Stuart. Is there a strong resemblance between the two?'

'There is a strong resemblance between Jim Stuart and this man. But Jim Stuart is at least two inches taller than the prisoner. And their eyes are a different colour.' This was entirely true. Tom's eyes were black, or very dark brown, while English Jim's were blue-grey. 'As for the expression of the eyes of the two men, they are quite different, also.'

'What of the way he moves, and holds himself?'

'Jim Stuart was much quicker in his motions than the prisoner. Jim Stuart's motions were very uncommon.'

'How so?'

'Stuart's motions are as quick as those of a wildcat.'

'How else do the two men differ?'

Stidger looked over at Tom, who had once more dejectedly leaned forward and let his head sag onto his chest. 'Stuart always held his head erect. Much more so than the prisoner. The real Jim Stuart is straighter in his personal formation. And he has a different, darker complexion.'

'Tell the court, how is it that you came to know Jim Stuart.'

'Stuart was often arraigned before me as a judge at Foster's Bar.'

'From this fact, your recollection of him is clear and distinct?'

'My recollection of him, from this and other facts, is clear and distinct.'

'So that you can say, without reservation, that the man in the prisoners' box is *not* Jim Stuart?'

'I can. I should also say that Jim Stuart has a stiff middle finger, but not such a one as the prisoner has.'

McAllister next called Benjamin Franklin Washington, Sacramento City's recorder. A Virginian, Washington was related to America's first president, George Washington. Once again, McAllister had Tom Burdue parade before the witness stand – more for drama than process.

'Mr Washington,' McAllister then asked, 'is it true that you know Jim Stuart?'

'It is,' Washington replied.

'From the fact that . . . ?'

'From the fact of his being a notorious character in Sacramento City, and from the fact that he has often been brought before me on different charges.'

'Is the prisoner at the bar Jim Stuart?'

'No, he is not.'

'Is there some resemblance between the two men?'

'There is some resemblance, but they are, to my eye, quite different men. Jim Stuart is an inch and a half, or two inches, taller than the prisoner.'[164]

Again the gallery was thrown into alarm.

Under cross-examination by District Attorney Goodwin, neither Stidger nor Washington exhibited the least doubt that Tom Burdue was *not* Jim Stuart. A succession of defence witnesses through the day likewise testified that Tom was not English Jim. But none of these other witnesses possessed the credentials, the credibility or the certainty of Judge Stidger or Recorder Washington. In fact, every one of them seemed terrified of recriminations at the hands of vigilantes – Marysville now had its own Committee of Vigilance – and were not at all convincing, doing more harm than good to Tom's defence.

When later asked about these witnesses by the press, Hall McAllister would concede, 'They seemed uneasy, in some trepidation, and acted in a manner most provoking to the defence.'[165]

Tuesday, July 1, 1851. San Francisco, California

If it hadn't been for English Jim Stuart, Joe Windred and Tom Burdue wouldn't have been at the centre of California's most infamous case of mistaken identity. And Stuart was about to again impact on their lives. During this Tuesday evening, the San Francisco Committee of Vigilance, at its new, rented headquarters on Battery Street, between Pine and Clay, received a report of a break and enter at a house on the sandy southern outskirts of the city. The five on-duty vigilante 'police' were despatched to investigate.

Finding no one at the house in question, the vigilantes fanned out along Mission Road carrying lanterns and with revolvers drawn. Here, in the sand hills, roughly where Powell and California streets would later intersect, vigilante Jim Adair stumbled on a figure lying on the sand, camouflaged by scrub oak branches. The man who sprang to his feet at Adair's challenge and dusted himself down had a neat moustache and beard, was reasonably tall, solidly built, and well-dressed in coat, vest and necktie, with a low, broad-brimmed black hat on his head. The man's clothes, Adair noted, were evenly creased, as if only recently taken, or stolen, from a suitcase or trunk.

'What's your name, and what are you doing here?' Adair demanded, covering the stranger with his revolver.

'William Stevens is my name,' said the man in a cultivated English accent. He said that he'd been taking a rest. 'I was walking back to San Francisco from the Mission,' he went on, adding that he had walked out to the Mission that morning.

'You've chosen a damned pretty way to come from the Mission,' said Adair.

Stevens replied that he had only recently arrived in California and was still finding his bearings.

Adair called for his four companions, then told Stevens that they would be taking him to the headquarters of the San Francisco Committee of Vigilance for questioning.

'Ah,' Stevens responded with a smile. 'I shall go there with pleasure. I'm interested to see that far-famed institution.'[166]

Now that Adair was joined by colleagues, who covered the Englishman with their revolvers, he relieved him of a revolver jammed in his belt and a sheathed, fourteen-inch Bowie knife. The first-floor Committee of Vigilance headquarters that Stevens was taken to had an official air to it. Its large, carpeted meeting room was equipped with chairs and a meeting table. Behind a lectern at one end hung a banner presented to the Committee by the ladies of Trinity Church. Handcuffs, leg-chains and the like decorated the walls. A door led to a corridor, off which opened several rooms fitted with barred windows and serving as cells to hold criminal suspects. In the meeting room, William Stevens was made to sit and answer questions from his captors.

Stevens was relaxed and friendly, even joking with the vigilantes. He answered their questions with alacrity, and made quite an impression on his questioners with 'his pleasing personality and apparent frankness'.[167] It was agreed by the questioners that Mr Stevens was innocent of involvement with the evening's break-in, but the Committee's rules specified that any man brought in for questioning could only be released on the authority of its 'chief of police', who would not be coming in until next morning. Stevens did not seem to mind when told he would have to spend the night in a Committee cell before being released next day.

As William Stevens was handed a blanket and locked in a cell off the meeting room for the night, not one of his captors knew to note the significance of the fact that the middle finger of his left hand was stiff and useless. Little did the vigilantes know who they were in fact locking up.

Wednesday, July 2, 1851. San Francisco, California

At dawn, a new roster of five volunteer 'citizen police' came on duty at Committee of Vigilance headquarters. One of these fresh men was John Sullivan. The boatman responsible for the trial and lynching of John Jenkins, Sullivan was now Committee of Vigilance member number 269. Only the previous day, he'd returned from testifying at the Marysville trial of Tom Burdue, where he had sworn that Burdue was in fact English Jim Stuart.

On his arrival, Sullivan asked executive committee member George E. Schenck whether there had been any action overnight. Schenck replied that an Englishman now occupied one of their cells after being found out in the sand hills, but he was due to be shortly released. Sullivan, curious, went to the cell, and, unlocking the door, looked in at the lone occupant. That occupant, sitting glumly in the far corner of the room, looked up.

Sullivan, to his astonishment, recognised the prisoner. 'Hello, Jim,' he exclaimed. 'How did you come here?'

The prisoner frowned, and, saying that his name was William Stevens, claimed to have never seen Sullivan before in his life.

'You needn't pretend not to know me,' Sullivan retorted. 'I know who you are. I worked for you six months at Foster's Bar.' From this response, it's unclear whether Sullivan had knowingly misidentified Tom Burdue as Jim Stuart, or genuinely thought that Stuart had been the man in court at Marysville and must have recently escaped to San Francisco.

Still the prisoner feigned ignorance, but Sullivan was convinced he knew him. Going back out to George Schenck, Sullivan said, 'Mr Schenk, do you know who you've got here?' When Schenck asked him what he meant, Sullivan said, 'Why, you've got English Jim.'

'English Jim?' responded the startled Schenck.

'Jim Stuart. The man who murdered the sheriff.'[168]

Sullivan's certainty convinced George Schenck to summon Jake Van Bokkelen, a fulltime Committee employee paid $350 a month as its 'chief of police'. After Van Bokkelen arrived at headquarters, he sent vigilante 'police' to scour the city for men who had known English Jim and bring them in to view William Stevens. Former policemen Andy McCarthy and Rob McIntyre were among them. Unbeknownst to the vigilantes, both had been in league with English

Jim in criminal pursuits, and both swore that they didn't know the Committee's prisoner. Stevens in turn showed no sign of recognising them. But every other man to whom William Stevens was shown declared that he was the real Jim Stuart. All the while, the prisoner stuck to his story that he was Stevens.

Finally, Charles Jansen, the victim of the robbery for which Joe Windred and Tom Burdue had been convicted, was sent for. Jansen had by this time defied his doctor's prognosis by recovering fully from the injury sustained from the business end of Jim Stuart's slung-shot.

'Is this man James Stuart, the man who attacked and robbed you?' Jansen was asked by Van Bokkelen.

After careful consideration, Jansen replied that he believed that this was indeed the man. When reminded that he had previously identified Thomas Burdue as that man, and that Burdue was being tried in Marysville as a consequence, Jansen replied, 'I am now convinced of my mistake in identification. Although, the resemblance is close.'[169]

Still the prisoner steadfastly refused to admit that he was English Jim. Confidently maintaining that he was new arrival William Stevens, he asked for pen and paper then began to fluently write his life story; the life story of William Stevens. Van Bokkelen now sent for lawyer Frank M. Pixley. Just twenty-six years of age, New Yorker Pixley had been elected San Francisco's city attorney in the April elections. But Van Bokkelen knew that, in private practice in Sacramento the previous year, Pixley had acted for the real English Jim Stuart. If anyone knew Stuart, Pixley should.

After Pixley climbed the stairs to the Committee rooms, members thronged around him, excited by the thought that they had nabbed the real English Jim. Van Bokkelen asked, 'Pixley, will you say, on your word of honour, if this is the man whom you have defended in the lower courts?'

'I will, gentlemen,' Pixley affirmed.

Armed with that guarantee, Van Bokkelen unlocked the cell door, then he and several Committee members accompanied Pixley into the cell while the others crowded around the door. William Stevens looked at Pixley, and, with a broad smile, came to his feet. But he didn't speak, and neither did Pixley.

'Is that Stuart, or not?' said Van Bokkelen to Pixley.

'You have no authority to ask me any questions,' Pixley abruptly came back. 'You are an illegal body.' He then demanded, in his capacity as city attorney, that the prisoner be handed over to the legitimate authorities.

This prompted a chorus from the men gathered out in the corridor: 'Hang him! Hang him! Hang him!'[170]

With the vigilantes refusing to give up their prisoner, Pixley rapidly took his leave, and immediately prepared a petition to the California Supreme Court seeking a writ of habeas corpus to force the Committee to give up William Stevens. Pixley was to come under severe criticism for having helped James Stuart in Sacramento and for now attempting to circumvent the vigilantes by observing the law of the land. Many American histories dealing with this period would even neglect to point out that Pixley was now San Francisco's city attorney, denigrating his official position by merely describing him as an attorney. Despite this criticism, Pixley would go on to lead an illustrious career, serving as Attorney General of California, during the US Civil War fighting alongside General Ulysses S. Grant, and later becoming an influential California newspaper owner.

By his actions, Pixley had left the vigilantes convinced that he had recognised the prisoner and that they did indeed hold the real English Jim Stuart. But, for the moment, they were not entirely sure what they should do with Stuart. Now, the Committee was reminded that Thomas Burdue was currently on trial for his life at Marysville. It was agreed that Captain Hartford Joy should go to Marysville as Committee envoy, to inform the Marysville Committee of Vigilance that the real English Jim Stuart was in custody in San Francisco and that Thomas Burdue was an innocent man. But time was fast running out for Tom Burdue.

Wednesday, July 2, 1851. Marysville, California

The Marysville court, ignorant of events in San Francisco, resumed sitting in the Moore murder trial. By mid-morning, both chief defence counsel McAllister and District Attorney Goodwin had delivered their final addresses to the jury. McAllister again stressed that his sole goal was to prove that the accused was not James Stuart, and that the wrong man was on trial. He stressed the evidence provided by his unimpeachable leading witnesses, Judge Oliver Stidger and Recorder B. F. Washington, who had testified that, without the shadow of a doubt, Thomas Burdue was not James Stuart. As a consequence, said McAllister, the jury could make just one finding, that Thomas Burdue was not guilty of murder.

District Attorney Goodwin reminded jurors of all the witnesses who had identified Burdue as Stuart, without doubt or hesitation, while all but two of the witnesses for the defence had been far from convincing in offering a counter view, and the jury could well draw the conclusion that they were lying. As for the two learned gentlemen who had stated on oath that Burdue was not Stuart, the district attorney did not believe for a moment that they were lying. Rather, Judge Stidger and Recorder Washington were, said Goodwin, merely mistaken.

Judge Mott gave the jury their instructions and sent them out to decide whether Tom Burdue was guilty of robbery and murder. The accused was taken away to a cell to await the jury's verdict.

Day gave way to night, and still the jury remained out.

Thursday, July 3, 1851. San Francisco, California

Armed vigilante guards hauled John Gough into Committee of Vigilance headquarters for interrogation. His principal 'crime' was having been a friend of prison escapee Joe Windred and his wife. Furthermore, the Committee had learned that Gough had served time as a convict in Australia. Said his accuser Charles Marsh, a former convict overseer at Government House in Sydney who now worked in a San Francisco store, 'He worked his seven years out, then went to Windsor. From there he came here. He is a bad character. He runs the Panama Restaurant.'[171]

When the executive committee questioned Gough, Brannan began by demanding, 'Tell this Committee how you came to California, and name those who came with you and state where they now are.'

Gough told of transiting the Pacific to San Francisco in the *Victoria* with his wife and a party from Windsor. Joseph Wright was dead, he said, and he had lost contact with James Smith, who was at the diggings. 'Burdue, the man now being tried at Marysville for murder, also came in the ship.'

'Was Burdue also a convict and a bad character?'

'No. And I never heard any harm of him at home. He was quiet on board the ship. He had a wife at Sydney.'

'How often have you seen Burdue here since?'

'I have seen him several times since he has been here. He brought four or five pounds of gold dust, which he left at my house.'

'Who else accompanied you here on the ship *Victoria* from Australia?'

It must have now dawned on Gough that the Committee was compiling a list of 'undesirables', Sydney Ducks who they wanted to eject from California. 'I don't recollect the names of any others,' he guardedly responded.

'You have said that you don't recognise the prisoner William Stevens.'

'Yes. I never saw Stevens before. He is not Burdue. There is some slight likeness. Burdue is a shorter man.'

'When was it that he left the gold dust with you?'

'It is about ten months since Burdue deposited the gold dust with me.'

After Gough denied that he had known either lynch victim John Jenkins or an associate of English Jim's named Byrnes, and stated that his only source of income was the Panama House, the Committee asked about Tom Burdue's wife, Elen.

'Burdue sent back for his wife,' Gough replied, before producing the page from his letter book in which Burdue had written his contact details at Auburn, for Elen's information on her arrival.

'Do you know Joseph Windred?' he was then asked.

'Yes. I lived near Joe at Windsor.'

'Have you been on intimate terms with Burdue and Windred in this country?'

'Yes.'

'Do you know where Windred is now?'

'He has gone home. I received a letter from Windred's wife just before they left.'

'What did she write in that letter?'

'She writes to say that we must excuse her for not calling on us. I will produce the letter. She sends an order to draw $600 or $700 on the lawyer Mr McAllister.'[172]

Gough was permitted to leave the Committee's headquarters, and the next day he would hand in Mary Windred's letters of May 5 and May 6, as well as her invoice to Tom Burdue and its note to Hall McAllister. But Gough had done nothing to satisfy the Committee of Vigilance that he was a fit and proper immigrant to California. Like so many 'Australians' in the state at this moment, his fate was now in the balance.

Thursday, July 3, 1851. Marysville, California

Late in the day, Tom Burdue's jailers came for him. The jury had reached a verdict. As the gallery filled and the jury filed back into court, Tom was returned to the prisoners' box. Now, too, the judge appeared. Finally, with the courtroom silent and tense, Tom was required by Judge Mott to stand, and the jury's verdict relating to the major charge was announced. 'On the charge of murder, we find the prisoner . . . guilty.'

All that was left to Tom now was to write to Elen and his children to tell them of the outcome of his trial, and to say goodbye to them. For, as Judge Mott adjourned the sitting until next day to permit him to determine what sentence he would hand down, Tom knew full well what his fate must be.

Friday, July 4, 1851. Marysville, California

It was Independence Day, the first to be celebrated by Americans with California a state of the Union. In the streets of San Francisco, there would be a grand parade. In Marysville, Tom was back in court. The jury box was empty, but the gallery had again filled. Judge Mott announced, in as grave a voice as he could muster, 'Thomas Burdue, alias James Stuart, it is the direction of this court that, seven days from this date, you be hanged by the neck 'till you are dead. So help you God.'

It was a sentence to generate cheers from the gallery.

22

THE HANGING OF 'ENGLISH JIM'

Tuesday, July 8, 1851. San Francisco, California

LATE IN THE DAY, Hartford Joy, the San Francisco Committee of Vigilance's envoy to their vigilante colleagues in Marysville, stepped off a riverboat and hurried to Committee of Vigilance headquarters. Despite Joy's protestations that the authorities had the wrong man, his Marysville colleagues had not believed him, and were counting the days until they saw Tom Burdue swing as English Jim.

Several members of the San Francisco Committee of Vigilance felt that something more substantial should be done to try to save Burdue. With Marysville's vigilantes unwilling to use their guns to force Burdue's release from jail, the only legal way of preventing his execution now was for the Governor of California to pardon him. Governor John McDougall had been in San Francisco since the state legislature ended its latest sitting at California's temporary state capital, Vallejo, in early May. A plot was now hatched to convince William Stevens to confess to being James Stuart, with the confession being presented to the governor for immediate action.

In the mid-evening, led by John F. Spence, the man who'd sat as principal judge in the February lynch trial of Burdue and Windred, several members of the executive committee began to question William Stevens. The prisoner, wearing handcuffs and leg-irons now, continued to steadfastly adhere to the story that he was William Stevens.

A little after 10.00 p.m., a deal was proposed to the prisoner. If he were to admit to being James Stuart and make a full confession to all his crimes, he would not be the subject of summary justice by the Committee, but would be handed over to the legitimate legal authorities to be tried in a proper court of law. To the astonishment of all present, William Stevens suddenly changed his tune. Yes, he said, he was James Stuart. As he was.

As he now informed his questioners, English Jim had returned to San Francisco on June 29, and had been given a bed by James Kitchen. While in Monterey, Stuart had boldly entered the witness-box in the custom-house robbery trial, and, as James Carlisle, had given false evidence which had helped secure the acquittal of his cronies. In the subsequent carve-up of the $13,000 haul from the robbery, Stuart had walked away with a share, as had the defence attorneys, the prosecutors and a juror who had held out for a guilty verdict. But Stuart was soon penniless and forced to dig for gold – this man accused by the Committee of Vigilance of being a master criminal had ineptly allowed his rented horse to be stolen and was bailed up by Mexican bandits who took his revolver and silver watch. On his return to San Francisco, Stuart had been warned by Mary Ann Hogan to leave town again, fast, and make himself scarce, as Sam Whitaker had done. Whitaker, said Hogan, was being hunted like a dog by both vigilantes and legitimate lawmen.

Going into hiding was easier said than done. It would require money, and Stuart was near broke. On July 1 he had gone out to Mission Dolores to see his cousin, who proposed robbing a Spaniard living near the Mission. But after sizing up the house of the prospective victim, Stuart had decided against the job. He had been walking back to San Francisco when he'd spotted vigilantes on patrol, and had gone to ground, only to be found by Jim Adair.

Stuart agreed to dictate a full confession of all his crimes. At 10.30 p.m., he began. Candidly, and with obvious delight at times, English Jim regaled his audience with his story, starting with his birth in England, his first conviction and transportation to New South Wales, before moving to his exploits in California. William T. Coleman was one of the executive committee members listening, fascinated yet appalled, to the detailed confession. He would later write, of Stuart at this time, 'It was curious to see his eyes brighten and twinkle, and a smile play around his facile countenance.'[173]

As Stuart spoke, he named close to thirty criminal associates, including Sam Whitaker and policemen McCarthy and McIntyre, and detailed all their roles in his many enterprises. The possibility of saving his neck had him giving up all pretensions of honour among thieves. He even implicated Mary Ann Hogan, although exonerated her estranged husband Michael from any crime. At one point, Stuart's confidence grew and he aired a boast that had some of his listeners fearing that he was careless in naming his cronies because he was confident that Sydney Duck friends would break him out of jail. 'I have heard hundreds remark here that the day would soon come when this country would be taken by the Sydney people.'[174]

It was the early hours of the morning by the time Stuart finished his confession. Committee members now sent for Governor McDougall. The governor, who was aged just twenty-nine, was nicknamed 'I John', because of a propensity for issuing proclamations seemingly at the drop of a hat, proclamations which began, 'I, John McDougall'. Short, redheaded and handsome, a son of Irish immigrants, McDougall had a feisty temperament and a liking for hard liquor. He had initially been highly popular with his constituents, but his support had recently begun to haemorrhage since he'd welcomed Chinese immigrants and aired disapproval of the illegal activities of the Committee of Vigilance.

For the benefit of the governor, the vigilantes had Stuart again identify himself and repeat the key elements of his confession. John F. Spence then conducted a 'cross-examination', as he styled it, while the governor listened.

'Did you know John Jenkins?' Spence asked Stuart.

'Yes, I knew him,' Stuart replied.

'Do you know Joseph Windred?'

'Yes, I know him. I think he is gone out of the country now.'[175] It is possible that Stuart had met Joe Windred, but it is more likely he merely knew of him, through Sam Whitaker, who would have told him how he'd arranged for Joe and Mary's escape from California.

And so the questioning went, with Stuart acknowledging a list of men brought before the courts or wanted by the police. When Spence asked whether the men arrested for striking and robbing Charles Jansen – Burdue and Windred – had any connection with that crime, Stuart declared that both were innocent, adding, 'We should certainly have fired the town in three or four places, should the men arrested for striking Jansen been hung.'

Suspecting that Stuart was implicated in Joe Windred's escape from the *Waban* when it was anchored off Angel Island, even though Stuart had been at sea aboard the schooner *H. L. Allen* at the time of Joe's escape, en route from Trinidad Bay, Spence asked if Stuart had ever visited the island.

'Yes, I have been to Angel Island,' Stuart replied. 'I generally stop at Daniel Wilder's. I think that there are no robbers there.'[176] But he would not admit to any knowledge of how Joe had made his escape, or name men who had helped him in that escape.

Despite confessing to numerous crimes, Stuart continued to deny that he'd had anything to do with the robbery and murder of Charles E. Moore in Yuba County. Many Committee of Vigilance members would say that this was because the Moore case was a capital crime, involving the death penalty, while, under California law, all the crimes that Stuart had confessed to did not involve the death penalty. Stuart, it was believed, was intent on saving himself from an appointment with the hangman.

The sun was beginning to rise when the questioning of English Jim came to an end. Governor McDougall came to his feet and announced that he would at once pen a pardon for Thomas Burdue and send it with dispatch to Marysville. And, he said, he expected the Committee of Vigilance to hand the real Jim Stuart over to San Francisco's legitimate legal authorities for the proper process of law to be followed.

Not long after the governor departed, copies of the morning's newspapers were brought in, and they were found to contain the news that City Attorney Pixley had succeeded in obtaining a writ of habeas corpus from the California Supreme Court, which he was expected to serve on the Committee of Vigilance that morning, with the aim of taking James Stuart into lawful custody. Even Ed Gilbert, editor of the *Alta California*, who had been supportive of the Committee of Vigilance up until now, voiced the opinion in this morning's edition of the *Alta* that Stuart should be handed over to the legally constituted authorities, with the law thereafter permitted to take its course.

This caused consternation among Committee ranks. For, many vigilantes had no intention of abiding by the deal struck with English Jim by handing him over to the legitimate authorities. Fearing that he would escape the noose, they decided to hide Stuart away from the city attorney. To disguise him a little, Committee secretary Isaac Bluxome teamed with merchant George Oakes to dress English Jim in a long cloak and a slouch hat.

Showing their prisoner that he and Oakes had pistols in their belts, Bluxome said, 'If you attempt to run, we will shoot you.'[177]

Stuart made no attempt to escape as the two vigilantes hustled him downstairs and out into the street. Via back ways, Stuart was taken to the First Street store which Oakes then operated in partnership with George Endicott, and was locked in its cellar.

At 11.00 a.m., City Attorney Pixley walked in the door of the Committee of Vigilance rooms, accompanied by the city's new mayor, Charles Brenham, master of the *McKim*, and San Francisco's recently elected sheriff, Jack Coffee Hays. The thirty-four-year-old sheriff was the eldest of the three men. Short, suited, with a moustache and goatee, Hays was a popular former captain with the Texas Rangers. After Pixley served the expected writ of habeas corpus on the vigilantes, Hays searched high and low throughout Committee premises. But, of course, he found no sign of James Stuart. Not only did Jake Van Bokkelen and other Committee members present deny any knowledge of Stuart's whereabouts, the Committee would tender an affidavit to the Supreme Court declaring that it didn't have James Stuart. Technically, this was true. But several leading Committee members knew where he was being held.

Unrewarded, sheriff, city attorney and mayor departed. Sheriff Hays and his deputies subsequently scoured the city looking for English Jim, issuing a warning that anyone harbouring him was liable to arrest and prosecution. Late in the day, George Endicott came puffing into Committee headquarters in search of Oakes and Bluxome. Endicott, who was also county treasurer, had only just learned that the man being sought so urgently by the authorities was being kept in *his* cellar.

'This won't do,' Endicott blustered. 'I'm a city official, and have taken the oath to support the government.' He demanded that Stuart be removed from his premises.[178]

Bluxome now asked Committee members present if any of them would hide Stuart away, and Eube Maloney put up his hand. So, Bluxome, Oakes and Maloney hurried to the Endicott and Oakes store, took Stuart from the cellar, and walked him to Maloney's house in the higher parts of the city. A little before midnight, looking worried, Maloney reappeared at Committee headquarters. The fear that Sheriff Hays would find out that he was holding Stuart and arrest *him* now gripped Maloney.

'I can't keep him any longer,' said Maloney to Bluxome.[179]

Bluxome was forced to remove Stuart from Maloney's house. 'He was shifted around to keep him from the sheriff,' Bluxome would later say.[180] This became like a manic game of chess, with English Jim the constantly castled king.

Thursday, July 10, 1851. San Francisco, California

True to his word, the previous day Governor McDougall had written a pardon for Thomas Burdue and sent it urgently to Marysville. Now, just a day before Tom was due to be hanged as English Jim Stuart, the pardoned man was on his way to San Francisco by river steamer after being freed from Yuma County Jail. But Burdue was coming in handcuffs and escorted by police. For, while the governor had quashed Tom's Marysville murder conviction with his pardon, Tom's San Francisco conviction for the Jansen robbery still stood. No one had thought to do anything about that, and, as far as the authorities were concerned, Tom still had to serve out his fourteen-year sentence in the state penitentiary for that crime. And his mate Joe Windred remained a wanted man.

This same day, twenty-one-year-old Alfred Dolen arrived in San Francisco from Auburn, where he had mined in the same ravine and lived in the same camp as Joe and Mary Windred and Tom Burdue. From Plymouth, Massachusetts, Dolen had a married sister living in San Francisco, and he was staying with her during this visit to the 'big smoke' – as San Francisco had become in more ways than one. Despite the activities and boasts of the Committee of Vigilance, San

Francisco appeared no safer than the last time Dolen had visited, prior to the existence of the Committee. 'We took a turn about the town,' Dolen wrote in his diary. 'There does not seem to be quite so much gambling going on as formerly, but thieves, pickpockets and assassins abound.'[181]

Friday, July 11, 1851. San Francisco, California

As this was the day on which Tom Burdue had been due to be hanged at Marysville for a crime attributed to English Jim Stuart, the executive committee of the Committee of Vigilance had decided to put the real Stuart on trial, then hang him.

At midday, the Monument Engine Company's fire bell began to toll twice every two minutes, summoning Committee of Vigilance members to their headquarters. While the executive committee met in the Committee's rooms, the rank and file membership and numerous other interested parties gathered outside in Battery Street. Chaired by president Sam Brannan, the Committee's trial of English Jim Stuart now took place. Stuart himself, who was being concealed close by, was not permitted to be present for his own trial. No one was delegated to represent him. No defence was offered. The trial consisted of a reading of his July 8–9 statement, after which Brannan proposed that the statement be accepted as a confession of Stuart's guilt. A vote was taken of executive committee members, who voted unanimously in favour.

A little before 1.00 p.m., executive committee member 'Colonel' Jonathan D. Stevenson came out to the waiting crowd. The former commanding officer of the 7th New York Volunteers, in which Ed Gilbert and Edward Buffum had served as lieutenants, fifty-one-year-old Stevenson had become involved in real estate in California after initially mining for gold. His age, background and reputation were thought by the executive committee to add authority to the announcement that he had been delegated to make – that the Committee of Vigilance had tried James Stuart for his many crimes, had found him guilty, and had sentenced him to be executed, by hanging, at 3.00 p.m. that day. This brought a huge cheer from the crowd. Stevenson also urged all Committee of Vigilance members to attend, and to come armed with pistols at 2.30 in preparation for the event.

THE HANGING OF 'ENGLISH JIM'   199

At 1.00 p.m., Committee supporter the Reverend Flevel S. Mines was ushered into the latest hiding place of English Jim. It was Mines who informed the prisoner of his sentence. Stuart took the news calmly. He had been expecting it. The Presbyterian minister tried hard to convince the condemned man to seek God's forgiveness for his crimes, but English Jim was not interested.

'I have not thought of God for fifteen years,' said Jim, 'and I cannot expect that He would think of me in the few moments that are left to me now.' And if Hell existed, he said, and he was to burn forever more, then the life he had led would undoubtedly take him there.

'You might yet be saved,' said the clergyman. He meant saved by God, not by mortals.

Stuart shook his head. 'It's too late. Too great a work could not be done in so short a time. Besides, I hardly know any longer whether the religion of my youth is true.'[182]

Stuart sent Mines away. Twice more during the next hour Mines returned and again attempted to steer Stuart toward a reconciliation with his maker. And twice more Stuart sent him away, on the last occasion refusing Mines' offer to accompany him to the scaffold.

By 2.30 p.m., four hundred Committee of Vigilance members had formed up in ranks ten abreast in Battery Street, many of them armed with pistols. Thousands of spectators expectantly lined the sidewalks. English Jim now materialised, his arms bound at the wrist behind him. Standing inches taller than the guards either side of him, and wearing the same black hat, blue coat and buff trousers he had worn since his July 1 capture, Stuart was marched down to the Battery Street Wharf in the midst of the vigilante phalanx. He walked upright, with firm steps, showing no fear. Having asked one of his guards for a quid of tobacco, he was chewing on that. As the crowd flooded along behind, some spectators manned small boats to watch proceedings from the water.

Battery Street Wharf was the city's longest wharf, and one of its newest. Along its edges stood several rudimentary wooden derricks – two wooden uprights three metres high linked by a crossbeam, from which rope and tackle were strung to unload dockside craft. The derrick at the very end of the wharf had been chosen to act as the scaffold for Jim Stuart's execution. Moored close by was the retired brig *Euphemia*, a hulk serving as San Francisco County Jail. Its rails were lined with men watching proceedings. One of those men was Tom Burdue. Tom's keepers thought it a kind act to allow him to watch the execution of the man for whom he himself had very nearly swung.

Every window and rooftop of nearby waterfront buildings was precariously crowded with spectators, but *Alta California* reporter Edward Buffum had a box seat for the execution. With his contacts in the Committee of Vigilance, Buffum had found a place in a rowboat with the Committee's appointed surgeon, Dr Matthew P. Burns, whose role was to certify life extinct in the condemned man. The boat, containing Buffum, Burns, County Coroner Edward Gallagher and several oarsmen, was manoeuvred into place just metres from the scaffold.

An eerie silence descended when the execution party reached the end of the wharf. Row after row of committeemen occupied the wharf, ready to repel any attempt by the authorities to seize Stuart. But, in the face of hundreds of armed and determined vigilantes, not a single legitimate lawman would make an appearance. Edgar Wakeman was again the Committee's hangman. The noose was ready, and strung up over the derrick's crossbeam. A party of committeemen took hold of the rope's other end. Once English Jim was standing beneath the derrick, Wakeman, himself wearing a peaked cap typical of his seafaring profession, removed the prisoner's flat black hat and looped the noose around his neck and fastened it, then replaced the hat.

Wakeman's and Stuart's eyes met. 'Be firm,' the executioner said, ''t'will soon be over.'[183]

Stuart seemed resigned, and prepared. 'I die reconciled,' he said in a strong voice. 'My sentence is just.'[184]

Wakeman stepped back, reached for his fob watch, and, folding his arms, consulted the timepiece. Members of the crowd began shaking their fists and calling for the hanging to proceed. But Wakeman, determined to conduct an orderly lynching, was waiting for the execution's appointed time. Stuart, stony-faced, was looking straight ahead. A sudden gust of wind sprang up, blowing off his hat. No one moved to retrieve it; the hat lay where it had fallen. As the minute hand on Wakeman's watch reached 12, signifying 3.00 p.m., the hangman looked over to the executive committee, and received a nod.

'Haul away,' Wakeman commanded, and the men on the other end of the rope heaved.

Jim Stuart was dragged into the air. With his feet just a metre off the ground, he was left dangling there, choking and convulsing. For minute after minute. Many spectators, seeing the victim meet his death resolutely and bravely, removed their hats in respect. In the view of a later Committee of Vigilance member Lell Hawley Woolley, Stuart's execution was botched. 'This was a sorry spectacle,' he would remark, 'a human being dying like a dog.' Still, Woolley reckoned Stuart deserved his fate.[185]

English Jim took a long time to die. Some onlookers, too embarrassed to continue watching, melted away. By 3.30, Stuart had stopped moving, and he was lowered into the boat containing physician Burns, coroner Gallagher and reporter Buffum. This boat took the body to an engine house on a nearby wharf, where Gallagher proposed to carry out an autopsy, with an eye to a fee, in the opinion of Buffum. Burns agreed, and two more surgeons were sent for – a total of four doctors were registered members of the Committee of Vigilance. In the meantime, Burns and Gallagher stripped Stuart and lay him out, naked, on a table. When the two additional physicians arrived, the autopsy began.

'The neck is not broken,' Dr Burns pronounced as the post-mortem examination proceeded. Clearly, Stuart had asphyxiated as a result of slow strangulation.

When a vein was lanced, Stuart's blood flowed freely.

'With a good galvanic battery,' one of the doctors commented, with an amused smile, 'we could restore the villain to life.'

In this mood of levity, reporter Buffum said, 'Being fond of dramatic situations, I propose that we should send for Thomas Burdue.'

The others thought this a capital idea, and thirty minutes later a handcuffed Tom Burdue was being brought into the engine shed by his jailers, who placed him beside the table where English Jim lay.

'There is your rival, Burdue,' said Buffum, as the others gathered around to observe his reaction. 'What do you think?'

Gazing down at Stuart's frozen face, Tom did not reply, could not reply. Now, he could see why he had been mistaken by so many people for this man. Buffum was to later say of the scene at this moment: 'It was like a man looking at his own corpse. I never before or since saw such a resemblance. Stuart was, perhaps, a trifle the stouter. But, having seen either one, I think I should have unhesitatingly, at any time thereafter, been willing to swear to the other as that one. It scarcely seems possible that the men could have so perfectly resembled each other.'[186]

Still, the sufferings of Tom Burdue were not yet over. Led away from the site of the autopsy, shaken by the experience of seeing his mirror image dead on the surgeon's table after suffering the fate that had very nearly been his own, he was placed in a boat and sent out to the *Waban*. There, he would begin his fourteen-year sentence for the armed robbery committed by the man who now lay lifeless in the engine shed.

Consider the statue of Justice, with her scales. She is often blindfolded. And in the case of Tom Burdue at this moment, justice was blind to the fact that he and Joe Windred had been wrongly convicted of the Jansen robbery. Joe had possessed the pluck to escape. And the luck – to have been broken out of prison by Sam Whitaker, a man with the means and the contacts to organise his escape. But, now, even as, from the deck of the *Herculean*, Joe and Mary Windred caught sight of the coast of New South Wales, Whitaker's own store of luck was running out.

23

LIFE AND DEATH

Sunday, July 13, 1851. Sydney, New South Wales

TWELVE SHIPS ENTERED SYDNEY Harbour this midwinter Sunday. Most were from ports in the Australian colonies. Several were from England. One was from San Francisco, California – the schooner *Herculean* – and aboard were Joe and Mary Windred. The couple had succeeded in escaping across the Pacific and back home to Australia.

A New South Wales government health inspector came aboard once the vessel was in the harbour, inspecting vessel and passengers to ensure no disease was aboard. When he completed the necessary forms that enabled the *Herculean* to land her passengers and cargo, the inspector would write the names of the vessel's four passengers: Mr Woods, James Mackay, and Mr and Mrs Johnson. Joe Windred was anxious not to be caught on the verge of safely landing back home. Was it possible the Americans had sent word to Sydney by fast ship that Joseph Windred was a prison escapee who was expected to flee back there? Had they asked the New South Wales authorities to arrest and return him? Joe would have reasoned that a ship leaving San Francisco after the *Herculean* might have found better winds and reached Sydney first. In fact, the schooners *Creole* and *Rattler* had done that very thing. Sailing from San Francisco on May 16, nine days behind the *Herculean*, they had reached Sydney days ahead of it, on July 7 and 8 respectively. So, to be on the safe side, Joe and Mary would remain Mr and Mrs Johnson for the time being, and keep a very low profile.

The inspector gave the *Herculean* a clean bill of health. As soon as Captain Hickens went ashore to arrange for a berth for his vessel and an agent for his cargo, Joe went in the ship's boat with him, to make his own arrangements. He and Mary had arrived back in Sydney with not a penny to their name. The only way they would reach Windsor would be if his family sent him money.

Joe walked into the Sydney pub that served as terminus for Ridge's Windsor coaches, planning to send a letter to his mother, Sophia, asking her to arrange coach tickets home for Mary and himself. Known at this pub from his boxing days, Joe learned, to his astonishment, that his family had seemingly scattered from Windsor en masse, like chaff before the wind. It was as if Joe's departure the previous year had unsettled them all. Joe's middle brother, Jack, his former partner in the fight training game, had taken his butchering skills to Bathurst, west of the Blue Mountains, joining Dargin relatives there. In Bathurst, opposite the Scots Kirk church, Jack had opened his own butchery. Meanwhile, in September 1850, Joe's brother William had taken over the licence of a Sydney pub, the Shamrock Inn, on Pitt Street. And the boys' mother, Sophia, had left Joe senior in his Windsor cottage and moved to Sydney to help William run his pub.

William's move to Sydney had happened almost by accident. Within days of Joe's April 1850 departure for California, owner George Freeman was offering William Windred's Australian Inn at Windsor for lease, after William sought to license other, cheaper premises in Windsor. But the licensing magistrates had considered the new place unsuitable, and on April 27, Joe's birthday, they had turned down William's application. Overnight, William had neither home nor business. Come the spring, he'd moved to Sydney, joining the city's legion of publicans.

It was to William's Shamrock Inn that Joe redirected his steps this Sunday, to rap on the closed door and be reunited with his surprised brother, his mother and an astonished little Isabel Walwyn. Following this family get-together, Joe hurried back to the *Herculean* to collect Mary, and he brought her ashore for a tearful reunion with her excited daughter. From this day forward, Mary would make sure, she and Isabel would never again be parted. From this day forward, too, Joe, Mary and Isabel would live together as a loving family.

For the moment, no one in New South Wales knew a thing about Joe's Californian trials. The fear that the Americans might convince the New South Wales Government to return him to California for trial and imprisonment would hover over him like a sword of Damocles. It suited Joe that he now had family in Sydney. Here in the big city, anonymity could be maintained. And here, Joe, his wife and stepdaughter now set up home.

Thursday, July 24, 1851. Windsor, New South Wales

Leaving Mary and Isabel with William and his wife and mother in Sydney, Joe had travelled out to Windsor to visit his father and those siblings who also still lived there, and to tell them his terrifying tale of trial, imprisonment and escape in San Francisco. It may be that Joe ended up in one of the local pubs telling his tale, perhaps the Windsor Common pub of his uncle James Cullen. And perhaps, well oiled and with an eager audience, Joe had said that the great San Francisco fire of May 3–4 had been started to cover his and Mary's escape.

A version of this story soon reached Windsor's chief constable, William Hobbs. Appointed the previous year, Hobbs was an officious man who, in April, had been praised in the press for the efficient way he ran his little police force. Hobbs had learned of San Francisco's great May fire after the *Sydney Morning Herald* first reported it on July 12, the details coming from San Francisco newspapers landed by the *Creole* following its recent arrival in Sydney. On July 17, it was further reported that the businesspeople of San Francisco were blaming Sydney men for the fire, and had resolved in a public meeting to demand that the US consul in Sydney be instructed to require every person leaving Sydney for California to provide him with proof they had not been a convict in Australia, with any subsequent Australian arrival in California not producing a consular certificate to that effect to be refused entry into the US, and deported.

Now, on July 24, Chief Constable Hobbs sat down to write to his superior in Sydney, newly appointed Inspector General of Police John McLerie. Hobbs informed McLerie that a local named Windred had recently returned from San Francisco boasting that he'd escaped from prison there, and had started the May 4 fire. It seems that, by the time it reached Hobbs' ears, Joe's retelling of Sam Whitaker's claim that the fire had been started to cover Joe's escape had been misconstrued into a boast by Joe that he himself was responsible for the fire.

Hobbs told McLerie that he knew Windred, who, according to him, had a bad name in the Windsor district for robbing his aunt when younger. This was Joe's wrongful conviction in the Barker case coming back to haunt him. If Joe had a bad name because of that case, it was with the Fancy, not the everyday men of the district, with whom Joe retained great popularity for his boxing exploits. Hobbs asked McLerie for authority to arrest Windred, so that he could be handed over to the US Government for return to California and trial there.[187]

Joe had by this time returned to Sydney, but Hobbs knew that Joe's father lived just a short distance from his office. Through the father, Hobbs could track down the son when he needed to.

Sunday, August 17, 1851. San Francisco Bay, California

As the bow of the 159-ton New York schooner *Veto* sliced through the waters of the bay, John Gough, his wife and children looked back at San Francisco with mixed feelings. The Goughs were departing this city that had turned against them, leaving behind the money and time they had invested in creating a profitable restaurant business.

Finding that the lynching of English Jim had not provoked any steps against it by San Francisco's legitimate law enforcers, the Committee of Vigilance had been flexing its muscles and ejecting 'Australians' from their city. But first, it had jettisoned Sam Brannan from its presidency. Lynch-obsessed Brannan had proven too impetuous and mentally unstable even for the more radical vigilantes. He had not only been voted out, he had been banned from Committee headquarters. Two new leaders had been elected in Brannan's place, city merchants both. Selim Woodworth was president of the overall body, while twenty-five-year-old Stephen Payran, an Irishman from Inniskilling, was elected president of the executive committee, and as such he wielded the true power. Both men were considered 'better balanced and more orderly' than Brannan.[188]

Although English Jim Stuart had not named John Gough as an associate, the fact that Gough was a known friend of Windred and Burdue marked him as an intimate of criminals. For, even though Stuart had confessed to the Jansen robbery and exonerated Windred and Burdue, Burdue was at this moment serving time for that crime, breaking rock on Angel Island and helping build San Quentin Penitentiary. Meanwhile, were Joe Windred ever to be caught in the United States, he could be tried for his prison break, and face an additional sentence.

The Committee of Vigilance had issued Gough with a Notice to Quit, requiring him to quit the Panama House, quit San Francisco and quit California, within five days. By one estimate, the Committee would force, or frighten, as many as eight hundred Sydney Ducks into leaving California and returning to Australia in July and August, branding them all escaped convicts.[189] Annoyingly, to the Committee, there had been protests in support of Gough and his ailing wife from some San Franciscan men and their wives. 'As there has been a sympathy [for the Goughs] excited in the breasts of some persons in this community', said the Committee, it released the transcript of its examination of Gough to the San Francisco press, which eagerly printed it in full.[190]

Said the San Francisco *Courier* on July 18, in introducing the transcript, 'We have been furnished by the Vigilance Committee with the following, which will go far to show what kind of people we have had to deal with in this city. We never doubted the correctness and propriety of the course adopted by them in re-shipping the escaped convicts to the Colonies. This shows a state of facts, too, in relation to the officers in the British penal colonies, that we have long expected was the case. The idea of sending men among us, whom they would not permit to live in their own country, is an insult, and should be promptly resisted by our government.' The *Courier* also published Mary Windred's letters to John Gough, and her invoice to Tom Burdue, inclusive of her note to Hall McAllister.

In the San Francisco *Herald*, William Walker had employed his trademark sarcastic wit in a scathing editorial about John Gough. Walker was a strong supporter of Irish political prisoners then languishing in Van Diemen's Land. One of these men, Terrence MacManus, had arrived in San Francisco on June 5 after escaping the island penal colony, receiving a hero's welcome from Americans and fellow Irishmen. Hence Walker's declaration in his editorial: 'If Mr Goff [sic] had been a political prisoner in Van Diemen's Land it would be different. But we are not aware that housebreaking comes within the catalogue of political offenses. We would strongly advise Mr Goff therefore to avail himself of the Committee's suggestion, and depart as soon as possible.' To Walker, Gough's record spoke for itself. 'He has done San Francisco the honour of choosing it as his place of residence, and has, since his arrival, it appears, kept up an intimacy with such men as Windred and others of that description.'[191]

Gough was damned. So too was Joe Windred, an innocent man now branded the worst of the worst in California because he had succeeded in escaping this prejudiced, primitive and predatory corner of the world. Following the protests in support of the Gough family, the Committee had delayed their deportation to give the ailing Mrs Gough time to recover. Now, together with two other families and eight crew, they were Sydney bound aboard the *Veto*. Many other Sydney Ducks were not being treated so politely by their vigilante evictors.

Monday, August 18, 1851. San Francisco, California

Mary Ann Hogan sat stiffly in front of the assembled members of the Committee of Vigilance's executive committee. Found hiding out on a ship in the harbour, she'd been brought to the Committee's rooms for questioning.

'The famous Mrs Hogan', as the *Herald*'s William Walker called her, was considered 'one of the leading spirits of the gang'. Walker would editorialise, 'We consider one such woman at large in a community worse than half a dozen burglars.' Women of her kind, said Walker, were 'frequently the great incentives to crime'.[192]

Mary Ann was read a statement made by Sam Whitaker. For, slippery Sam had been apprehended, on August 8. He'd been recognised in Santa Barbara, more than 500 kilometres down the coast from San Francisco, by the town's sheriff, V. W. Hearne. Sheriff Hearne had brought Whitaker by sea to San Francisco, and handed him over to the Committee of Vigilance in return for a handsome sum, supposedly to cover his expenses.

Under interrogation, Sam had emulated English Jim by freely admitting crimes and naming cronies. Over the past month a number of these men, including Dab, Jemmy-from-Town, Jemmy Roundhead, George Arthur and George Adams, had been located throughout northern California and handed over to the San Francisco Committee of Vigilance. Most had been passed on to the legitimate authorities to be charged and tried. This, in the opinion of William Walker, had made the Committee more acceptable to many of its Californian critics. But Sam Whitaker was a different matter. He was the jewel in the Sydney Duck crown, and the Committee wanted to make an example of him.

Mary Ann Hogan, after responding to Whitaker's statement — but, like Whitaker, keeping quiet about the May 3–4 fire and Joe Windred's escape, or their part in either — was confronted with her lover. Whitaker was being held in a Committee cell along with Bob McKenzie, who'd been captured by committeeman Julius Schultz in Sacramento on July 29.

After Mary Ann was absolved of any wrongdoing, Whitaker was hustled away. Both must have known they would never see each other again. Mary Ann would later be released by the Committee, which considered her only crime to be that of loving a bad man. But Whitaker's fate was to be much more grim.

Sunday, August 24, 1851. San Francisco, California

The Committee of Vigilance had been outsmarted. One Australian newspaper commented that the Governor of California was 'evidently anxious to do his duty, but has no force at his command which will enable him to do so'.[193] To make up for his lack of forces, pugnacious Governor McDougall had employed the element of surprise. In the early hours of August 20, McDougall and City Attorney Pixley had called on Myron Norton, associate justice of the superior court, with an affidavit requesting a writ of habeas corpus for Sam Whitaker and Robert McKenzie. Armed with that writ, McDougall and Pixley had collected Sheriff Jack Hays.

The trio had subsequently burst into Committee of Vigilance headquarters with drawn pistols, and rescued Whitaker and McKenzie. The two crooks had been removed to the new county jail on Broadway, to await proper trial. That same day, Governor McDougall issued a proclamation, denouncing the Committee of Vigilance as a despotic and unlawful body which defied the Constitution of California, and calling on 'all good citizens' to 'aid public officers in the discharge of their duty'.[194] It was a call destined to fall on deaf ears.

At 2.30 p.m. this Sunday, Divine Service for prisoners began at the county jail, conducted by the Reverend Albert Williams from the First Presbyterian Church. Apart from all the prisoners in the jail other than two or three who were sick, the service was attended by Judge R. H. Waller and the jail's commandant, San Francisco Police captain William Lambert. Sam Whitaker and Bob McKenzie were among the congregation.

Because the jail had yet to be completed, no assembly hall was available, so the service was held in an open passageway between jail wall and cell doors. As the Reverend Williams began, the bell of the Monument Fire Engine Company could be heard to ring, away in the distance, summoning Committee of Vigilance members. Ever since the recapture of Whitaker and McKenzie, all talk in the city had been of hangings. On Friday, in Sacramento, two Sydney Ducks, Gibson and Thompson, had been legally hanged by that town's sheriff after their conviction in a legitimate court of law. A third condemned man, Robinson, an American citizen, had received a stay of execution from Governor McDougall. This had angered the Sacramento mob, and, urged on by Sam Brannan, who had come from San Francisco to watch the executions, that mob had seized Robinson and lynched him.

A few minutes before 2.45, as the church service continued at the jail, commandant Captain Lambert was alerted by a sentry on the roof that a mob of armed men was rushing toward the jail. In moments, both gates were smashed open, and upward of forty armed vigilantes charged into the jail. At the main gate, Captain Lambert was knocked from his feet and held down. Judge Waller rushed to help him.

'Shoot! Shoot!' Lambert urged his jailers.[195]

Those jailers would claim they were too afraid of hitting Lambert and Judge Waller to open fire. Vigilantes surged past captain and judge. The storming of the jail had been carefully planned – timed to coincide with the church service, and with the feared Sheriff Jack Hays lured away that morning by an invitation to a Sunday bullfight taking place a long ride south of San Francisco.

The Committee of Vigilance had come for two prisoners, and two prisoners only – Sam Whitaker and Bob McKenzie. Vigilantes seized the pair and dragged them out onto Broadway. There, a two-horse carriage waited, escorted by armed horsemen. As Whitaker and McKenzie, dressed in white cotton shirts and buff-coloured pants, were bundled into the carriage, pistol shots were fired into the air, to signal to committeemen waiting at headquarters on Battery Street that the snatch had been successful. With its mounted escort, the carriage raced away.

Taken from the carriage at its Battery Street destination, Whitaker and McKenzie were dragged to a doorway above which a sign declared 'Vigilance Committee Chambers', and upstairs to first-floor rooms that extended above commercial premises. Here, the executive committee, fearing that Captain Lambert might raise a force of armed police to recapture the prisoners, did not even bother with a farcical kangaroo court. Two tall French windows facing Battery Street were thrown open. Below, the street was filling with a large crowd, 'perfectly wild with excitement'.[196] One eyewitness would calculate that the crowd numbered fifteen thousand.[197] All eyes lifted expectantly to the open windows.

Above the Committee-room windows, two large beams equipped with block and tackle extended out over the street. As ropes were attached to each, a round of applause ran around onlookers below. The Committee's usual hangman, Edgar Wakeman, had recently taken a new maritime command and was now at sea. In 1853, Wakeman would sail into Sydney, where he would be recognised by former Sydney Ducks who would call for his arrest for the lynching murder of British citizens Stuart and Jenkins in San Francisco. The New South Wales Government would not act, considering those crimes a matter for Californian authorities.

In Wakeman's stead, plenty of others were eager to have a hand in dispatching Whitaker and Mackenzie. Nooses were quickly knotted. Sam Whitaker, knowing what was coming, stood, silent and resigned. His stoicism impressed one of the Committee members present, who described him as being 'as brave as Caesar'.[198]

Pathetic McKenzie, on the other hand, was whimpering and sobbing, and he impressed no one. He kicked and struggled as, with the noose around his neck and his arms strapped by his side, he was manhandled to an open window, then shoved out. McKenzie fell a short distance before the rope pulled him up with a jerk. He then crashed back against the side of the building with a thud. A cheer went up from the onlookers. Struggling at the end of the rope, McKenzie was hauled to the top of the block.

Then, it was Whitaker's turn. From the second window, he too was pushed out into space, and suffered the identical fate to McKenzie. A cheer also accompanied Whitaker's drop, followed by another when a member of the Committee leaned out one of the windows and waved the blue banner presented by the ladies of Trinity Church. Whitaker, suspended above a sign advertising provision merchants Bullitt, Patrick and Dow, was drawn up to hang just below the pulley. Just seventeen minutes had elapsed since the seizure of the two men at the jail. Both men would struggle at the end of their ropes. They would not be cut down for forty-five minutes.

The entertainment was over. So too were the criminal careers of two Sydney Ducks. In New South Wales, Joe Windred, once he learned of the lynching of Whitaker and McKenzie, would not lament McKenzie's passing. He didn't even know the youth. But Joe and Mary Windred had reason to be thankful to Sam Whitaker, without whom Joe would never have made it home to Australia.

24

HIDING OUT

Sunday, August 31, 1851. San Francisco, California

IN A SPECIAL COURT sitting, in a temporary courtroom in a San Francisco hospital that had been used since City Hall's destruction in June, Tom Burdue was brought in chains before Judge Alistair Campbell after being rowed ashore from the state prison hulk *Waban*. Also in court were Tom's attorney, Hall McAllister, and several members of the San Francisco Committee of Vigilance. McAllister now applied to the court for the conviction of Thomas Burdue and Joseph Windred in the Jansen robbery to be 'vacated', and, in support of that application, the Committee's representatives tendered James Stuart's signed confession, in which Stuart had accepted responsibility for that crime and exonerated both Burdue and Windred.

It did not take thirty-one-year-old Judge Campbell long to rule in the matter. He accepted the application, and vacated Tom and Joe's convictions. The judge went further. Born in Jamaica, of Scottish parents, Campbell had completed legal studies in New York City. Perhaps it was his British background, or his youth in cosmopolitan New York, but Campbell now expressed sympathy to Burdue for what he had been put through, and urged the Committee of Vigilance to raise a benevolent fund for Tom and his family. Tom thanked the judge, shook hands with his attorney, and walked out the door a free man, to reunite with Elen and their children. It was assumed in San Francisco that Tom would follow Joe Windred's example and return to Australia.

Even though the court had vacated Joe's conviction, because jailbreak was a crime, and despite the fact that he had been innocent of the crime for which he had originally been imprisoned, as far as the State of California was concerned Joe was still a wanted man and subject to arrest, trial and conviction for his escape.

Friday, September 5, 1851, Sydney, New South Wales

An item in the morning's issue of the Sydney *Empire* would have caused Joe Windred growing trepidation. Living with his brother William at the Shamrock Inn and helping him out in the pub, Joe and Mary were trying to restart their lives and leave behind their nightmare year in California, with the wide blue Pacific acting as a buffer between the recent traumatic past and their future. But that was easier said than done.

The previous Monday, September 1, the *Empire* had printed a letter from Captain Isaac Harris, master of the 300-ton London-registered barque *Timandra*, who wrote bitterly of being almost lynched during San Francisco's June 22 fire. Harris landed in San Francisco from the *Timandra* that very day, and was helping with the fire-fighting when accused of being a Sydney Duck, and of lighting the fire. Stripped and battered, he had only been saved from being lynched from a lamppost when, dragged before the Committee of Vigilance, he was recognised by leading member Felix Argenti, who was Harris' shipping agent in the city.

Neither Joe nor Tom Burdue were mentioned in Harris' letter, but it was still enough to unsettle Joe. He had first learned of the Committee of Vigilance's existence in reports of John Jenkins' lynching that had appeared in the Sydney press in late August. But this letter from Captain Harris brought Joe's Californian experience uncomfortably close to his Sydney doorstep. As did the editorial in the same issue from *Empire* editor Henry Parkes. A future knight of the realm, eventually five-times Premier of New South Wales and father of the federation of the Australian colonies into the sovereign nation of Australia, Parkes had founded the *Empire* the previous December with the objective of making it the liberal voice of New South Wales. In his editorial, Parkes had lambasted the Americans behind the Committee of Vigilance with all the vitriol he could muster.

On page three of its Friday edition, the *Empire* reprinted English Jim Stuart's confession, taken from a recently arrived San Francisco paper. And there, toward the end of the long report, were the words, from Stuart's own mouth, 'Knew Windred; think he has gone out of the country.' This was the sole reference to Joe by name, and only used his surname. But Windred was not a common name. Joe could only hope that nothing more would appear in the local press about the sad and sorry affair.

Little did Joe know that a letter about him was at that moment on its way across the Pacific to Governor McDougall of California from James Hartwell Williams, US consul in Sydney. The report about Joe from Chief Constable Hobbs at Windsor had been passed on to Consul Williams by the New South Wales Government, and Williams had now written to the governor to seek his instructions to make a formal approach for Joe's extradition to California.[199]

Wednesday, September 24, 1851. San Francisco, California

A short letter from Tom Burdue appeared this morning in San Francisco's *Courier*, addressed to the Committee of Vigilance:

> I have kindly to thank those gentlemen for what they have done for me. Certainly, through their vigilance and the kind providence of Almighty God, they have succeeded in capturing the criminal for whom I have suffered so much.
> Thomas Burdue

Ironically, Tom was thanking the men who had originally been so keen to lynch him. Equally ironically, the Committee no longer existed. Eight days earlier, Joseph Bluxome, on behalf of the Committee of Vigilance, had presented Tom with the proceeds of the benevolent fund established on Judge Campbell's recommendation. Those proceeds totalled just $302. The largest contributor was Charles Jansen, whose false identification had led to Tom and Joe's wrongful conviction. Jansen also returned the $1700 confiscated from Tom back in February.

As for the rank and file members of the Committee of Vigilance, they had melted away like snow in the sun. On September 15, the organisation had voted to disband, announcing that it considered its work done. This proffered reason for the Committee's sudden demise would be repeated by the California press and by writers to this day. In fact, while the legally constituted authorities of California had proven powerless to defeat it, the Committee of Vigilance had been routed by a single man, a Sydney Duck – forty-three-year-old drayman Peter Metcalfe, a native of Manchester, England and formerly a cabinetmaker in Sydney.

Back in July, Committee leader Felix Argenti and fifty vigilantes had forced their way into Metcalfe's home at midnight, supposedly looking for stolen goods, and turned out Metcalfe and his family. Employing veteran attorney Rufus Lockwood, Metcalfe had sued the Committee of Vigilance for trespass in civil court, for $20,000 damages. When the jury in the case could not agree, Lockwood immediately relaunched the suit, increasing the damages claim to $50,000.[200] Now, the Committee of Vigilance received two rude shocks. Firstly, the lawyers representing them in the case, whom the vigilantes had assumed were volunteering their services, sent them a bill for $1000. Then it was realised that, under the law, every single member of the Committee was responsible for its debts. If the Committee lost the Metcalfe case, every member would be liable to contribute to the $50,000 award.

President Stephen Payran resigned. He would not only leave the organisation, he would leave San Francisco. He was followed out the door by seven hundred members trying to protect their own pockets. The Committee's treasury was empty. It couldn't even pay the rent on its proud headquarters, let alone the salary of its 'chief of police'. The Committee's few remaining loyal members hastily folded the organisation.

While the rump of its executive committee would continue to meet in secret into 1853, no longer did the organisation wield any power or influence. It would briefly and dramatically re-emerge in 1856, but to lynch political opponents, not Australians. Meanwhile, to paper over the cracks in Californian society, the legitimate authorities chose not to prosecute Committee members for its crimes, which included kidnap and murder. Ex-members who sought to trade off its notoriety failed at the ballot box. Democrats would soon sweep back into city government power.

Meanwhile, Bob Collyer, a self-proclaimed doctor, had few attendees to his ghoulish lecture 'The Anatomy of Crime', during which he displayed the skulls of English Jim Stuart, Sam Whitaker, Bob McKenzie and John Jenkins, having purchased their decapitated heads from the coroner then boiled away their flesh and brain matter.

Friday, September 26, 1851. Sydney, New South Wales

Joe must have been feeling uneasy. Since Wednesday, letters and editorials had been appearing in the *Empire* and *Sydney Morning Herald* about San Francisco's Committee of Vigilance. Ignited by Captain Harris' letter earlier in the month, pages of newsprint were being devoted to claims and counterclaims about the Committee, and about how Australian immigrants were being ill-treated in California.

Colonial correspondents were both for and against the Committee of Vigilance. In the *Sydney Morning Herald*'s letters column, W. B. Allen defended the Committee's members as men of honour. A correspondent calling himself An Old Miner had countered by saying he'd spent twelve months in California and knew the leading members of the Committee of Vigilance. 'The whole of the Committee are devoid of honesty or honour,' he thundered.[201] Now, in a letter printed in today's *Sydney Morning Herald*, a correspondent signing himself A Sydneyite came to the defence of the Committee of Vigilance, declaring, 'The Committee would not wilfully do any man an injury did he not deserve it.'

These exchanges had not mentioned Joe Windred. But Thursday's *Empire* had printed John Gough's testimony before the Committee of Vigilance. And there was Joe's name, and Mary's name. The *Empire* had even published Mary's May letters to Gough and invoice to Tom Burdue. Anyone in Sydney who frequented William Windred's pub and read this could only deduce that the publican's recently arrived brother Joe and sister-in-law Mary must be the Windreds mentioned in the press. Joe began to think that Mary, Isabel and himself should leave town and go into hiding, but the pragmatic Mary, not wanting to take Isabel out of school in Sydney, where she was settled, would have counselled waiting to give the affair a chance to blow over.

Saturday, October 11, 1851. San Francisco, California

In the morning's issue of the *Alta California*, Edward Buffum wrote that Tom Burdue had lost his $302 donation from the Committee of Vigilance 'in an unfortunate mining venture'. To have lost that money in less than a month suggests that Tom had in fact gambled it away at a mining camp. And Buffum, who had developed sympathy for Tom, probably knew it, hence the wording of his report.

According to the *Alta*, Tom was now devoid of money 'and his friends were trying to raise more'. Tom's situation was made worse by the fact that his time in damp prison cells had severely damaged his health. Plus, Tom had received a bill from lawyer Hall McAllister for his legal services and expenses during his three trials, amounting to close to $4000.

Saturday, October 25, 1851. Sydney, New South Wales

Joe's dread of the American government seeking his arrest continued to grow. Through October, the Sydney press had continued to publish articles from California, and in the *Sydney Morning Herald* on October 20, there was Joe's name again. 'We have the Californian newspapers to the 1st September,' began a long report. A host of familiar names now leapt from the page – Stuart, Whitaker, McKenzie, Jenkins, Mrs Hogan. Here were the details of Tom Burdue's trials. And then, 'A young man named Windred (a native of this colony), who was convicted of the robbery with Berdue [sic], was also by Stuart's confession declared to be innocent. Windred escaped from prison, and we believe arrived in Sydney some months since.'

Through the week, Sydney's newspapers had reprinted vast slabs verbatim from the California press about Sydney Duck episodes, as each paper vied with the other to grab the reading public's attention. This morning, under the headline 'Yankee Christianity', a detailed and highly censorious account of the lynching of Whitaker and McKenzie appeared, in, of all publications, *Bell's Life in Sydney and Sporting Reviewer*. Through it, Joe and Mary learned the grisly fate of their saviour, Whitaker.

Every newspaper in the Australian colonies covered the situation in California, adding outraged editorials. Typically, in Melbourne, the *Argus* labelled the Committee of Vigilance 'murderers', 'demons', 'scoundrels' and 'wretches'.[202] Inevitably, people who knew Joe were now asking him if he was the Windred involved in the sensational goings on in California and who had recently returned to Sydney from there.

Fearing that the United States Government must surely now try to secure his arrest and return to California, Joe decided to leave Sydney. Fast. And he knew just the place to hide. Younger brother Jack Windred had recently relocated to Sofala, a remote frontier settlement which, only months before, had blossomed overnight in the Turon Valley, forty kilometres north of Bathurst, with the discovery of gold. There, at virgin Sofala, where everyone was anonymous, Joe and his family could lay low for a while with Jack.

Joe's fears were not, it turned out, exaggerated. At that moment, a letter was on its way from Governor McDougall in California to US Consul Williams in Sydney, replying to Williams' earlier correspondence and asking him to make a requisition to the New South Wales Government for the arrest and surrender into US custody of Joseph Windred.

Saturday, December 13, 1851. Sofala, New South Wales

Joe, Mary and Isabel had joined Joe's brother Jack at Sofala, 300 kilometres west of Sydney and a six-hour coach ride from Bathurst. To those who might say that Joe could not keep away from gold diggings, Joe would say that he had come to visit his brother. In this remote place, men were too busy digging for gold to read newspapers and to connect Joe with the story of an Australian who had escaped from prison in distant California.

The camp here was just as primitive as the one at Auburn in California, but much larger. As in California, the backdrop was a rugged mountain range, while gold mining was confined to a ravine through which the slim, stony Turon River wound. Sofala possessed a single, narrow main street filled with canvas and slab pubs and shops, while thousands of tents spread in disorganised fashion beside the river. There would be 60,000 gold-seekers in the Turon Valley by 1852 – almost twice the population of San Francisco, and greater even than the population of Sydney. Many gold-seekers had in fact come from Sydney, while Australians who had gone to the California rush returned at the flood to try their luck at home, bringing many American gold-seekers with them.

At Sofala, Jack Windred, like his neighbours, lived in a tent. In September, Jack had chased two robbers on foot through the tent city. He caught them, too, handing them over to the authorities, who offered their warm thanks. With Jack making a good living here as a butcher, brother Joe, with memories of the cut-throat Auburn diggings still raw, seems to have guaranteed to wife Mary that he would not become involved in mining for gold. Joe now erected a tent for his little family, and went to work with Jack, whose largest problem was maintaining a reliable supply of beef to feed famished miners. Together, the brothers fenced off a stockyard on the settlement's fringe. From now on, it would be Joe's task to source cattle from across the colony for his brother's butchering business, and then drive them to Sofala.

Joe's new job would see him riding far and wide, and would conveniently keep him out of circulation. For, the California affair had not left the press. Through December, *Bell's Life* published every snippet of information it could find about Sydney Ducks and the Committee of Vigilance, and in this Saturday's edition reprinted statements by Mary Ann Hogan and James Whiting. Not only did Whiting mention Joe Windred, he also referred to Mary Windred, speaking of 'the times I went to Mrs Hogan's house with Mrs Windred to see about witnesses'.[203] On learning of this, Joe and Mary would have been pleased with their decision to leave Sydney.

The editor of *Bell's Life in Sydney*, who had once been a firm supporter of Young Joe Windred the boxer, now railed not so much against the Committee of Vigilance as against 'the misdeeds of those who roused them to fury, [and] brought the very name of Sydney into disrepute with the Californians'.[204] Innocent though Joe was, by being in the wrong place at the wrong time he had been tarred with the same Sydney Duck brush as the true wrongdoers.

Thursday, January 1, 1852. Sofala, New South Wales

It was New Year's Day, and the Windreds had joined the miners of the Turon Valley for a rare day off, enjoying the very first meeting of the Sofala Races. The gold diggings at Sofala were unlike any

Joe and Mary had experienced in California. Rather than leave the administration of law and order to each individual community, as was the American way, the central government in Sydney appointed a Gold Commissioner to administer affairs in the Turon, backed by a small detachment of uniformed New South Wales Police.

Even though the police force here was small, and vastly outnumbered by the thousands of miners, such was the respect for, or fear of, the authorities, that the crime rate at the diggings was low. Murder was almost unheard of, although, just two days before this, on a night when Sofala was hit by a storm 'which sent the tents flying in every direction', a man had been killed with a tomahawk. The Windred brothers knew the victim, John Donnelly, who came from the Windsor area and had once done a little boxing under the name Mick Power's Johnny. This violent death was the result of jealousy, not a robbery, for, according to the press, 'some woman was the cause of the unfortunate affair'. That woman was now in police custody, while the murderer was on the run.[205]

There was another unusual aspect to the Turon goldfields. Over Christmas, two thirds of the thousands of gold diggers had gone home to spend the holidays with their families, leaving their claims unattended without fearing they would be jumped by others. Such was the atmosphere of trust and camaraderie on the goldfields here. By January 1, many of these miners had returned, and 'a great muster of people' turned out for Sofala's inaugural race meeting, a day for a picnic, a tipple and a wager or two. Jack Windred was one of the organisers, and also entered two horses in the races. The meeting was held 'on a miserable little piece of a flat', in the opinion of one local newspaper correspondent, 'situated on one of the ranges behind Sofala, on the Bathurst road, and the course did not exceed three quarters of a mile'.[206]

Short the course may have been, and the runners only advertised as saddle horses, but the big crowd enjoyed the day's racing. Jack Windred's hack Charley lost the first race, but his fine black mare Miss Flirt easily won the next event, the £10 Hack Stakes. Charley ran in the next race, the Turon Welter Stakes, and again lost, before Miss Flirt easily took out the £20 Sofala Plate for Jack.

Just as Jack was celebrating his win with Joe, Mary and little Isabel, a protest was lodged, claiming that Miss Flirt was a trained racehorse and ineligible for the event. She was indeed a trained racehorse; Jack had recently bought Miss Flirt from coach operator John Minehan with the idea of taking her around the colony's race meetings and cleaning up. Jack lost the protest, lost both races, and lost not only Miss Flirt's £30 race winnings but his entry fee. In a huff, Jack declared that he ought to go to Victoria to buy several more racehorses, and show the colony what real horseracing was about.

Wednesday, February 25, 1852. Sofala, New South Wales

Joe had found himself running little brother Jack's butchery business. By February 4, Jack was aboard the brig *Melbourne Packet* and sailing from Sydney to Melbourne. Joe, meanwhile, had decided to stage a prize fight, in a ring he set up behind the Windred brothers' Sofala stockyards. Gambling on professional boxing was still frowned on by the authorities, so the bout would have to be a once-only affair – for old times' sake, Joe would have told Mary. Not only was he the fight's promoter, Joe trained one of the two combatants.

Jack Windred arrived back from Melbourne just in time for the fight. Despite a purse of only £10, this fight, on a Wednesday afternoon in the February heat, attracted a thousand eager diggers otherwise starved of entertainment. It was the largest crowd Joe had ever seen at a boxing match. The fighters were Jack the Waiter, an employee of Sofala's Golden Point Hotel trained by Joe, and Billy Frost, a fighter from Penrith who had accepted Joe's offer to come out to Sofala for the event. Joe also organised a knowledgeable referee, and, remembering how much George Pickering, editor of *Bell's Life in Sydney and Sporting Reviewer*, enjoyed a boxing match, also invited him out to Sofala.

Frost's father and younger brother were his seconds, and Joe and Jack Windred once again teamed up, to occupy Jack the Waiter's corner. Before the fight, Joe, determined to keep his location secret in case the US Government was looking for him, took George Pickering aside and asked him not to identify his brother or himself as Jack the Waiter's trainers.

When Pickering asked how his report of the fight should identify the men in the Waiter's corner, Joe replied, 'Just call us "two Australians".' Which he did.

At 2.20 p.m., the two combatants stepped onto the ring, to an enormous, good-hearted cheer from the crowd. Both fighters weighed much the same. Frost was the taller of the two, the Waiter the more solid. The 'mill' was soon underway, with Frost scoring the first knockdown. Betting in the crowd was strongly on Frost. But as the rounds progressed, Jack the Waiter began to follow Joe's shouted instructions and land some good punches. After Frost was floored to end round seven, the betting was 2 to 1 on the Waiter. Frost regained his feet, and his corner, where his bloodied face was sponged by his father. Frost gamely came out for round eight, but was soon freely bleeding from nose and mouth. Both men, obviously weakened, were in a clinch, when a uniformed horseman came barging into the crowd.

'The Gold Commissioner!' went up an alarmed cry.

A thousand spectators, four trainers, two boxers and a referee scattered in all directions, abandoning the fight rather than face arrest, and taking all evidence of gambling with them. Less than an hour later, word circulated that the fight was to be resumed behind the Golden Nugget Hotel. There was no boxing ring there, but a large earth bank was ideal for spectators. The crowd flooded back, and before long, without ropes or corners now, the bout resumed, at the foot of the bank. This time, the fight ran its course. Another eight rounds were fought before Frost's corner literally threw in the sponge. With victory came new strength; the Waiter bounded up onto the bank and ran up and down with his arms in the air. Frost, meanwhile, seemingly impervious to the fact that his face looked like raw steak, remonstrated with his father for yielding the fight.[207]

For Joe, it had been a good day's sport. As usual, he had not wagered a penny. A good contest was all that interested him, spicing up a life that had become a little tame. Jack the Waiter's later victory celebrations at the Golden Point Hotel provided Joe with an opportunity to chat with newspaperman Pickering. Whether Pickering knew that Joe was *the* Windred in the California story is unclear. He may have worked it out, or Joe may have told him. Even if he was ignorant of Joe's secret, Pickering would now have told Joe that the demise of the Committee of Vigilance meant the Sydney Ducks episode had become stale news by the new year.

In fact, since December, nothing more had appeared in the New South Wales press about anti-Australian activities and lynchings in California. With no more sensational news to print, Pickering and his fellow editors had lost interest, and moved on.

What was more, nowhere had Joe heard of any attempt by American authorities to seek his return to California. This gave him pause for thought about his immediate future, and his little family's future. With few children on the goldfields, primitive Sofala was devoid of a school. This was no place to raise a child, and Joe, who had come to love little Isabel as his own, began to think that the California business might be over, permitting him to come out of hiding and move his family to another, more established place where he wasn't known, and start life anew.

But the danger, while lessened, had not passed. From Sydney, US Consul Williams had written back to Governor McDougall before Christmas to say that the extremely negative reaction here to recent news from California of the lynching of Australians had convinced him that any application locally for the extradition of Joseph Windred to face trial in San Francisco would be futile. In Williams' opinion, the New South Wales Government would not surrender any Australian while there was a possibility he might be lynched on reaching California. Instead, Williams recommended that McDougall ask the US Secretary of State in Washington to approach the British Government in London for Joseph Windred's extradition, as a matter of US foreign policy.[208] For, while the New South Wales Government was independent of London in most respects, in matters of foreign affairs London ruled.

Joe knew nothing of any of this. Had he known, he would probably have sought an even more distant hiding place. But as unlucky as Joe was in many ways, luck never completely deserted him. By the time that John McDougall received Consul Williams' recommendation, in early 1852, the situation in California had changed significantly. With Californians now anxious to forget the excesses of the brief reign of the Committee of Vigilance, putting those dark days back in the headlines by extraditing and putting on trial for jailbreak a man whose original conviction had now been overturned seemed devoid of political sense, or natural justice. McDougall would decide not to pursue the Windred affair any further.[209] Nonetheless, Joe's status as a wanted man in California remained unchanged.

Sunday, September 26, 1852. Bathurst, New South Wales

Joe was devastated.

By the spring he, Mary, Isabel and Jack had all relocated to Bathurst, where the Windred brothers rented houses next door to each other in Piper Street. Here, Mary would be happier, as would eight-year-old Isabel, who was able to return to school. Jack had opened a new butchery in the town, and Joe was continuing to act as his stock agent. In the autumn, Jack had run Miss Flirt and several new racehorses at meetings around the colony, with mixed success, and Joe had accompanied him. At the Mudgee races, Joe had seen a big, handsome, grey gelding called Captain win a race, after which the owner put him up for sale. Falling in love with the horse, Joe bought him. He was still struggling to make a living, so his excuse to Mary was that he would use the mount as his day-to-day saddle horse in the stock business, racing him on the side.

Joe renamed the horse Ariosto. This was the name of a famous racehorse in England, taken from Renaissance Italian poet Ludovico Ariosto, who had written about Bayard, a magical flying horse that moulded himself to the size of his rider. With Joe's affinity with horses, it was as if his new horse did just that, and big horse and tall rider became one. For their first outing together, Ariosto had run at the Hawkesbury Races at Windsor, in front of Joe's brothers and father. Ariosto had lived up to his mythological connections; as fast as lightning, he'd carried Joe's colours to victory.

But now, disaster! Just the night before, a Saturday night, Joe had proudly ridden Ariosto down to Patrick Sullivan's Shamrock Inn on Bathurst's George Street. Tethering Ariosto outside, Joe had gone inside for a convivial drink with friends. When he later emerged, it was to find that Ariosto had disappeared. After fruitlessly looking for the horse, and hoping that Ariosto had only strayed, Joe sat down to write a press advertisement offering a £10 reward, all he could afford, for Ariosto's return or for the conviction of his thief.

The powerful grey racehorse was too distinctive to go unnoticed, and Ariosto would be restored to Joe within a week, with no theft charges laid.

Monday, January 3, 1853. Vallejo, California

In the vestibule of California's temporary capitol building, at the corner of Vallejo's York and Sacramento streets, Tom Burdue shook the hand of state senator Daniel B. Kurtz, and handed him a one-page document.

Contrary to expectations in both California and Australia, Burdue had not followed Joe Windred back to New South Wales. Determined to receive restitution from the government for what he had been put through, he had remained in California right through 1852 with his wife and family. But no one in San Francisco had been prepared to take up his cause, which had the potential to resurrect the embarrassments of the lethal reign of the Committee of Vigilance. Kurtz, who had been the second mayor of the city of San Diego in Southern California, was elected to the senate in 1852. A carpenter by trade, Kurtz was now studying law. Those studies perhaps helped him appreciate the travesty of justice in Tom Burdue's case. And, divorced as he was from the heated atmosphere in San Francisco, the senator from San Diego didn't have to worry about a political backlash in his own bailiwick.

With the Californian legislature about to commence its fourth session, Senator Kurtz agreed to present a 'memorial', or petition, from Tom, to the body. In that memorial, Tom sought financial reparations for the two prosecutions that had resulted in his wrongful conviction and imprisonment. Hall McAllister probably helped draft his memorial, in which Tom said, in part, that he had resorted to this step 'after suffering the ignominies of a prison cell for the space of nearly nine months, contracting disease, and suffering both mentally and physically'. His family's situation, he said, was dire. 'In order to defend himself,' he said, 'and procure the necessary counsel and witnesses, your petitioner had expended all his own and his friends' means, amounting to nearly four thousand dollars. That, in consequence whereof, his wife and children have been reduced from comparative affluence to a state of beggary and want.'

Tom was not asking for a fortune. 'Your petitioner therefore prays your honourable body will pass a joint resolution of both Houses, authorizing the Comptroller of the State to draw warrants on the Treasurer for the sum of four thousand dollars, to be paid out of the General Fund, for the relief of your petitioner, to reimburse him for the actual outlay of cash, and injury sustained in consequence of prosecutions.' At the time his ordeal had begun, almost two years earlier, he said, he had been 'pursuing his ordinary avocations as a good and peaceable, law-abiding citizen'.[210] More than the money, an award would, to Tom, be proof that the government acknowledged it had failed him at his time of greatest need.

Tabled by Kurtz, Tom's memorial would be referred to the California Senate's Judiciary Committee on January 21. Meanwhile, Tom would return to Elen and the children in San Francisco to await the outcome. Once again, his fate was in the hands of a committee.

Thursday, January 19, 1853. Sydney, New South Wales

Riding Ariosto into Sydney for a visit, Joe was able to stay with his brother William, now licensee of the substantial, eight-roomed Sir Richard Bourke Hotel, opposite the Victoria Theatre in Pitt Street. The boys' mother was now also a publican in her own right. The previous year, using her legal name of Sophia Brady, she'd held the licence of Sydney's Railway Tavern. By September she had moved to the Royal Oak, in George Street, before selling her lease in December. Later this year, Sophia would pay the publican of the Albion Inn on the corner of Sussex and Market streets a considerable sum for its licence.

On Joe's latest Sydney visit, a fellow patron in the bar at the Sir Richard Bourke, Noah Bent, challenged him to a race, on their saddle horses. Each would put up £25, winner take all. 'Always a sportsman and an enthusiast in horse-racing', in the opinion of one relative, Joe had readily accepted the challenge.[211] They raced five miles along Old South Head Road, and *Bell's Life in Sydney* would chortle that Mr Windred 'won easily'.[212] Mr Bent paid the price of not inquiring into the background of the grey saddle horse that now left him in its dust. For, Joe was aboard Ariosto, and rode away with the £25 prize.

Thursday, May 19, 1853. Benicia, California

During its latest sitting, the state legislature had relocated to the small northern Californian town of Benicia; it would finally take permanent root in Sacramento in 1854. By the time the two houses of the legislature rose on this spring day, at the conclusion of their fourth session since California had become a state, the nine-member Senate Judiciary Committee had delivered its findings on Tom Burdue's petition for restitution of $4000.

'To grant the prayer of the petitioner would establish a precedent which, if carried out in all cases of the kind, would more than exhaust the entire revenue of the State,' declared the Judiciary Committee in its written finding. 'We know of no legislative precedent for such appropriation. The most that has been done was to refund fines illegally collected from innocent parties, leaving them responsible for their own expenses. In Society, it too often happens that the innocent are wrongly accused of crime. This is their misfortune, and government has now power to relieve them.'

The Committee denied Tom's petition. What's more, it scolded him for having the gall to apply for restitution in the first place. 'He should rejoice that the laws have afforded that protection to him when wrongfully accused, rather than seek remuneration for his expenses from the government whose justice has protected him from ignominious death.'[213] In other words, Tom should be grateful to be alive, and leave it at that.

Many years later, US legal commentators would declare the Judiciary Committee wrong in its determination. The state's laws had not protected Tom when wrongfully accused. And, irony of ironies, it had not been government that had protected him from ignominious death, it was the unlawful and otherwise abhorrent Committee of Vigilance that had saved Tom's life, by bringing in Governor McDougall to hear James Stuart's confession and prompt the pardon which McDougall wrote for Tom just two days before he was due to be executed.

So, Tom Burdue was denied financial restitution. From this point, he disappeared from history. One colourful, fanciful and inaccurate California book had him playing cards at the end of a San Francisco wharf when last seen. Perhaps that was factual, perhaps not. What happened to Tom next is uncertain. What is certain is that within eight years he was dead, with his wife Elen back in Northumberland, England and listed as a widow.

There is no record of Tom's death in California, Australia or Britain. But, many San Francisco records were destroyed in the 1906 earthquake, making his death in San Francisco an unrecorded possibility. In his memorandum to the state legislature, he mentioned that his time behind bars had damaged his health, and possibly this resulted in his early death. It seems that his youngest child, the unnamed baby thrust into his arms by Elen during the February 1851 mob trial, also perished in California before 1861. Elen's three elder children were with her back in Northumberland by 1861, but not a younger child.[214] Equally, there is no record of Joe and Mary Windred having any contact with Tom or Elen Burdue after 1851.

While Tom Burdue lost the battle to start his life over again, Joe Windred did not. Joe had once before started over, after the wrongful conviction in the Barker affair and his years as a convict in Van Diemen's Land. Like a Hawkesbury River gum tree, Joe was made of tough stuff. Just as he had pulled himself up from the depths in earlier times, he could do it again.

25

THE RACEHORSE OWNER

Friday, December 16, 1853. Bathurst, New South Wales

JOE'S FORTUNES WERE SLOWLY improving. In October, he had gone into business as a stock agent. In addition to supplying brother Jack's cattle needs, he'd offered for public sale 400 to 600 head of cattle then running at Narromine, west of Dubbo. Joe told potential clients he was prepared to drive those cattle into Bathurst or as far south as Port Phillip in Victoria. To date, he'd sold just sixty head, but that sale was his entree into the competitive stock trade.

Horseracing was meanwhile proving a lucrative sideline. In March, Ariosto had won two races for Joe at Orange, out west. With just a population of twenty-six at the beginning of 1851, Orange was growing fast, and its inaugural annual races were a statement of its intent to become a town of note. Joe took away £32 in prize money, and next month entered Ariosto in the Albert Stakes at Bathurst's annual races. There was a catch to the Albert Stakes. The winner had to offer his horse up for sale after the race. Joe still sent Ariosto to the start line, and the grey won the £33 prize for him. To Joe's relief, no one bid for Ariosto; the opinion in horseflesh circles was that Ariosto was now past his prime.

With Christmas looming, sportsman Joe entered a gruelling harness match race. Over a distance of twenty-seven kilometres from Roberts' Inn at Green Swamp to his uncle John Dargin's Coach and

Horses Inn at Kelso, on the Sydney Road outskirts of Bathurst, the race involved a stake of £50 each, winner take all. Joe had trained a bay mare in harness, while his opponent came to the race with a chestnut horse. A crowd of drinkers stood outside the Coach and Horses, a long, single-storey brick building on the Sydney side of the Macquarie River, and raised their tankards with a cheer as the first horse and driver came in sight. It was not even a contest. 'The mare had it all her own way,' *Bell's Life in Sydney* would report. Joe won easily, taking home the £50 prize.[215]

Saturday, September 16, 1854. Bathurst, New South Wales

Joe was riding Ariosto down Bathurst's Durham Street, with his thoughts on the lot of land he'd purchased in the town just two days previously for £75. Ariosto's winnings had contributed to Joe's savings for that plot, where he intended building a new home for Mary, Isabel and himself. As for the money to build that home, it looked as if Ariosto would not be contributing much to that. The so-called judges of horseflesh seemed to have been proven right. Joe had taken Ariosto to numerous race meetings in the autumn, and while his now-famed grey gelding had won at the Hawkesbury Races and again taken out the Albert Stakes at Bathurst, he'd been defeated at every other start. Joe's brother Jack had even less luck, running three horses in various meetings, with just a single win for a £5 prize.

Sudden screams jerked Joe from his thoughts. Ahead, a bread cart had been standing outside Dupen's Bakery with a large, heavy dray drawn by two horses close by, also stationary. Two young children sat on the dray's bench seat, while their father, the drayman, was busy in a nearby shop. For no apparent reason, the baker's horse shied, and bolted down the street, taking the baker's cart with it and sending bread in all directions. The baker's cart spooked the big dray horses, and they also set off, in wild panic, taking the dray and its young passengers with it. The children screamed. Women on the footpath screamed.

Joe, kicking his grey to the gallop, set off in chase. The dray had gathered a furious pace, with its horses careering blindly, their erratic course and speed 'threatening every now and again to overturn the dray'. But Joe, aboard his racehorse Ariosto, was soon abreast of the dray. The two children, being jolted and tossed about on the dray's hard wooden seat, looked over at Joe with terrified expressions.

'Hold on with all your strength!' Joe yelled to the pair, before urging Ariosto to greater speed.

Once Joe had drawn level with the charging horses, he leaned Ariosto in against them, guiding them around the next corner and up a cross-street, then gradually wheeled them into an empty allotment. With fences looming up in front of them, the two horses came to a halt. The *Sydney Morning Herald* reported the drama the following Tuesday. 'How the matter would have terminated, it is difficult to say,' said the paper, 'had not Mr Windred, mounted upon Ariosto, happened to be convenient.' But, it was certain, the 'two children very narrowly escaped being either seriously injured or killed'.[216]

Joe and Ariosto were heroes.

Thursday, May 31, 1855. Homebush, New South Wales

The crowd roared, and the Australia Plate, main event of the prestigious Australian Jockey Club's Homebush Races for 1855, was run, and won. In the crowd watching the race were Joe and Jack Windred, racehorse owners both.

Joe had retired Ariosto from racing, and was now using him exclusively as his saddle horse. But Joe himself had not retired from racing. He had acquired two more racehorses, Ranger and Comet, and during the summer and autumn had run them at various meetings around New South Wales. In January, he and Jack had returned to Sofala, to compete in the annual meeting which Jack had helped inaugurate when Joe was hiding out at the gold diggings. The Sofala Races had grown in stature, and so too had their prize money. But neither Joe nor Jack was able to ride away with a single prize. Still, as with all meetings, the post-race celebrations were exuberant; at 'a first rate dinner' at the Sofala Inn, 'toasts, songs and glasses circulated until the dawn of morning'.[217]

At the Bathurst Races in April, Ranger and Comet had both won for Joe. Chestnut gelding Comet was particularly impressive, winning a £75 race and attracting heavy betting support. This success had encouraged Joe to venture for the first time to Homebush, home of Australia's premier horseracing meeting. Over the three days of the Homebush Races, Joe entered Comet in the £100 Queen's Plate and the £100 Australia Plate. His runner attracted no interest from punters, and won no prizes. The star of this meeting was Cooramin, a horse Joe had seen win at Windsor earlier in the season. By Plover from Dudu, an elegant, six-year-old brown stallion from Bukkulla, near Inverell, Cooramin had turned heads by winning the AJC St Ledger at Homebush two years earlier. Now, rated by aficionados one of the three best racehorses around, he turned Joe Windred's head as he left Joe's Comet in his wake and won the Australia Plate.

Now here, thought Joe, was a racehorse! But it would take a king's ransom to acquire a horse like that. Or, a lot of luck.

26

A WEDDING RING, A HORSE THIEF AND A GOLD STRIKE

Saturday, January 19, 1856. Sydney, New South Wales

JOE AND MARY COULD not legally marry while Mary's first husband, James Walwyn, was still alive. But Mary had come by an old report from a London newspaper. Dated December 1852, it briefly told of the death of James Walwyn in West London. This meant that Joe and Mary could wed after all.

Now, on this January day, at Scots Presbyterian Church in Margaret Street, Sydney, the Reverend John Dougall of St Andrews Church married the couple. It was a discreet affair, for, as far as Joe and Mary's friends and neighbours in Bathurst were concerned, the couple had been married since 1848 – likely the year they'd consummated their relationship at Windsor. Joe's best man was his father, Joe senior, who came in from Windsor for the occasion. Mary's maid of honour was Isabella Risley, a Sydney friend who had herself gone through a hurried wedding ceremony, to William Risley, in this same church ten years before, when she was pregnant.

Mary had achieved her greatest dream, to formalise her union with Joe. Joe was still working on his dreams.

Friday, May 2, 1856. Windsor, New South Wales

Just when Joe was beginning to think that 1856 was his year, things began to turn sour.

'What do you mean?' he said to the Windsor police constable. 'The horses are stolen?'

Twelve months had passed since Joe had watched Cooramin win at Homebush. So disillusioned had he been by Comet's defeat, Joe had sold both Comet and Ranger. There was another reason for selling his two racehorses. He needed the money. In the past year, Joe had briefly gone into partnership with another stock dealer named Austin. But Austin had cheated him out of hundreds of pounds. Joe had sued Austin, settling out of court for £100. The £100 had recently been paid to Joe's solicitor in Bathurst, but the solicitor's clerk had stolen the money. The clerk had been tried and convicted, but Joe's money was never recovered.

While Joe was having a financial struggle, his younger brothers William and Jack were thriving. Since March, William had been licensee of Sydney's Whitehaven Castle, on the corner of Goulburn and Sussex streets. Jack was now also a publican, this year taking over the licence of the Coach and Horses at Bathurst, where his uncle John Dargin had made his fortune. The boys' mother had moved out to Bathurst to help Jack. What was more, Jack was engaged to be married, to a Sydney girl.

Joe would also have loved to follow the family trade of pub-keeping. But, struggling financially, he couldn't afford a lease on a public house, let alone the cost of fitting out a pub as he would want, as a haven for sports lovers like himself. And, would not his criminal record prevent him from being awarded a publican's licence by the licensing magistrates? He had thought that horseracing might help him financially, but that dream, like his youthful dream of success as a prize fighter and trainer, had come to nothing.

He still followed the horses, and it had been while in Windsor for this year's Hawkesbury Races that he had heard that local auctioneer George Seymour was auctioning off thirty-seven horses and foals for William Scott Ross, nephew of a local dignitary and political candidate.

According to Seymour, devil-may-care young Mr Ross seemed ambivalent about the price he received from the auction, and would not even be attending. Auctioneer Seymour was the same George Seymour who, fifteen years before, had employed as his bookkeeper old Frederick Lahrbush, who in turn had paid Joe's nemesis, the vile 'Fagin' of Windsor, Henry Nichols, for the attentions of his young sister-in-law Jane. When Joe turned up at the Windsor auction the previous Wednesday, he'd succeeded in buying three fillies for £11 and 10 shillings; a bargain. He would be able to resell them for double that amount back in Bathurst.

This morning, Joe had seen Mr Ross receiving his £201 proceeds of the sale from auctioneer Seymour. Ross was a surprising sight for the nephew of a gentleman: 'a young man of rather wild appearance, with an exuberant beard'.[218] Ross had then mounted up and ridden out of town, heading toward Parramatta. Now, as Joe went to collect his three fillies from Seymour, he was met by Constable William Grainger of the Windsor Police, who told Joe that the horses he had purchased were on a list just received detailing horses stolen from three properties on the Paterson River. Two of the three victims of the theft were Charles Reynolds and William Zuill, and, sure enough, two of the horses that Joe bought had the brand 'CR' on one shoulder, while the third was branded 'WZ'.

Joe said that he had seen Ross riding out of town a little earlier, and urged giving chase. Constable Grainger agreed, and promptly deputised both Joe and John Wood, another victim of the auction, as special constables, arming them with loaded revolvers. How ironic that, just five years before, Windsor's chief constable had been all for arresting Joe and sending him back to California. Joe mounted Ariosto and joined the others as they headed out after William Scott Ross at the trot. He was soon way out in front. 'I was better mounted than the other two pursuers,' Joe would later say, 'and pushed on ahead of them.'[219]

In his eagerness to catch the horse thief, Joe soon left his companions behind as he galloped down the Parramatta road. The man he was chasing was not William Scott Ross. Unbeknownst to Joe, he was a brazen young criminal by the name of Johnny Garbutt, member of a gang of very active horse thieves which included his brother James and their uncle Fred Ward. This same Fred Ward, later in his career, would gain lasting bushranging fame under the name Captain Thunderbolt. On April 25, Garbutt, Ward and an aboriginal youth had boldly ridden into Windsor, where, sitting drinking on a pub veranda, they had sent for auctioneer Seymour. Because Ward had grown up in the Windsor district and ran the risk of being recognised, he kept his hat pulled down over his eyes and let Garbutt do the talking with the auctioneer, in the inn's parlour. Garbutt, a confident and convincing liar, had arranged for the April 30 auction of the stolen horses.

Eleven miles from Windsor, at a point where the road passed through thick bushland, Joe overtook Garbutt, alias Ross, who was riding nonchalantly along.

'Good morning,' said Joe, drawing Ariosto up alongside the fair-haired, thickly bearded young man.

'Good morning,' said Garbutt with a smile.

'Would you not be Mr Ross?' Joe asked.

'That I am.'

Joe promptly reached over with his left hand and grabbed Garbutt's reins, at the same time drawing the revolver from his belt and pointing it at Garbutt. 'I'm a special constable,' Joe announced, 'and you're my prisoner.'

'What for?' Garbutt responded, feigning complete innocence.

'Because the horses you sold in Windsor were stolen,' Joe advised.

The young man's blue eyes widened. 'Really? Who claimed them as stolen?'

'I couldn't say. There are other constables behind me, and they will take charge of you.'

Joe turned Garbutt's horse around, and they set off back toward Windsor, with Joe beside and a little behind Garbutt's horse, keeping his pistol trained on the thief.

'Did you buy some of the horses?' Garbutt asked as they rode.

'I did,' Joe replied.

'How many?'

'Three.'

'What price did you pay for them?'

'Not a heavy price.'

'I tell you what,' said Garbutt, 'I'll pay you £150 if you'll let me go.'

Joe shook his head. 'Even if I wanted to, the other constables are very close behind, and you wouldn't get far.'

They continued riding a little way further, until Garbutt suddenly reined in his horse.

'I'm going no further!' Garbutt announced. Reaching to his belt, he removed a money bag and threw it onto the road. The bag landed with a heavy clink.

'What are you doing?' Joe demanded.

'There's your money.'

'I told you . . .'

Garbutt threw one leg over his horse and slipped to the ground.

'If you run, I'll shoot you,' Joe warned.

'Well, shoot away, Mr Special Constable!' said Garbutt with a grin, before turning his back and dashing toward the post and rail fence that bordered the road.[220]

Joe lifted his revolver, and, cocking it, took aim. Garbutt was bending, and climbing between two rails. But Joe Windred was not a cold-blooded killer. There was no way he could shoot a man in the back. Within seconds, Garbutt was through the fence and disappearing into the bush. Cursing, Joe dropped to the ground and took up the money bag. It would later be found to contain £51. Garbutt had a little more on him, and had hidden the rest of the auction haul for Ward to find.

After stuffing the money bag under his belt, Joe tethered the man's horse, removed the roadside fence's top rail, then remounted. Taking Ariosto a little way back, he then urged him forward. Ariosto cleared the fence at the jump, and Joe went in search of the runaway in the bushland.

Garbutt managed to evade Joe, and by the time Joe returned to where he had left the man's horse, Grainger and Wood had arrived on the scene. It would soon be dark, so, with Grainger continuing on to Parramatta to warn the police there to be on the lookout for Garbutt, Joe and Wood returned to Windsor with the captured horse and the £51. That evening, when Constable Grainger reached Parramatta, there was a train standing at the railway station, preparing to set off for Sydney. Just to be sure, and taking a lantern, Grainger searched the train. Sitting in a first-class carriage was none other than Johnny Garbutt.

Garbutt would be tried, and Joe Windred would appear in court – on the witness stand, not in the dock, for once. Garbutt would be sentenced to five years with hard labour. Fred Ward would also be captured, receiving a ten-year sentence. Ward would escape from Sydney's Cockatoo Island Prison seven years later, and commence his bushranging career as Captain Thunderbolt.

Joe Windred now had a colourful tale to tell patrons at his brothers' pubs. But, he still lost out as a result of the episode. The three fillies Joe had paid for were returned to their owners, and not all the proceeds of the horse sale were recovered.

Saturday, July 5, 1856. Bathurst, New South Wales

There was another Windred family wedding, this time in Bathurst. Jack Windred was marrying Elizabeth Kearey, daughter of John Kearey, owner, since 1840, of a successful carriage-building business in Pitt Street, Sydney. The wedding, an intimate affair, was held at the Manse, residence of Presbyterian minister Reverend James Laughton on Commonwealth Street. Jack's mother and father were there, and his in-laws, as well as Joe, who was his best man, and Mary and Isabel, plus Jack's other siblings.

Inevitably, at the wedding reception that followed at the Coach and Horses, the conversation turned to the news that had been the talk of the town since first appearing in the *Bathurst Free Press* on Wednesday. There had been a new gold strike, at Stoney Creek, not far from Bathurst. Even as the Windred clan celebrated Jack and Elizabeth's nuptials, parties of gold-seekers were passing the pub's door, heading for the new diggings. Some drove carts, some rode, some were on foot. The *Sydney Morning Herald* would report that a party of carpenters took eight days to walk from Sydney, across the Blue Mountains, to the Stoney Creek diggings.

The Stoney Creek strike had been accidental. One wet June night, local drunk 'Bothered Harry' had kicked the ground beside Stockyard Creek, a small tributary to Stoney Creek, and unearthed a golden nugget weighing 28 ounces; just over half a kilogram. Taking the nugget to the nearest pub, Harry had shouted drinks for the house. Next morning, when Harry woke up, and sobered up, he went back to where he'd stumbled on the nugget, to find three other men there ahead of him, digging furiously. Harry and those other first diggers tried to keep the find a secret, but word seeped out, and with it claims that numerous other nuggets had been found, including one weighing 54 ounces and worth a good £200.

As the Windred brothers drank champagne and talked and laughed about the gold waiting to be found just a few hours away, Joe looked at Mary. In the days that followed, he would make Mary a proposition. If she agreed, he would go to the Stoney Creek diggings and dig for gold. For one month. No longer. After their experience in the Californian goldfields, if anyone knew what geological conditions to look for, it was Joe. Meanwhile, Mary and Isabel would remain in Bathurst. If Joe was successful, his gold finds would set them up for the future. And he would be able to finance his dream, that of owning the best racehorse in Australia. Despite her misgivings after their horrific experiences chasing gold in California, Mary agreed.

Wednesday, July 16, 1856. Stoney Creek Diggings, New South Wales

Around Joe, twelve hundred damp diggers were spread through gullies and flats for thirty kilometres. Joe had chosen the location of his claim with care. Many men, expecting gold to be lying on the ground, were literally only scratching the surface. Others were digging holes as deep as two metres, only for them to fill with rainwater. Many gold-seekers were standing, or sitting, shivering with hands in pockets and looking at the inhospitable wet ground with despair written on their faces.

Rain and mud were constant companions. It was a particularly bitter winter. When Joe made his way to the diggings with a cart-horse and heavily loaded cart, it had been a nightmarish struggle through rain, and snow, over roads that had become quagmires. On his way he'd passed drenched, dispirited young men already heading home after only digging for a few days before giving up. Still, glowing stories of the discovery of large nuggets met Joe on arrival. 'A man from Orange pounced upon one of 44 ounces,' he was told, 'and a Chinaman another of 13 ounces.'[221] On the other side of the ledger, Bothered Harry had already worked out his claim, and the third man to start work here after Harry's initial find had gone home with just 10 ounces of gold. The man working alongside Bothered Harry's claim hadn't found a thing.

Joe had come with all the mining equipment he would need, plus a large tent, 20 feet by 10 (6 x 3 metres). He had thought that, if worse came to worst, he might use the big tent as a shop or pub. But others had already thought of that. 'Of stores and public houses,' Joe wrote home from the diggings, 'there are so many now open that it would be undesirable for anyone to speculate further in that way.' So, Joe chose his ground with care, and quietly dug and sieved. 'The number of fresh arrivals increases daily,' he wrote, 'many foolishly expecting to find gold almost without labour. And on the day of their arrival come totally unprepared to work. Others, from accounts they hear on the roads and on the ground, never even get to work.'[222]

Wednesday, July 23, 1851. Bathurst, New South Wales

Joe had ridden back into Bathurst on Tuesday, with gold nuggets in his saddlebag. For, after digging for just a short while, he'd struck gold. Spending the night at home with Mary and Isabel, he discreetly sold his finds to locals. On other goldfields at other times, Joe had seen that some diggers who broadcast news of their success had attracted the attention of thieves, so he was determined to keep his success under his hat. Now, he heard that a local businessman named Wise was telling all and sundry that the previous day he'd purchased a gold nugget weighing 9½ ounces from Joe, for £35. Unhappy that news of his strike was out, Joe mounted up and headed back to the diggings.

Tuesday, July 29, 1856. Stoney Creek Diggings, New South Wales

Joe, back at his claim, learned that the *Bathurst Free Press* had told of his nugget sale to the obviously loudmouthed Mr Wise. This prompted Joe to sit down in his tent that night and pen a letter to the paper's editor, to play down his own success and discourage others from making their way out here to the goldfields. 'A sad affair occurred here last night,' he wrote, 'which terminated on the death of one person, and may possibly prove fatal to another. A young man named George Bansley, who has been married but four months, and has been on this field but a few days, had reason to suspect his wife's fidelity, went home and cut her throat, and his own afterwards.' Bansley was expected to survive, and face a murder charge.

242   MISTAKEN IDENTITY

'Another poor fellow who was unwell for two days died last night and was buried today.'

This death rate was reminiscent of the California diggings, yet the atmosphere here was less threatening, even if it was rambunctious. 'Owing to the want of any Commissioner or police,' Joe continued, 'society here is in a very disorderly state, many employing themselves on Sunday gambling the entire day. The diggers are, however, very honest among themselves, very few cases of robbery having as yet taken place.'

Joe had a piece of advice for prospective prospectors. 'It is perfectly ridiculous for anyone to come to these diggings unless he is prepared to give them a fair trial, say, a month at least.'[223]

Sunday, August 24, 1856. Bathurst, New South Wales

Keeping his word to Mary, Joe put in his month at the Stoney Creek diggings, plus a few extra weeks for good measure, then upped stakes. He had just returned home. It was evening now, and he had unhitched and stabled his carthorse, and was walking wearily up the path to the rear of his house when he noticed, next door, someone skulking beneath the bedroom window of his brother Jack and his new bride.

Determined to find out what the fellow was up to, Joe set down his bags and hurried around his house to Jack's front door. Like all country people, Jack left his front door unlocked, so Joe went in through it, then, 'gliding through the house as nimbly as a greyhound', as he himself would later relate, slipped out the back door. He pounced on the prowler before the man 'had time to look about him or to bless himself'.

'Who are you?' Joe demanded. 'And what's your business here?'

The man jumped up, staggered back, and squealed, 'My name's Mr Paul Pry, if you wish to call upon me.'

To which Joe replied by boxing the prowler around the ear. The prowler turned to run, enabling Joe to plant a boot on his rear end, speeding the man's departure.[224] Joe then returned to his own house, to be welcomed home by Mary and Isabel, and to share the news with them that in the final tally-up he had done rather well at the Stoney Creek gold diggings. Very well. Joe had struck it rich.

Thursday, September 18, 1856. Liverpool, New South Wales

Call it a late honeymoon. It was 12.30 p.m., and Joe and Mary were in pride of place in the grandstand at the Liverpool Racecourse, south-west of Sydney. Joe had just bought himself a racehorse, the famous Cooramin. The sleek brown horse had experienced an outstanding season through the first half of the year, at Windsor twice beating favourite and great rival Veno, the champion Sydney gelding, winning at Parramatta, and at Homebush in May taking the AJC's prestigious Queen's Plate. After returning from Stoney Creek in August, Joe had made Cooramin's then-owner Thomas O'Shaughnessy an offer. The amount was undisclosed, but would have run to several hundred pounds. Joe, now the proud owner of one of the best racehorses in Australia, had become a racing identity.

These Liverpool Races were Cooramin's first outing in Joe Windred's colours. And the first race of this third day brought the largest crowd ever seen at the Liverpool course. Hundreds arrived from Sydney by train to join the locals to witness the meeting's Railway Cup, a special three-mile event put on to celebrate the opening of the new Liverpool Railway. To compete for a silver cup worth £100 and containing 100 gold sovereigns, the field included the three top horses in New South Wales – Cooramin, his great rival Veno, and Akbar, an imported English stallion. Having paid his £10 entry fee, and employed one of the best professional jockeys in Australia, Mick O'Brien, Joe could almost taste the victory champagne as the runners lined up.

And they were off! The *Sydney Morning Herald* would report: 'On first passing the stand, a sheet could have covered the field, so closely did the horses lay together. Veno then took the lead, and kept it, with Cooramin following hard.'[225] After three closely contested circuits of the course, Veno won by a length. Second prize wasn't the wedding present that Joe was hoping for, but with good grace he took a sip of champagne from the Railway Cup when Veno's owner, George Rowe, proffered it, and wished Rowe good health. *Bell's Life in Sydney* concluded its report of the race, 'the running of Mr Windred's horse sadly disappointing his admirers'.[226] It also sadly disappointed Cooramin's new owner.

It was not the prize money that interested Joe. A life of bitter and unjust defeats had made victory especially sweet for him, on the few occasions he was permitted to taste it. Money he had aplenty now, courtesy of his gold finds at Stoney Creek; finds that he had managed to mostly keep confidential. Not tens of thousands of pounds worth, but enough to change his life, and Mary's life. Joe now filled his Bathurst house with the best furniture, crockery and cutlery, and with a fine Thompson piano from England for Isabel, who was learning to play. He decorated the walls with paintings of racehorses and hunting dogs, as befitted the home of a sportsman, and prints depicting recent Crimean War events, especially the suicidal Charge of the Light Brigade of two years earlier, with its dashing cavalry horses.

In October, Joe would pit Cooramin against Veno again, at the Camden Races last meeting of the year.

27

THE PRICE OF SUCCESS

Tuesday, January 13, 1857. Sydney, New South Wales

THE CROWDED BATHURST COACH pulled into the yard behind the pub that served as its Sydney terminus, and Joe Windred stepped down then helped his wife and thirteen-year-old stepdaughter to the ground. All three looked haggard. It was not the journey that had done this to them, nor Cooramin's loss to Veno, again, at the Camden Races the previous October. Joe no longer cared about horseracing. For, in December, his brother Jack had been diagnosed with a virulent form of cancer.

Jack's doctors had suggested that he stay in Sydney. Not that he would receive better treatment there. There was no reliable treatment for cancer in these times. It was because Jack's new wife, Elizabeth, was expecting the couple's first child, which was due in April, and was experiencing a difficult pregnancy. By staying with Elizabeth's parents at their Pitt Street home, Jack would enable Elizabeth's mother to care for both Elizabeth and himself.

On hearing Jack's news, Joe had decided to sell up and go into Sydney to be with his little brother. He, Mary and Isabel would stay with William and his wife Sarah at the Whitehaven Castle, for however long it took. In December, Joe had put all the contents of his Bathurst home up for auction, even his prized racehorse paintings, his gold diggings tent and his caged canary. Mary had asked if they could keep Isabel's piano, perhaps storing it at the Coach and Horses, which the boys' mother was running in Jack's absence. But in the end, Joe even put that up for sale, promising to later buy Isabel an even better piano. The auction had taken place the previous Saturday, at their Piper Street house. Now, Joe and his family had arrived in Sydney to be close to Jack and do what they could to help.

Every day, Joe, Mary and Isabel would walk around to Pitt Street to spend time with Jack, who, increasingly weak, would soon be confined to his bed. While Mary helped care for Elizabeth, Joe would share the newspapers' sporting columns with Jack, and the brothers would talk about boxing and racehorses, as they recalled their youth together and their joint exploits in the ring and on the turf. Joe and brother William were close; Joe had been William's protector, virtually bringing him up when they were infants at Port Macquarie and Windsor. But Jack was special to Joe. Butchers, boxers and horse-lovers together, Joe and Jack always had a unique bond.

In one of the strange ironies and coincidences that attended the life of Joe Windred, on this same January day, John Gough, his wife and daughter visited bushrangers Fred Ward and James Garbutt at Sydney's Cockatoo Island Prison. The Goughs, who had arrived back in Sydney in November 1851, were related to Ward and the Garbutts, the same men Joe had helped convict of horse-stealing.

Tuesday, March 24, 1857. Sydney, New South Wales

After a short and severe illness, Jack Windred was dead, at just twenty-nine years of age. Joe Windred, like the rest of his family, was shattered. Jack's wife, Elizabeth, would give birth to a daughter just weeks later. In June, that frail daughter, Mary Ann Sophia Windred, would also pass away.

Wednesday, December 16, 1857. Sydney, New South Wales

Trying to forget Jack's death, Joe had been throwing himself into life, and throwing money around. In April, he had taken Cooramin to the Hawkesbury Races, where he was twice beaten by his nemesis, Veno. At April's Liverpool Races, Cooramin was beaten by the unfancied Eureka. But, at Homebush in May, Cooramin had won the £100 City Plate, beating Akbar by two lengths.

In July, Joe took a step in a new career direction. On his daily visits to Jack at the Keareys' 290 Pitt Street home, sometimes also putting his head in George Pickering's door at the *Bell's Life in Sydney* office across the road, Joe would pass a large, vacant pub at 256 Pitt Street. Between Market and Park streets, it was adjacent to Tattersall's, hostelry to the rural elite when they visited Sydney. It was as if this rundown, boarded-up place were calling out to Joe every time he passed, for it was named, of all things, the Gold Digger's Arms. Joe began to see potential here, for a pub of his own. Out at Bathurst, his mother, using her de facto name of Windred now, was taking over Jack's lease at the Coach and Horses. William, meanwhile, had been making a small fortune in his Sydney pubs for years. Why couldn't Joe and Mary make a go of a pub of their own?

Flush with thousands of pounds from his gold finds and his Bathurst household sale, Joe signed a three-year lease with building owner George Hill of Surry Hills, and applied for a publican's licence. But he would have to wait for the magistrates to conduct their customary inquiries into the hundreds of licensing applications received, and that could take months. Renting a house at 4 Pitt Street, and buying Isabel her new piano, Joe confidently began making plans for his pub.

Joe intended renaming the pub the Sportsman's Arms, and was determined to make it the centre of sporting life for Sydney's drinking public. As a first step, he'd purchased a painting on show at the Fine Art Exhibition at the Sydney Mechanics School of Arts. By noted colonial artist Joseph Fowles, it was of his racehorse Cooramin. This painting would have pride of place in the bar of the Sportsman's Arms. As for Cooramin himself, Joe this month put him out to stud. And, just as his horse was retiring from racing, so too was Joe. Running a pub would allow no time for flitting around country race meetings.

On this December day, the licensing magistrates' decision was published; Joe's application was approved. With great excitement, he, Mary and Isabel immediately began the redecoration and refit of the Gold Digger's Arms, to create the Sportsman's Arms.

Thursday, December 30, 1858. Sydney, New South Wales

Joe was celebrating a successful year. During that period, the Sportsman's Arms had become a rip-roaring success. As Joe had planned, it was now Sydney's sporting headquarters. He spared no expense in fitting it out. Prints of boxers, racehorses and hunting dogs joined the celebrated Cooramin painting on his walls. The eight bedrooms were in regular use by country visitors from Bathurst, Windsor, Richmond and Camden, where Joe had celebrity status as a former boxer and racehorse owner. The Sportsman's Arms offered luncheon daily, with Mary in charge of kitchen and dining room. The noisy bar overflowed with sportsmen and their fans. With professional boxing again on the rise, local champion John Perry made Joe's bar his daily headquarters, and negotiated all his fight contracts here. Acquiring a white bullterrier as the Sportsman's Arms' mascot, Joe gave the dog pride of place in the bar. Adding to the profitability, the pub was now booking agent and starting point for Samuel Jenner's Royal Mail coach line on the Sydney to Windsor run.

'To the Sporting Public,' Joe advertised in the press: 'J. W. need say no more than that all newcomers may depend upon finding everything as it should be at the Sportsman's Arms.'[227] Joe, now a Sydney identity, was in his element. Not only was he enjoying playing the convivial host, he was making money. Lots of it. Emulating brother William, he donated rare wildlife specimens to the Australian Museum and Botanic Gardens. A lover of exotic birds since childhood, he could now afford to keep rare bronze-wing pigeons and silver and golden pheasants in cages behind the pub, and display a beautiful rose-coloured cockatoo in the bar. The fact that he'd been fined ten shillings, plus court costs, for opening the Sportsman's Arms on Christmas Day was a minor distraction. Joe's future seemed assured.

Friday, December 16, 1859. Sydney, New South Wales

In financial terms, Joe's second year at the Sportsman's Arms had proved just as successful as the first. And, a member of the Sydney Poultry Club, he was winning first prize with his birds at their shows. Meanwhile, he'd acquired his father's half share of the thirty-acre Peninsula Farm at Windsor. Here, where Cooramin and the now-retired Ariosto were running, there was a barn, stables and apple orchard. Here, too, Joe grew vegetables, including a giant 200-pound (90-kilogram) pumpkin that he displayed in the Sportsman's Arms bar. Joe had also become quite the businessman, taking a share in a harness-making business and a butchery at Windsor and a blacksmith's shop at Camden, fifty kilometres south-west of Sydney, as well as purchasing a fourteen-seat drag, an open carriage, to hire out.

But he'd had problems too. In July 1858, Joe had ejected gamblers from his saloon bar, sending them into the yard outside. They were playing 'three-up', tossing a trio of threepenny bits and betting on their fall. It would eventuate that one of the players was cheating, using a 'grey', or double-sided coin, and this resulted in a legal case in which Joe gave evidence that helped bring a conviction. The following February, Joe's bullterrier had been stolen from the bar. In March, his much-admired cockatoo was pilfered, and then two of his prize pigeons were allowed to escape. Someone had it in for Joe, and it was likely this was related to the gambling affair, although nothing was ever proven.

In May, Joe had been convicted in the Police Court of having a gambling implement on his licensed premises. Foolishly, especially considering his aversion to gambling, he had brought a toy roulette wheel into his bar, and permitted patrons to use it. Joe had been fined 10 shillings, plus £3 and 3 shillings costs. In the end, Joe had profited from the affair, successfully suing the publisher of the *Era* newspaper for £100 damages for libelling him, after the *Era* reported the case under the inaccurate headline of 'A Charge of Fraud'.

But then, in September, Joe had again been fined for trading out of hours. This was his third conviction as a publican. The licensing court rarely gave wrongdoers much leeway, and Joe now worried that he would be considered an habitual offender and his licence would not be renewed come the end of the year. So rather than wait for bad news, he'd immediately put the pub's lease, contents and goodwill up for sale while he still had something to sell. But no one would come at his high price. Keeping at the pub trade, he raked in even more money, with the Sportsman's Arms now also becoming the booking office for the American Coaching Line, which served all of western New South Wales. With Christmas and licensing court decisions looming, like a condemned man awaiting word of his execution date Joe waited for the court to bring the curtain down on his career as a publican.

28

ANOTHER NARROW ESCAPE

Monday, July 22, 1861. Lambing Flat, New South Wales

WITH A LOADED REVOLVER in his belt, and prepared to use it, Joe planted his feet as he faced off against a mob of angry miners.

'No!' he declared. 'Back off!'

Joe was still running the Sportsman's Arms, but it was a different Sportsman's Arms, in a very different place. A very dangerous place. Up until July 1860, when the lease had run out, Joe had continued to run his 'celebrated hostelry' in Pitt Street without anyone making an offer for lease or goodwill. 'Mr Windred, who is about retiring into the country,' said Sydney auctioneer Robert Muriel, 'is retiring from business.' Muriel auctioned off the pub's entire contents 'cheap' that June, taking what he could get for Joe.[228] Simultaneously, Joe sold all his other business interests. With Joe taking Mary and Isabel to live in a rented rural house at Camden, the lease and licence of Sydney's Sportsman's Arms were taken over by one of Joe's former patrons, boxer and 'champion of the lightweights' John Sullivan, who announced his retirement from the ring while also advertising 'private lessons in pugilism daily, at any hour'.[229]

Come Joe's thirty-ninth birthday on April 27, 1861, he was still at Camden, and bored stiff. From newspaper reports, he'd been learning about New South Wales' newest goldfield, at Lambing Flat, 150 kilometres south-west of Bathurst. Since the previous year,

Lambing Flat, a former sheep run, had been attracting tens of thousands of gold-seekers, including many Chinese. As in California, the Chinese had become widely unpopular on the Australian goldfields. The Chinese, by keeping to their ethnic group, working as a team, tolerating primitive conditions and speaking their own language, alienated European miners, who were suspicious of them and envied their discipline and success.

The previous June, white miners had rioted against the Chinese, killing two and injuring ten. The press had played this down. In December, Sydney's *Empire*, which was no longer under the stewardship of Henry Parkes after he'd been forced to sell the paper in 1858, had declared the reported riots a fiction, stating, incorrectly, 'No Chinese have been killed, or even attacked.'[230] This past January, forty miners had attacked and driven away 200 Chinese, but this had been passed off in the press as inconsequential. And it certainly did not deter Joe Windred. It truly seems that he could not resist the lure of gold.

Deciding that there was an opportunity to make a handsome profit by opening a pub at the goldfields, calling it the Sportsman's Arms, and trading on the fame of his original establishment, Joe somehow talked Mary into the move. But she was able to wring one promise from Joe – to stand above the gold-seeking madness and focus totally on being a publican, without raising a shovel in the quest for gold. So, Joe, Mary and the now eighteen-year-old Isabel had relocated to Lambing Flat, on Joe's fourth venture to a goldfield.

By the last week of June, they had staked out a standard mining claim, 120 feet by 60 (36 x 18 metres), on flat ground above a gully in the Alandale area, scene of the latest gold finds and called New Rush by the miners. There, on the only real street, the Windreds built themselves a rough and ready hotel with timber and canvas, the new Sportsman's Arms. But its location was not ideal. 'At present, the main street of the New Rush is about twenty inches deep in mud,' Sydney's *Empire* would report on July 25, and was 'most inconveniently narrow, in some places just wide enough to allow two teams to pass'.

But Joe Windred never did anything by halves. 'I have gone heart and soul into the matter,' he had written the previous year.[231] For Joe, it was all or nothing, and, full of optimism, he had advertised in the *Sydney Morning Herald* on June 29: 'Sportsman's Arms, New Rush, Alandale, Lambing Flat. Joseph Windred, formerly of the Sportsman's Arms, Pitt Street, Sydney, wishes to acquaint his numerous friends that he has resumed business under his old flag. Visitors from Sydney are specially invited to call upon their old friend.'

Joe's timing was not good. The very next morning after that advertisement first appeared, Sunday, June 30, Lambing Flat diggers had gone on the rampage, setting fire to the tented camp of Chinese miners at Burrangong Creek and driving the Chinese out. Police had promptly arrested three ringleaders. That evening, at eight o'clock, led by miner William Spicer, an estimated 2000 white miners, many of them armed, set courthouse and gaol alight as they demanded the three prisoners' release. At the new Sportsman's Arms, Joe and Mary emulated many Lambing Flat shopkeepers, arming themselves and standing guard at their door to protect their premises from the mob.

Meanwhile, Captain William Zouch, with a small force of foot police and seventeen mounted troopers, faced off against the miners, as the Riot Act was read aloud by the Gold Commissioner. After some miners opened fire, the police charged miners' ranks with naked swords, sending the rioters fleeing. One miner, William Lupton, was shot dead. A number were injured. Several police were wounded, with four police horses shot from under their riders. Next morning, 5000 miners attended the funeral of Lupton, as an agitated air hung over the diggings. It was not a great launch for the Windreds' latest business venture.

A full-scale rebellion in the 1854 Eureka Stockade mould was feared by the government, and Premier of New South Wales Charles Cowper would lead military reinforcements from Sydney to Lambing Flat, including infantry, sailors from HMS *Fawn* and artillerymen.

On July 17, a miners' meeting took place at the Cosmopolitan Hotel at Tipperary Gully. The hotel's owner, James Torpy, a fiery twenty-nine-year-old Irishman, joined eleven others in forming a committee of vigilance on Californian lines, electing William Spicer their president. Calling themselves the Miners' Protection League, they agreed to send two delegates to Sydney to present a petition to Governor Sir John Young, asking for all Chinese to be removed from the diggings. The governor would refuse to see the two delegates, and on August 5 they would be arrested. One of those delegates was

James Torpy. Before long, Torpy would change the lives of Joe and Mary Windred.

By the second week of July, gold was found in the gully below Joe's new Sportsman's Arms, generating a flurry of claims. But, reported the *Empire*, 'the rush to the gully at the back of Windred's public house is not turning out as successful as first anticipated'.[232] Seeing no mining taking place on the ground immediately behind the Sportsman's Arms and an adjacent store, miners had also started digging there.

Now, Joe and his shopkeeper neighbour appeared, armed, to clear their land. Joe was well known as a former boxer, and he clearly meant business. Complaining bitterly, the diggers withdrew. 'Much dissatisfaction had been expressed by the miners at the conduct of a certain publican and a storekeeper who prevented several parties lately from digging on the ground held under their business licences,' the *Empire*'s correspondent would report. 'It does seem very absurd that publicans and storekeepers should be allowed to plant themselves down on any part of the diggings and claim their 60 feet by 120 on ground which may be the best on the field.'[233] Absurd it may have seemed, but Joe had vowed not to mine, and Joe never broke his word.

Sunday, June 7, 1863. Young, New South Wales

As Joe Windred prepared to board Grieg's Royal Mail coach for the early morning run from Young to Forbes, the ground was a sea of puddles from a downpour that had blanketed the district on Saturday night. It was just before 2.00 a.m., in the settlement that had originally been known as Lambing Flat. Following the anti-Chinese riots, Charles Cowper's New South Wales Government paid out £15,000 compensation to affected Chinese, and, hoping to wipe away the slur of the riots, had renamed the place Young, after the colony's governor.

While mail bags and luggage were loaded into the coach's rear boot and onto its roof, a small crowd of locals farewelled one of the passengers. As Joe's coincidence-ridden life would have it, this was none other than William Spicer, leader of the Miners' Protection League. The previous year, Spicer had been arrested in Forbes, where he'd settled following the riots. Tried for his leading role in the affair, Spicer had been sent to prison for two years. Just ten days ago, it had been announced that Queen Victoria was granting Spicer clemency on her birthday. Spicer was heading home to Forbes after serving just a year at Berrima Gaol. Arriving in Young on Thursday, he had spent several days with friends. Now, he was embarking on the last leg of his journey home.

Joe Windred and William Spicer had several things in common. They were of a similar age, both had been born in Australia, and both had spent time in the California goldfields. But Joe had no time for Spicer's bigoted politics. As he watched, Spicer shook hands with friends then walked to the coach. Near penniless after his legal battle the previous year, Spicer could only afford to sit outside, and now, breath steaming on this bitter winter's night, he clambered up onto the box seat beside George the driver and Henry Godfrey, a young man from Yass.

Joe was prepared for the cold, wearing a Californian poncho over his coat – quite possibly a poncho worn during his escape from San Francisco. He would be riding out of the weather, inside the coach, having paid for a first-class seat. Business at the new Sportsman's Arms didn't compare with the roaring trade that Joe had done at the Sydney original. Most miners didn't spend like Sydney sportsmen. On top of that, Joe had alienated himself from many diggers with his antagonistic attitude to their committee of vigilance. But he was determined to travel in comparative comfort.

Extending his hand to Mrs Margaret Alexander, a Young resident, Joe helped her climb up inside the coach, then followed her in, closed the door, and took a seat opposite. They would be the only inside passengers. The driver released the brake, lashed the reins along the backs of his four horses, and set the coach in motion. In a way, Joe's visit to Forbes was connected with William Spicer. For, on June 3 the previous year, Joe's stepdaughter, Isabel, had married James Torpy, one of Spicer's fellow leaders of the Miners' Protection League.

Torpy had never been tried following his arrest. Nobody would testify against him, and charges were dropped. After his return to Young, Torpy had, to Joe's surprise, become a regular visitor to the Sportsman's Arms. Joe had found the Irishman an absolute charmer;

argumentative, but warm and chivalrous, except when it came to Chinese. When Joe learned that Torpy had subsequently sold his mining claim to Chinese, he let Torpy know how hypocritical this appeared. To which Torpy had replied, 'I would rather make a profit out of an enemy than a friend.'[234]

A father is often the last to know when it comes to a daughter's affairs of the heart, and only when Isabel confessed that she had fallen in love with Torpy did it dawn on Joe why he had patronised the Sportsman's Arms, and Joe realised that the glib Irishman was to become his son-in-law. After marrying in Goulburn, the couple had settled in Forbes. Now, Joe was on his way to help them celebrate their first wedding anniversary. He would be a few days late, as the good pub trade produced by the previous week's fledgling Young Races had detained him. Joe and Mary hadn't been able to have children of their own, so Joe had become very attached to his step-daughter, and was determined to raise a glass to his darling Isabel and her Irishman. Isabel was equally attached to Joe; when the first of the eight children she would bear Torpy was born, she would name him James Walwyn Joseph Torpy, after James Walwyn, the father she hadn't seen since she was three, and her stepfather Joe.

Out into the darkness rolled the coach, along the Lachlan Road, leaving Young behind. Freezing rain now began to tumble down, quickly soaking the driver and outside passengers. Had the coach been carrying a gold shipment, an armed guard would have been sitting up with the driver. Noted bushrangers Frank Gardner, Johnny Gilbert and their gang had been active in the district in recent weeks, robbing stores and bailing up coaches, but not even they were known to venture out at this hour, in this sort of weather.

In the coach's cabin, Joe and Mrs Alexander soon nodded off. Up on the box, driver George followed a route through the torrential rain that he knew like the back of his hand. Before long, the coach came to White's Creek, which the coach would normally cross at a ford. But, with the creek badly swollen by two days of rain, George decided to wait for daylight to assess the situation. There, the coach sat, until the sun rose and the rain cleared. With daylight, George decided that it was safe to cross the creek, and, although water rose to the cabin floor, the coach made it across without difficulty, then continued on its way over the muddy road.

Shortly after 11.00 a.m., forty kilometres from Young, the coach came to Brewers Creek. At the usual fording place, George reined in and studied the fast-moving water. After passengers Spicer and Godfrey agreed that this creek did not seem as deep as the last, the driver urged his horses forward. The coach rolled into the creek and its team pushed gamely through the dirty, swirling waters.

When the coach was halfway across, its wheels left the ground. In a matter of seconds, the force of the water swept the vehicle over onto its side, sending George, Spicer and Godfrey flying. The two leading horses broke free from their harness and kept going toward the bank on the Forbes side of the creek. The ringbolt giving way, the second pair of horses, the 'wheelers', were also set free. Dragging the coach's pole and front wheels, the wheelers turned completely around and swam back toward the Young bank. William Spicer, who could not swim and was floundering, grabbed desperately at the passing wheelers, and getting a hold of the harness on one, was dragged to safety. George and Godfrey, meanwhile, swam for the Forbes bank.

Joe and Mrs Alexander were trapped inside the coach, which, on its side, was being carried down the swift-flowing creek. Joe threw off his poncho, then, stretching up, opened the door on the top side of the coach. After climbing up through the opening, he knelt on the side of the bobbing vehicle and reached back down to the terrified Margaret Alexander. She, wearing a bonnet, a flowing, ankle-length dress and high, lace-up boots, was frozen in place.

Yelling above the noise of the surging creek, Joe told Mrs Alexander that, with water now rising inside the cabin, she could not stay where she was. She raised her hands to him, and, with a monumental effort, Joe hauled her up onto the coach's exterior. There was no possibility of remaining where they were – their weight on top made the coach topple over. Grabbing for Joe, Margaret Alexander was propelled into the creek with a shriek. Joe went in after her. In a moment, both were in the water and being swept along.

George the driver had succeeded in reaching the Forbes bank. Dripping wet, he set off at the run, trying to keep pace with the floating coach and observing, with horror, the fate of his two inside passengers. 'Mr Windred, who is a splendid swimmer,' the *Empire* would report on June 7 after speaking with driver George, 'struggled hard to save Mrs Alexander. He was seen bearing her up far down the stream, endeavouring to gain the bank.' At one point, Joe grabbed unsuccessfully at the low bough of a tree standing beside the swollen creek. Then he tried to grasp a log floating past, to support the woman and himself, but it was too slippery. Suddenly, Joe lost his hold on her.

'Oh, my poor children!' Mrs Alexander cried, wide eyed, as she reached out to Joe. Then, in an instant, she disappeared beneath the surface, as her long dress caught on an underwater obstruction. The flow dragged her under.

Joe never saw Margaret Alexander again. Days later, her body would be retrieved from the creek. 'It was only with great difficulty that he secured his own safety,' Young paper *The Miner* would report, of Joe.[235] Several kilometres downstream from the scene of the accident, Joe succeeded in gaining the riverbank. The battered coach would come to rest five kilometres from the fatal ford. *The Miner* would reserve most praise for driver George, who spent several days retrieving lost mailbags from Brewers Creek. Mail, to the parochial *Miner*, was apparently more valuable than a woman's life. In contrast, Sydney's *Empire* said on June 9, 'Windred made great efforts to save the woman', and gave Joe maximum credit. Once again, Joe Windred was hailed the hero.

EPILOGUE

THE ORANGE DAYS

Two years later, in June 1865, Joe Windred rode to Bathurst to meet a visiting preacher. That preacher was William Taylor, the American minister sent to Joe in the cells beneath San Francisco's City Hall by Mary Windred in February 1851, as the lynch mob outside bayed for Joe's blood.

Joe rode to this meeting, not from Young, but from Orange, where he and Mary had relocated a year earlier. With the gold at Young playing out, the Sportsman's Arms was no longer a paying proposition. Joe's twenty-nine-year-old brother, Henry, had settled in Orange, as had the boys' mother, Sophia. So, when Henry wrote to tell Joe that Orange's largest and grandest hotel, the Royal, was under construction in Byng Street, Joe had jumped at the chance of securing the lease and licence. In June 1864, after selling much of what they owned to finance the move, Joe and Mary had opened the Royal Hotel, and it had quickly become Orange's social hub and local booking office for Cobb and Co coaches.

Joe had learned that 'California Taylor', as the well-travelled William Taylor was being called in Australia, was touring New South Wales and sermonising on the Sodom and Gomorrah that had been California in the gold-rush days. Joe rode fifty kilometres to reacquaint himself with Taylor, and to tell him that he had made good back home in Australia.

The surprised American remembered Joe. 'Did you succeed in clearing yourself?' the now bushy bearded Taylor asked him when they met following his well-attended Bathurst event.

'Oh, yes,' Joe assured him. Although, he didn't add that, fearing arrest for his prison break, he would never venture back to California.[236]

In Orange, Joe would tell patrons at the Royal that he had spent time on the California goldfields in his younger days, but he never revealed what had happened to him there. All he would say was, 'We found the gold fever at its height, with a great amount of rowdyism and lawlessness.'[237]

Although owning racehorses had proven an expensive hobby for Joe, he was still a dedicated lover of horseracing, and in August 1865 he convened a meeting at the Royal Hotel which formed the Orange Jockey Club, with Joe inaugural secretary and official starter. Other members of the first OJC management committee included Joe's brother Henry and son-in-law, James Torpy, who this year also relocated to Orange with wife Isabel. The jockey club acquired land on the town's outskirts, and five committee members, including Joe, guaranteed a £2000 loan to create a fine racecourse. As Orange's leading publican and now jockey club founder, Joe had again made himself a local identity.

But, as so often happened with Joe, just when he was riding high, he fell at a hurdle. The first two seasons of the Orange Races were grand affairs, as the OJC attempted to create the finest race meeting outside Sydney. But prize money was too high, attendances too low. The loan was called in. Four of the guarantors paid their £400 share, but Joe Windred could not. Joe, once comfortably well-off, had lost much of his small fortune at the ill-starred Sportsman's Arms on the Young goldfields. With liabilities of £1585 and assets of £512, Joe's creditors commenced insolvency proceedings against him in February 1867. Having to surrender the Royal Hotel lease, Joe and Mary moved into the Commercial Hotel, whose licensee was now their generous son-in-law, James Torpy.

From this new low point, in his forty-fifth year, Joe had once again to fight his way back to prosperity. And he did it. Resurrecting his selling skills, as a stock and real estate auctioneer now, and financed by partner Charles Casey, a young Irishman running Young's largest flour mill, Joe slowly rebuilt his career. And he still waved the red flag as starter of the Orange Races every year, with his limp becoming more pronounced as he grew older. Joe also served as an Orange alderman for many years, and in 1877 was a popular candidate for Mayor of Orange. The press reported: 'Mr Joseph Windred was elected. There was great excitement among those present.'[238] Joe's one regret was that his parents did not live to see him don the mayoral chain. Seventy-five-year-old Sophia died, in Orange, in 1871. Joe senior died, aged eighty-seven, at his Windsor cottage in July 1872, just a month after a mineral discovery again restored his eldest son's fortunes.

For, in partnership with son-in-law James Torpy, Joe junior had struck copper twenty-five kilometres outside Orange. This find would fund Joe and Mary's old age, and enable Torpy to establish Young's *Leader* newspaper and successfully run for the New South Wales Parliament. Joe was again elected mayor of Orange in 1883, and is credited with laying out its Cook Park and spurring the growing city's development.

In one of the many turnarounds in Joe Windred's life, in 1884, at the age of sixty-two, he became a justice of the peace, sitting as a magistrate on the bench of the Young Police Court, judging others as he had been judged so often in the past. He proved a just, fair and outspoken judge. In one case, Orange Municipal Council's officious 'nuisance inspector' brought the city's two town criers and Salvation Army band to court, charged with blocking the footpath.

'The Army does a lot of good,' said Joe, in dismissing the prosecution. 'In a town like Orange, there is plenty of room for everybody to pass. The police might be better occupied in clearing larrikins off the street corners on Saturday nights.' When the nuisance inspector 'warmly resented' Joe's comments, Joe responded, 'I don't care whether my remarks please the inspector or not!'[239]

In September 1890, Joe had a run-in with colourful, loose-lipped Irishman Daniel O'Connor, Postmaster-General in the latest New South Wales Government of Sir Henry Parkes. On the bench, Joe had raised a matter where letters containing money had gone missing, and, in Parliament, O'Connor dismissed Joe's complaint. Joe subsequently provided documentary evidence of the crime, and declared, 'In justice to myself, an apology should certainly be made to me, as my character is as of much importance to myself as Mr O'Connor's is to him, and I think I should have been treated with a little more courtesy.'[240]

That character, which meant so much to Joe, ensured a vast crowd at his funeral in January 1901, which was led by the then Mayor of Orange. Loyal Mary had preceded Joe, dying in 1896 at their Byng Street, Orange home. Seventy-nine-year-old Joe himself died from a heart attack while visiting a nephew at Molong on January 11, just ten days after celebrating the birth of the sovereign nation of Australia on January 1. Joe was laid to rest at Orange in a railed enclosure which also included the graves of Mary, Joe's mother, Sophia, and his brother William and sister-in-law Sarah, who had also relocated to Orange.

Joe was not a rich man when he died, although he had tasted wealth during his lifetime. Yet, as shown by his determinations from the bench, his life of struggle had imbued him with the happy gift of wisdom. Son-in-law James Torpy, writing a long obituary in the *Leader*, described Joe as 'a strong ally' and 'fearless foe' who, 'by his strength of character, was always a prominent figure'.[241] Torpy mentioned that Joe had been born on the banks of the Hawkesbury and that he and Mary had gone to the California goldfields, and described Joe's later days in Orange. But Torpy gave away none of the secrets that Joe had kept from most of his acquaintances until his dying day.

Little did the good people of Orange know that the man they had twice elected their mayor was the son of a convict, and was himself an ex-convict, one who was twice convicted of crimes he did not commit, on the second occasion featuring in what Harvard Law professor Edwin Borchard would describe as a landmark case in American history. Little did the people of Orange know that, technically, Joe was still a wanted man in the US. And, little did the people of Orange know that Joe's wife, Mary, was herself an ex-convict, or that Joe's parents never legally married, making him a 'bastard'.

Tough, determined, fearless, indestructible Joe, the archetypal Aussie battler who faced so many trials during his life and several times escaped violent death by a hair's breadth, always rising from adversity to shine like the gold that played such a part in his life, had kept all these secrets close to his chest. Yet, there was one secret about Joe Windred that it seems not even Joe himself knew. In 1856, when Joe and Mary married, they firmly believed that Mary's first husband was dead. But the James Walwyn who had died in London in 1852 was not Mary's first husband. It was yet another case of mistaken identity. Not only was Mary's James Walwyn still alive when she married Joe Windred, Walwyn lived until 1889, when he died at Doverage, Derbyshire at the age of seventy-nine, with Mary shown as his spouse on the death certificate. In reality, Joe and Mary were illegally married for thirty-three years. Worse, Mary was guilty of bigamy, a crime that would have sent her to prison had the authorities known of it.

Was the couple aware of this? Almost certainly not. Thankfully, for Joe and Mary, a bigamy case was one additional trial they didn't have to face.

BIBLIOGRAPHY

Books

Asbury, H., *The Barbary Coast*. Garden City, NY, Garden City Publications, 1933.

Atherton, G. F. A., *California: An Intimate History*. New York, Harper & Brothers, 1914.

Baxter, C., *Captain Thunderbolt And His Lady*. Sydney, Allen & Unwin, 2011.

Bancroft, H. H., *Popular Tribunals, Vol. II: San Francisco*. San Francisco, The History Coy, 1887.

Barry, T. A., and B. A. Patton, *Men And Memories of San Francisco*. San Francisco, Bancroft, 1873.

Bateson, C., *Gold Fleet for California: Forty-niners from Australia and New Zealand*. Sydney, Ure Smith, 1963.

Binney, K. R., *Horsemen of the First Frontier, and the Serpent's Legacy*. Neutral Bay, NSW, Volcanic, 2005.

Bookspan, S., *A Germ of Goodness: The California State Prison System, 1851–1944*. Lincoln, University of Nebraska Press, 1991.

Borchard, E. M., *Convicting the Innocent: Sixty-five Errors of Criminal Justice*. Garden City, NY, Garden City Publications, 1932.

Coblenz, S. A., *Villains & Vigilantes*. New York, Wilson-Erickson, 1936.

Dando-Collins, S., *Pasteur's Gambit*. Sydney, Vintage, 2008.

Dando-Collins, S., *Taking Hawaii*. New York, E-Reads, 2012.

Dando-Collins, S., *Tycoon's War*, Cambridge, Massachusetts, Da Capo, 2008.

Eldridge, Z. S. (editor), *History of California, Vol. 4*. New York, Century, 1915.

Ellison, W. H., *A Self-Governing Dominion: California, 1849–1860*. Berkeley, California, University of California Press, 1950.

Fergusson, C. D., *Experiences of a Forty-Niner*. Cleveland, Ohio, Williams, 1888.

Fowles, J., *Sydney in 1848*. Sydney, Fowles, 1848.

Hargraves, E. H., *Australia And Its Goldfields*. London, Hargraves, 1855.

Hope, R. J., *Colours, Battle Honours & Medals of a Staffordshire Regiment: 80th Regiment of Foot*. UK, Churnet Valley Books, 1999.

Kimble, C. P. (editor), *San Francisco City Directory, 1850*. San Francisco, Journal of Commerce press, 1850.

Lay, R. F., *Lessons of Infinite Advantage: William Taylor's California Experiences*. Lanham, Maryland, Lexington, 2010.

Madgwich, R. B., *Immigration into Eastern Australia, 1788–1851*. Sydney, Sydney University Press, 1969.

McGowan, E., *Narrative of Edward McGowan*. San Francisco, McGowan, 1857.

Monaghan, J., *Australians and the Gold Rush, California and Down Under, 1849–54*. San Francisco, University of California Press, 1966.

Morris, D., *Australian Dictionary of Biography, Vol. 6*, 'James Torpy'. Melbourne, Melbourne University Press, 1976.

Mullen, K. J., *Let Justice Be Done: Crime & Politics in Early San Francisco*. Reno, University of Nevada Press, 1989.

Parker, J. M. (editor), *San Francisco City Directory, 1852–53*. San Francisco, A. W. Morgan, 1852.

Paxton, P., *A Stray Yankee in Texas*. New York, Redfield, 1853.

Royce, J., *California: From the Conquest in 1846 to the Second Vigilance Committee in San Francisco*. Boston, Houghton-Mifflin, 1886.

Secrest, W. B., *California Desperados: Stories of Early California Outlaws in Their Own Words*. Fresno, California, Word Dancer, 2000.

Sheldon, P., *Rags or Riches: Passengers and Ships, Sydney to California, 1849–51*. Sydney, Blakehurst, NSW, Sheldon, 1992.

Sherer, J., *The Lion of the Vigilantes: William T. Coleman And the Life of Old San Francisco*. Indianapolis, Bobbs-Merrill, 1939.

Sherman, W. T., *Memoirs of General William T. Sherman*. New York, Appleton, 1889.

Shertzer, J. H., *A History of San Francisco, & Incidentals of the State of California*. San Francisco, Bancroft, 1878.

Shuck, O. T., *History of the Bench and Bar in California*. Los Angeles, Commercial Printing, 1901.

Soule, F., and J. H. Gihon, *The Annals of San Francisco: Containing a Summary of the History of California And a Complete History of Its Great City*. NY, Appleton, 1855.

Starr, K., and R. J. Orsi (editors), *Rooted in Barbarous Soil: People, Culture & Community in Gold Rush California*. Berkeley, California, University of California Press, 2000.

Stewart, G. P., *Committee of Vigilance. Revolution in San Francisco, 1851: An Account of the Hundred Days When Certain Citizens Undertook the Suppression of the Criminal Activities of the Sydney Ducks*. Boston, Houghton Mifflin, 1964.

Taylor, W., *California Life Illustrated*. New York, Carlton & Porter, 1858.

Taylor, W., *Seven Years Street Preaching in San Francisco*. New York, Carlton & Porter, 1857.

Taylor, W., *Story of My Life: An Account of What I Have Said And Done in My Ministry*. New York, Eaton & Mains, 1896.

White, S. E., *The Forty-Niners: A Chronicle of the California Trail & El Dorado*. New Haven, Connecticut, Yale University Press, 1918.

Williams, A., *A Pioneer Pastorate and Times: Embodying Contemporary Transactions and Events*. San Francisco, Wallace & Hassett, 1879.

Williams, M. F., *History of the San Francisco Committee of Vigilance: A Study of Social Control on the California Frontier in the Days of the Gold Rush*. Berkeley, California, University of California Press, 1921.

Williams, M. F., *Papers of the San Francisco Committee of Vigilance, 1851*. Berkeley, California, Academy of Pacific Coast History, 1919.

Woolley, L. H., *California, 1849–1913: Or, the Rambling Sketches of Sixty-Four Years' Residence in that State*. Oakland, California, DeWitt & Snelling, 1913.

Historical Journals

American Quarterly, Vol. 33, No. 5, Winter, 1981. 'Vigilance and the Law: The Moral Authority of Popular Justice in the Far West,' D.A. Johnson.

Pacific Historical Review, Vol. 42, No. 1, February 1973. 'The Sydney Ducks: A Demographic Analysis', S. I. Ricards and G. M. Blackburn.

Newspapers and Magazines

Alta California, San Francisco, 1849–56
Argus, Melbourne, 1851
Australasian Chronicle, Sydney, 1840
Bathurst Free Press, NSW, 1852–64
Bell's Life in Sydney and Sporting Reviewer/Chronicle, 1844–64
California Police Gazette, San Francisco, 1859
Century, New York, November and December 1891
Cornwall Chronicle, Launceston, Van Diemen's Land (Tasmania), 1851
Courier, Hobart, Van Diemen's Land, 1851
Courier, San Francisco, 1851
Empire, Sydney, 1850–58
Galaxy, New York, 1858
Goulburn Herald, 1861
Leader, Orange, NSW, 1901
Life, New York, 1959
Maitland Mercury & Hunter Valley General Advertiser, 1860–61
Miner, Young, NSW, 1861–64
New York Times, 1851
Sacramento News-Letter, 1851
Sacramento Union, 1851
San Francisco Evening Picayune, 1851
Shipping Gazette & Sydney General Trade List, Sydney, 1848–1852
Sydney Gazette & New South Wales Advertiser, 1840
Sydney Herald, 1840
Sydney Monitor & Commercial Advertiser, 1840
Sydney Morning Herald, 1850–91

Unpublished Letters and Journals

Bourke, Sir Richard, Letters, HRA Series I, Vol. XVII, State Library of NSW.
Journal of William Augustus Miles, Commissioner of Police, Sydney, 1840–1848. State Library of New South Wales, Sydney.
Letter from a Gold Miner, Placerville, California, March, 1850, S. Shufelt. Library of Congress, Washington, D.C.

Official Documents

Adelaide Proformat, Census of 1841. South Australian Records Office, Adelaide.
Birth record, James Frederick Walwyn, India Office Records, British Library, London, Ref. N/1/66 f.180.
Convict No. 77811, Windred, Joseph. Conduct Record CON31/12/48; Indent CON16/1/1, Archives Office of Tasmania, Hobart, Tasmania.
English Census, 1861, 'Slaley, Northumberland'. UK Public Record Office, RG10/5144, London.
Memorial of Thomas Berdue, *Journal of the Fourth Session of the Legislature of the State of California*. San Francisco, Kerr, 1853.
New South Wales marriage certificate, Joseph Windred junr. and Mary Walwyn, January 19, 1856, 2623 Vol. 73C, Registrar of Births & Marriages, Sydney.
Shipping Master's Office: Passengers Arriving 1826–1859. State Records of New South Wales, Sydney, Ref. NRS13278.

NOTES

CHAPTER 1
1. William Taylor describes this episode, in varying detail, in both *California Life Illustrated* and *Seven Years Street Preaching in San Francisco*.

CHAPTER 2
2. Taken from trial testimony of Eliza Barker and Thomas Keane. Reported in *Sydney Herald*, May 13, 1840; *Sydney Gazette & NSW Advertiser*, May 14, 1840 (which included the epithet 'bloody' when the other papers did not); *Sydney Monitor & Commercial Advertiser*, May 11 and 20, 1840; and *Australasian Chronicle*, May 19, 1840.
3. Eliza Barker's testimony, ibid.
4. Thomas Nichols' testimony, ibid.

CHAPTER 3
5. Thomas Wilson's testimony, *Sydney Herald*, May 11, 1840.
6. Thomas Nichols' testimony, ibid.

CHAPTER 4
7. Thomas Nichols' testimony, *Sydney Herald*, May 11, 1840.

CHAPTER 5
8. HRA, Series I, Vol XVII.
9. *Journal of William Augustus Miles.*
10. Orange *Leader*, January 16, 1901.
11. Regular instance recorded in *Sydney Morning Herald (SMH)*, January 7, 1852.
12. Eliza Barker's testimony.
13. Thomas Keane's testimony.
14. Thomas Nichols' testimony.
15. February 5, 1840 issue.
16. Thomas Nichols' testimony.
17. Elizabeth Nichols' testimony.
18. Thomas Wilson's testimony.
19. Thomas Bevan's testimony.
20. John Horan's testimony.
21. John Barker's testimony.
22. Frederick Lahrbush's testimony.
23. Eliza Barker's testimony on re-examination.
24. Thomas Nichols' testimony on re-examination.

CHAPTER 6
25. Foster's summation, *Sydney Herald (SH)*, May 11, 1840.
26. Purefoy's summation, ibid.
27. Downing's jury instructions, ibid.
28. *SH*, May 11, 1840.
29. *Australasian Chronicle*, May 19, 1840.
30. *SH*, May 11, 1840.
31. Ibid.
32. *Sydney Monitor*, May 20, 1840.

CHAPTER 7
33. *SH*, May 11, 1840.
34. *SH*, May 20, 1840.

CHAPTER 8
35. *Bell's Life in Sydney & Sporting Reviewer*, January 11, 1845.
36. Ibid.
37. Ibid.; full report of fight.

38. October 18, 1845.
39. Ibid.

CHAPTER 9
40. *Bell's Life*, January 20, 1847.
41. *Bell's Life*, March 6, 1847.
42. *Bell's Life*, May 22, 1847.
43. *Bell's Life*, October 30, 1847.
44. Ibid.
45. *Bell's Life*, December 4, 1847.

CHAPTER 10
46. *SMH*, May 21, 1849.
47. Ibid.
48. Ibid.
49. Ibid.
50. May 19, 1849.
51. May 25, 1849.

CHAPTER 11
52. July 21, 1849.
53. Ibid.

CHAPTER 12
54. Longfield's letter, *SMH*, February 14, 1850. The *SMH* reckoned, in its August 28, 1851 issue, that $1500 was the equivalent of £390, hence $900 equating to £233.
55. Advertisement, *SMH*, February 14, 1850.
56. *SMH*, April 5, 1850.

CHAPTER 13
57. *San Francisco City Directory, 1850*.
58. Monaghan, *Australians and the Gold Rush*; and Ricards and Blackburn, *The Sydney Ducks*.
59. *Galaxy magazine*, February 1868.
60. Ibid.
61. McGowan, *Narrative of Edward McGowan*.
62. Asbury, *Barbary Coast*.

63. Gough statement to Committee of Vigilance, San Francisco *Courier*, July 18, 1851. Reprinted Sydney *Empire*, September 25, 1851.
64. Ibid.
65. In America, the Handcock family would change the spelling of their name to Hancock.

CHAPTER 14
66. Taylor, *Seven Years Street Preaching in San Francisco*.
67. Ibid.
68. *Bathurst Free Press (BFP)*, August 30, 1851.
69. Shufelt letter, US Library of Congress.
70. Taylor, *California Life Illustrated*.
71. *Berdue Memorial*.

CHAPTER 15
72. Stuart's confession to Committee of Vigilance. Reprinted Sydney *Empire*, September 5, 1851.
73. Ibid.
74. Ibid.
75. Ibid.

CHAPTER 16
76. Mullen, *Let Justice Be Done*.
77. Joe and Tom's arrest described in Williams, *History of the San Francisco Committee of Vigilance*.
78. *Galaxy*, February 1868.
79. Ibid.
80. Ibid.
81. Ibid.
82. *San Francisco City Directory, 1850*.
83. Soule and Gihon, *Annals of San Francisco*.
84. *Galaxy*, February 1868.
85. Ibid.
86. Atherton, *California, an Intimate History*.
87. *Galaxy*, February 1868.
88. Ibid.
89. Ibid.

90. Atherton.
91. *Galaxy*, February 1868.
92. Taylor, *California Life Illustrated*.
93. Orange *Leader*, January 16, 1901.
94. Taylor, *California Life Illustrated*.

CHAPTER 17
95. *Galaxy*, February 1868.
96. Ibid.
97. Ibid.
98. Williams, *History*.
99. Ibid.
100. Ibid.
101. *Galaxy*, February 1868.
102. Ibid.
103. Ibid.
104. Atherton.
105. *Galaxy*, February 1868.
106. Ibid.
107. Ibid.
108. Ibid.
109. Whiting's statement to Committee of Vigilance. Reprinted *Bell's Life*, December 13, 1851.
110. *Galaxy*, February 1868.
111. Ibid.
112. Ibid.
113. Ibid.
114. Ibid.
115. Ibid.
116. Ibid.
117. San Francisco *Herald*. Reprinted *Cornwall Chronicle*, October 25, 1851.
118. *Galaxy*, February 1868.
119. Soule and Gihon.
120. Paxton, *A Stray Yankee in Texas*.
121. Mullen, *Let Justice Be Done*.
122. *Galaxy*, February 1868.

CHAPTER 18
123. Monaghan.
124. San Francisco *Herald*. Reprinted *Cornwall Chronicle*, October 25, 1851.
125. Whiting statement. Reprinted *Bell's Life*, December 13, 1851.
126. Stuart confession.
127. Stuart confession and Whiting statement.
128. Shuck, *History of the Bench and Bar in California*.
129. Read about Walker's Central American misadventures in Dando-Collins, *Tycoon's War*.
130. *Galaxy*, February 1868.
131. Ibid.
132. McKenzie statement. Reprinted *Argus*, October 28, 1851.

CHAPTER 19
133. Ellison, *A Self-Governing Dominion*.
134. Hogan statement. Reprinted *Bell's Life*, December 13, 1851.
135. Ibid.
136. Ibid.
137. Monaghan. It should be noted that the exact date of Joe's escape is not recorded, although the date shown is likely to have been close to the mark.
138. Stuart confession.
139. Ibid.
140. Ibid.
141. Williams, *History*. The exact date that this occurred is not recorded, but the date shown would be very close to the mark.
142. *San Francisco City Directory, 1850*.

CHAPTER 20
143. Letter reprinted, *Empire*, September 25, 1851.
144. Ibid.
145. Williams, *History*.
146. Reprinted *BFP*, August 30, 1851.
147. Jenkins' physical description, just prior to and after death, comes from an unidentified Australian who witnessed his ordeal and next day viewed his battered body in San Francisco's mortuary, and wrote an account which appeared in the Sydney *Empire*, October

10, 1851. As an aside, in 1851, Hobart merchant John T. Waterhouse and his family migrated to the Kingdom of Hawaii, on the way passing through San Francisco at the height of the lynch mania. See Dando-Collins, *Taking Hawaii*, for more on the Waterhouses.
148. Williams, *History*.
149. *Alta California*. Reprinted *BFP*, August 30, 1851.
150. Ibid.
151. Mines statement, Williams, *Papers*.
152. Reprinted *BFP*, August 30, 1851.
153. Williams, *Papers*.
154. A. Williams, *A Pioneer Pastorate and Times*.
155. San Francisco *Herald*. Reprinted *Cornwall Chronicle*, October 25, 1851.

CHAPTER 21
156. *Galaxy*, February 1868.
157. Borchard, *Convicting the Innocent*.
158. Ibid.
159. Ibid.
160. Ibid.
161. Ibid.
162. Ibid.
163. Ibid.
164. Ibid.
165. Ibid.
166. Adair statement, Williams, *Papers*.
167. Ibid.
168. Secrest, *California Desperados*.
169. Ibid.
170. Ibid.
171. Gough statement.
172. Ibid.

CHAPTER 22
173. *Century* magazine, November 1891, 'San Francisco Vigilance Committee, by the Chairman of the Committees of 1851, 1856, and 1877'.
174. Stuart confession.

175. Ibid.
176. Ibid.
177. Bluxome statement, Williams, *Papers*.
178. Ibid.
179. Ibid.
180. Ibid.
181. *Life*, April 27, 1959.
182. Mines statement, Williams, *Papers*.
183. Barry and Patten, *Men and Memories of San Francisco*.
184. Buffum, *Galaxy*, February 1868.
185. Woolley, *California 1849–1913*.
186. *Galaxy*, February 1868.

CHAPTER 23

187. Monaghan, *Australians*.
188. Williams, *History*.
189. White, *The Forty-Niners*.
190. San Francisco *Courier*, July 18, 1851
191. *San Francisco Herald*. Reprinted *Cornwall Chronicle*, October 25, 1851.
192. Ibid. Whitaker's name was, and is, consistently misspelled, as Whittaker, in US accounts.
193. *SMH*, October 21, 1851.
194. Ibid.
195. *Bell's Life*, October 25, 1851.
196. Ibid.
197. Quirot & Co, San Francisco, lithograph, 'Tremendous Excitement', 1851.
198. Williams, *Papers*.

CHAPTER 24

199. Monaghan.
200. Lockwood's closing address reprinted *Hobart Courier*, November 29, 1851.
201. *SMH*, September 25, 1851.
202. October 28, 1851.
203. Whiting statement.
204. *Bell's Life*, October 25, 1851.

205. *Maitland Mercury*, January 10, 1852.
206. Ibid.
207. *Bell's Life* (detailed report of fight), March 6, 1852.
208. Monaghan.
209. Ibid.
210. *Berdue Memorial*.
211. Orange *Leader*, January 16, 1901.
212. January 22, 1853.
213. Borchard.
214. Elen Burdue and her three children lived for a time in Northumberland with farmer Cuthbert Burdue, married younger brother of Tom Burdue. Elen had two illegitimate children to Cuthbert, before Elen moved her brood and herself in with Thomas Burdue senior, elderly father of Tom Burdue, at his 'Coalpits Farm', Slaley, where Elen and a daughter took in sewing while her sons worked at farming. Elen died there at Slaley some little time before 1891.

CHAPTER 25
215. December 17, 1853.
216. *SMH*, September 19, 1854.
217. *Bell's Life*, December 16, 1854.

CHAPTER 26
218. *SMH*, May 13, 1856.
219. Ibid.
220. Ibid.
221. *SMH*, July 5, 1856.
222. *BFP*, August 3, 1856.
223. Ibid.
224. *BFP*, August 27, 1856.
225. September 19, 1856.
226. October 18, 1856.

CHAPTER 27
227. *Bell's Life*, March 20, 1858.

CHAPTER 28

228. Advertisement, *SMH*, October 26, 1860.
229. Advertisement, *Bell's Life*, July 6, 1861.
230. December 15, 1860.
231. From a letter written by Joe Windred to the editor, *Bell's Life*, June 23, 1860.
232. July 25, 1861.
233. Ibid.
234. Morris, *Australian Dictionary of Biography*.
235. *The Miner*'s report reprinted *SMH*, June 13, 1856. The *Empire* repeated its report the same day.

EPILOGUE

236. Taylor, *Story of My Life*.
237. Ross Maroney, Orange City Database.
238. *Maitland Mercury*, February 5, 1876.
239. *BFP*, August 24, 1891.
240. *BFP*, September 15, 1890.
241. Orange *Leader*, January 16, 1901.

INDEX

Abercrombie 51, 62, 81
Adair, Jim 184–5, 193
Adams, George 102, 209
Addison, J. E. 148
Admiralty House 81
Agincourt 86
Albert Stakes 230, 231
Alexander, Margaret 254, 255, 256–7
Allen, W. B. 217
Alta California 111, 123, 138–9, 163, 164, 171, 173, 175, 195, 218
American Coaching Line 249
Argenti, Felix 214, 216
Armstrong, Thomas 81
Arthur, George 209
Ashcroft, Samuel 15, 16, 17, 29, 32, 33, 53
Australasian Chronicle 23, 45, 46
Australian gold rush 219–20, 250–1

Balmoral 80
Bansley, George 241
Barker, Eliza (nee Dargin) 6–8, 9, 16, 17, 26–8, 40, 42

Barker, John 6, 8, 9, 15, 18, 19, 39–40
Barker robbery 4–6, 23, 74, 104, 114, 137, 206
Bartol, Captain Abraham 2, 118–19, 121
Bathurst 225, 230–1, 234, 239, 258
Bathurst Free Press 241
Bathurst Races 232
Beebee, Ludlow and Condon Bank 143
Belcher Kay, Thomas 102, 157–8, 160
Bell's Life in Sydney and Sporting Reviewer 54, 55, 57, 58–60, 61, 67, 69, 70, 74, 76, 218, 220, 227, 231, 243
Benham, Calhoun 141, 148, 154, 167, 170, 177, 178
Benicia (California) 228
Bent, Noah 227
Bevan, Thomas 37–8, 43
Bicheno, James 52
Black Hole of Calcutta 66
Bluxome junior, Isaac 171, 196, 197
Borchard, Edwin 261

279

Bothered Harry 239, 240
Bourke, Sir Richard 20
Bowie, H. R. 126, 136
Brady, Patrick 24
Brady, Sophia *see* Windred, Sophia
Brannan, Samuel 117–20, 123, 134, 137, 146, 171, 172–5, 189, 198, 206, 210
Brenham, Captain Charles 111, 154, 166, 196
Bridges, Thomas 10, 15
Briggs, James 'Jemmy-from-Town' 97, 144, 145, 209
Brosnan, Charles M. 148
Buffum, Edward 88, 111–14, 116, 118–19, 120, 123, 124, 127, 129, 130, 131, 134, 135, 139, 149, 178, 198, 200, 201, 218
Burdue, Elen 78–9, 95, 96–7, 103, 108, 134–5, 140, 155, 161, 167, 168, 177, 190, 191, 213, 227, 229
Burdue, Tom 2, 78–9, 81, 89–90, 91, 93, 94–7, 103, 104, 108, 110, 167, 199, 202, 213, 215, 229
  arrest for Jansen robbery 110, 112–13
  children 134, 155, 177, 229
  conviction for murder, overturning of 213
  identification as English Jim 113–14, 149, 178–83
  kangaroo court 123–39
  murder charge 151, 154, 170
  murder trial 177–91
  pardon 197
  petition for restitution 226–7, 228
  sentence 150, 191
  trial for Jansen robbery 147–50
Burns, Dr Matthew P. 200, 201

Calcutta 66
California District Court 137
California Engine Company 171
Californian gold rush 1, 77, 80, 87, 117

Auburn diggings 93–4
  Australians and 87–9
  foreign miners tax 147
Camden 250
Camden Races 244, 245
Campbell, Judge Alistair 213, 215
Casey, Charles 259
Causzer, Captain William Henry 81–2, 85, 91
Chaulker, William 72, 73
Cheeke, John 10, 12, 15, 16, 17, 18, 19, 20, 22, 25, 26, 29, 37, 47, 48, 49, 50
Coffey, Edward 66
Coleman, Napoleon Bonaparte 124
Coleman, William Tell 124–6, 128, 129–32, 136, 148, 149, 193
Collyer, Bob 217
Cowper, Premier Charles 252, 253
Creole 203, 205
Crescent 146
Crozier, Robert G. 166, 175
Cullen, James 9, 37, 38, 53, 65, 67, 205
Cupitt, George 54, 67, 70
Cupitt, old George 54, 55–8, 61, 63, 67

Dargin, James 24
Dargin, John 230, 235
Dargin, Mary 7
Dargin, Thomas 54
Dargin senior, Thomas 7, 54, 68
Davis, Bill 60
Dawes junior, Bill 72–4
Dawes senior, William 72, 73
Deaf Bob 63
Dillon, John Moore 74
Dodge, Captain 98
Dolen, Alfred 197–8
Donnelly, John 221
Dougall, Reverend John 234
Dowling, Sir James 25–6, 44–7, 49–50

Echols, Sheriff 94, 99
Edwards, John 101, 102, 106, 155
80th Regiment (Staffordshire Volunteers) 64–6, 77
Ellison, William Henry 153
Emerson and Dunbar auction house 143–4
Endicott, George 196, 197
Euphemia 199
Eureka Stockade 252
Everard, James 91

Fairfax, John 23
Fallon, Marshall Malachi 109, 110, 114, 124, 138, 166
First Sikh War 66
Fitzroy, Sir Charles 78
Forbes 253, 254–5
Forty-Niners 77
Foster, William 25, 27–8, 34, 35, 38, 39, 42, 47
Foster's Bar 95, 96, 98, 100, 115, 144, 178, 181, 183, 186
Fowles, Joseph 247
Freeman, George 13, 76, 204
Frost, Billy 222–3
Froud, James 48, 50

Gallagher, Edward 200, 201
Garbutt, James 236
Garbutt, Johnny 236–8, 246
Gardner, Frank 255
Garven, Andy 10, 13–14, 15, 17, 18, 19, 20, 21–2, 25, 26, 43, 47, 48, 49, 50, 51, 65, 70, 115, 151
Geary, Mayor John W. 137–8, 154
Gelson, Captain 92
Gibbes, Colonel John 81
Gifford, Edward 98
Gilbert, Captain Edward 173
Gilbert, Edward 112, 123, 163–4, 195, 198
Gilbert, Johnny 255
Gladwin and Whitmore 144

Godfrey, Henry 254, 256
Goodwin, John O. 177, 178–9, 180, 181–2, 183, 188–9
Gorrick, 'Bungarribee Jack' Isaac 63, 72, 73, 103
Gough, Elicia (nee Bahan) 77, 89, 96, 103, 145, 167, 206, 208, 246
Gough, John 77–9, 81, 89–90, 93, 96, 103, 134, 140–1, 145, 150, 156, 167–8, 169, 170, 189–91, 206–8, 217, 246
Gough junior, John 89
Grainger, Constable William 236, 238
Greenaway, Francis 22
Griffiths, Johnny 157
Guichard, Eugene 149
Gwynne, William 93

Haig, Andrew 173
Hall McAllister, Matthew 126, 128, 129, 130–1, 132, 135, 140–1, 142, 145, 148, 149–50, 154, 167, 169, 177, 178, 179, 180–4, 188–9, 218, 226
Hammett, Samuel Adams 138
Hand, Jack 60–1
Handcock, Elizabeth 83, 91
Handcock, William 83, 91
Harris, Captain Isaac 214, 217
Hawkesbury Regatta 75
Hawkesbury Stakes 231, 246
Hays, Jack Coffee 196, 197, 209, 211
Hearne, V. W. 208
Henry Wellesley 64
Herculean 160–1, 163, 167, 169, 170, 177, 202, 203–4
Hetherington, Joseph 106, 133
Hickens, Captain William 160, 169, 204
Hill, George 247
H. L. Allen 145, 158, 159, 195
HMS *Fawn* 252
Hobbs, William 205–6, 215

282 MISTAKEN IDENTITY

Hogan, Andy *see* Garven, Andy
Hogan, Mary Ann 106, 133, 141–2, 145, 154–6, 159, 160, 161, 165, 167, 168, 193, 194, 208–9, 220
Hogan, Michael 106, 194
Homebush Races 75, 232–3, 235, 246
Horan, Watch-house Keeper John 15, 16, 18, 38–9
Hoskisson, John 75
Howard, William H. 174
Hughes, Bill 144
Hunt, George F. 149

Jack the Waiter 222–3
James Caskie 99, 109, 110
Jansen and Company 104–5
Jansen, Charles 104–5, 107, 109, 110, 112, 113, 120, 129, 130, 142, 148, 150, 187, 195, 215
  robbery 105–7
Jenkins, John 171–5, 190, 194, 211, 214, 217
Jenner, Samuel 248
John Munn 84
Jones, W. A. 126, 127
Joy, Captain Hartford 188

Keane, Thomas 5–6, 8, 9, 17, 18, 28, 42, 43
Kearey, Elizabeth *see* Windred, Elizabeth (nee Kearey)
Kearey, John 239
Kemp, Charles 23
Kimball, Charles 86, 114, 162
Kitchen, James 157, 158–9, 160, 168–9, 193
Kurtz, Daniel B. 226–7

Lahrbush, Frederick 34, 36, 40, 41, 236
Lambert, Dr Bernard 155, 156, 165, 166
Lambert, William 210, 211

Lambing Flat 250–3 *see also* Young
Langham, Ned 68
Laughton, Reverend James 239
Lewis, Ben 176
Liverpool Races 243, 246
Lock, 'Young Lock' John 69–70
Lockwood, Rufus 216
Longfield, John 80, 85
Lovett, Thomas 72, 73
Lupton, William 252

McCarthy, Captain Andrew 154, 155, 186–7, 194
McCormack, Edward 'Teddy' 101
McDougall, Governor John 192, 194, 195, 197, 209–10, 215, 219, 224–5, 228
McIntyre, Second Sergeant Robert 154, 186–7, 194
Mackay, James 169, 203
McKenzie, Bob 102, 152, 158, 209–12, 217, 218
McLerie, John 205–6
MacManus, Terrence 207
Maloney, Eube 197
Marney, Constable Dennis 71, 72, 73, 74
Marsh, Charles 189
Marysville 151, 170, 177–91
  Committee of Vigilance 188, 192
Mason, George 149
Melbourne Packet 222
Metcalfe, Peter 216
Methodist Episcopal Church 1–2
Miners' Protection League 252, 253
Mines, Reverend Flevel S. 174, 175, 198–9
Monterey 166, 193
Moore, Charles E. 100, 151, 171, 177–8, 195
Morgan, John 'Old Jack' 104–6, 129
Morgan, Morris 144, 145
Mortimer, Ben 52, 54, 55, 56–60

INDEX 283

Mott, Judge Gordon Newell 177, 179, 180, 189, 191
Muriel, Robert 250
Myers, Abraham 72, 73

New Orleans 146, 152
New South Wales Advertiser 23
New York Herald 111
Newcastle Gaol 50
Newcastle-upon-Tyne 64
Nichols, Elizabeth (nee Whitehead) 12–13, 15–16, 34, 35–6, 42–4
Nichols, Henry 10–11, 12–14, 15–17, 18, 28, 35, 47, 53, 236
   cross examination 32–5
   evidence 29–32, 40–1
Norfolk Island 49
Norris, Frank 55–7, 63, 67, 69–70
North, Samuel 18
Norton, Myron 209
Nugent, John 146

Oakes, George 196, 197
O'Brien, Mick 243
O'Connor, Daniel 260
Orange 258–61
Orange Jockey Club 259
Orange Races 259, 260
O'Shaughnessy, Thomas 243

Parbutt, George R. 142, 145, 160
Parker, James M. 165
Parkes, Sir Henry 214–15, 251, 260
Parramatta 65, 73, 77, 236
   White Hart Inn 60
Parsons, Levi 137, 146–7, 148, 150
Patterson, Captain Robert 103, 141, 149, 176
Payne, Theodore 107
Payran, Stephen 206, 216
Peate, James 'Dab' 158, 159, 209
Penrith 71–2, 73
Perry, John 248
Perry, Joseph 32

Pickering, George 69, 74, 222, 223, 247
Pitman, Isaac 23
Pixley, Frank 100, 187–8, 195, 196, 209
Platt, George K. 148, 149–50
Plunkett, John 25, 26–7, 28, 29, 35, 36–41
Port Macquarie 24
Prentiss, 'Colonel' James H. 180
Purefoy, William Alexander 25, 32–3, 40, 43–4, 74

Randolph, Edmund 147
Rattler 203
Read, Isaac 'Ike' 66–7
Reynolds, Charles 236
Richmond (England) 68
Richmond (NSW) 52, 69–70
   Farlow's Hotel 69
Ridge, Richard 38, 64, 75, 204
Risley, Isabella 234
Risley, William 234
Robinson, John (Paddy) 10–11, 12–14, 15–18, 19, 20, 22, 25, 26, 37, 43, 47, 48, 49, 50
Ross, Charles L. 126, 136
Ross, William Scott *see* Garbutt, Johnny
Roundhead, Jemmy 209
Royal City Theatre (Sydney) 77
Royal Saxon 64, 66

Sacramento 97, 99, 101, 107, 157, 210
San Diego 226
San Francisco 1, 78, 84, 85–9, 96, 97, 101–2, 109–11, 119, 203
   City Hall riots 116–22, 123–39, 138
   Committee of Vigilance 171–6, 184–5, 186, 189–91, 192, 195–6, 198, 206–12, 213, 214, 215–17, 224

earthquakes 161
fires 162–4, 168, 171, 176, 205, 209, 214
lynch mob 123–39
public hangings 175–6, 199–201, 211–12
San Francisco *Courier* 207, 215
San Francisco *Directory* 165
San Francisco *Evening Picayune* 139, 175
San Francisco *Herald* 142, 145, 176, 207
San Quentin Prison 3, 151, 207
Santa Barbara 208
Schenck, George E. 186
Schultz, Julius 209
Seymour, George 34, 235–6
Shattuck, D. O. 126, 128, 129, 130–1, 135
Shepheard, Justice Philip W. 112–15
Sheppard and Alger 82
Sherringham, Richard 'Gosh' 72–3, 73, 74
Shufelt, Sheldon 94
Silk, Sarah 67
Smith, James 78, 89, 189
Smith, John 12–13
Sofala 219–23, 232
  Golden Nugget Hotel 222, 223
Sparkes, Bill 60, 63, 68–9, 70
Sparkes, 'Sprig of Myrtle' Tom 69, 72, 73
Spence, John F. 126, 127, 128, 130, 131, 132, 135–7, 192, 194
Spicer, William 252, 253–4, 255–6
SS *McKim* 108, 111, 120, 154, 166
SS *Tennessee* 97
Stevenson, Colonel Jonathan D. 111, 198
Stewart, Constable Charles 71, 72, 73, 74
Stewart, Robert 40
Stewart, Samuel 99–100
Stewart, William 99–100

Stidger, Judge Oliver Perry 98, 182–3, 184, 189
Stokes, Frederick 23
Stoney Creek diggings 239–42
Stuart, James 'English Jim' 2, 97–100, 101–6, 109, 129, 133, 142, 143–5, 152, 157, 158–9, 166, 178, 184–5, 217, 228
  Committee of Vigilance trial 198–9
  concealment by Committee of Vigilance 196–7
  confession 193–5, 215
  execution 199–201, 211
  William Stevens as 184–8, 192–3
Sullivan, John 98, 115, 130, 149, 172–3, 178–9, 186
Sullivan, Patrick 225
Sydney Supreme Court 22–4, 48
Sydney Ducks 88–9, 97, 99, 101, 114, 116, 119, 124, 141, 147, 152, 164–5, 175, 190, 207–8, 211, 218, 220, 223
Sydney *Empire* 214–15, 217, 251, 253
Sydney Fives Courts 62–3
Sydney Gaol 20–1, 47, 51, 62
Sydney *Gazette* 23
Sydney *Monitor and Commercial Advertiser* 23, 33, 47
Sydney *Morning Herald* 23, 73, 75, 80, 205, 217, 218, 232, 239, 251
Sydney Orphans School 35
Sydney Poultry Club 248

Taylor, Isabel 90
Taylor, Reverend William 1–2, 90–1, 94, 120–1, 162–3, 165, 258–9
Taylor, Samuel 23
Teale, John 12, 36, 37, 65
Tilford, Franklin 116, 118, 137, 154
Timandra 214
Torpy, Isabel *see* Walwyn, Isabel

INDEX 285

Torpy, James 252, 254–5, 259, 260, 261
Torpy, James Walwyn Joseph 255
Townes, John E. 126, 137
Tredwen, William 82
Trinidad Bay 152, 158, 195
Turnbull, William 156
Turner, George Cooper 103, 149
Turon goldfields 220–1

Una 80, 81–4, 85, 86, 91

Vallejo (California) 226
Van Bokkelen, Jake 186, 187, 196
Van Diemen's Land 49, 50–1, 52, 55, 62, 65, 77, 102, 103, 141, 172, 173, 207
Veto 206, 208
Victoria 78, 81
Virgin, George 172, 173

Waban 151, 157, 195, 213
Wakeman, Edgar 174, 175, 200, 211
Walker, William 141–2, 145–7, 176, 207–9
Waller, Judge R. H. 210
Walton, Margaret 155–6, 158
Walton, William 155–6
Walwyn, Isabel 64, 65–6, 83, 204–5, 217, 219, 221, 224, 225, 240, 245–6, 250, 254–5, 259
Walwyn, James Frederick 66
Walwyn, Mary Anne (nee Douglass) *see* Windred, Mary Anne (Joe's wife)
Walwyn, Quartermaster Sergeant James 64–6, 82, 234, 262
Ward, Fred 'Captain Thunderbolt' 236, 238–9, 246
Warner, James 48, 50
Warner, Jonathan 48
Washington, B. F. 99, 183, 184, 189
Waterhouse, John T. 173
Watson, R. S. 135, 136

Whitaker, Sam 101–6, 133, 141–4, 145, 153–6, 157, 159, 160, 165, 166, 168, 193, 194, 202, 206, 208–12, 217, 218
White, Bill 63
Whitehead, Elizabeth *see* Nichols, Elizabeth (nee Whitehead)
Whitehead, Jane 34, 36, 40, 41
Whiting, Agnes 103, 133, 141
Whiting, James W. 103, 106, 133, 141, 142, 145, 153, 161, 220
Wilder, Daniel 157, 195
Williams, James Hartwell 215, 224
Williams, Reverend Albert 176, 210
Wilson, Thomas 12–13, 36
Windred, Charles 55
Windred, Elizabeth (nee Kearey) 239, 245–6
Windred, Henry 55
Windred, Jack 67, 68, 69–70, 81–3, 204, 219, 220, 221–2, 225, 230, 232, 235, 239, 242, 245–6
Windred, Joe (Joseph) 2–3, 4, 8–11, 13–14, 75, 219–20, 245–6, 253–7
    alias 169, 203–4
    Auburn diggings 92–3, 99, 108, 110, 197
    Barker robbery and 18–19, 20–51
    Bathurst 225–6, 230–2
    boxing 52–61, 62–3, 66–7, 68–75, 222–3
    conviction, overturning of 213–14
    escape 153–4, 157–8, 160–1, 169–70
    free pardon 52
    funeral 261
    heroic behaviour 231–2
    horse racing 225–7, 230–3, 235–8, 243–4, 246–7, 248, 259
    horse thieves and 236–9
    Jansen robbery and 110, 112–14, 140, 149–50
    kangaroo court 123–39
    Lambing Flat 250–3

marriage to Mary 234
Orange 258–62
return to Australia 203–5
San Francisco 85–7, 89–90, 103–4
Sofala 219–5
Sportsman's Arms 247–9, 251–4, 258
Stoney Creek Diggings 240–2
trial for Jansen robbery 147–50
Van Diemen's Land 52–3, 62, 65
Windred, John 24, 55, 258
Windred, Joseph (Joe's father) 9, 24–5, 45, 53, 55, 204, 260
Windred, Mary Ann (Joe's sister) 24, 83
Windred, Mary Anne (Joe's wife) 64–6, 67, 78, 82–4, 85–7, 89–90, 92–3, 103–4, 108, 110, 120, 134–5, 140–1, 145, 148, 153–4, 155, 158, 160, 161–2, 167–9, 203–5, 217, 219–20, 221, 225, 234, 240, 245–6, 250, 258, 259, 261
Windred, Richard 55
Windred, Sarah 245, 261
Windred, Sophia 9, 24, 45, 55, 68, 83, 204, 227, 258, 260, 261

Windred, William 24, 55, 67, 68, 76, 204, 227, 235, 245–6, 261
Windsor (NSW) 4, 8, 9–10, 12, 24, 64–5, 66, 204, 205
  Australian Inn 76, 204
  Coffey's Hotel 66
  Cricketer's Arms 67–8
  Green Dragon 68
  Horse and Jockey Inn 38, 75
  Peninsula Farm 248–9
  Red Lion Inn 54, 68
  Sir John Barleycorn Inn 68
  White Swan 68
Windsor Gaol 19, 21
Wood, John 236, 238
Wood, John S. 93
Woodworth, Selim 206
Woolley, Lell Hawley 201
Wright, Joseph 78–9, 89, 189

Young 254, 255 *see also* Lambing Flat
Young, Governor Sir John 252
Young's Bank 143

Zouch, Captain William 252
Zuill, William 236

ABOUT THE AUTHOR

STEPHEN DANDO-COLLINS IS THE author of the bestselling *Crack Hardy*, as well as the award-winning *Pasteur's Gambit* and *Captain Bligh's Other Mutiny*. He has also written a number of internationally successful books about Roman and American history, including *Legions of Rome*, *Nero's Killing Machine*, *Tycoon's War* and the bestselling *Caesar's Legion*. He lives and writes in Tasmania's Tamar Valley.